Hitler's Wehrmacht

Hitler's Wehrmacht

German Armed Forces
in Support of the Führer

JAMES STEINER

McFarland & Company, Inc., Publishers
Jefferson, North Carolina, and London

The maps used in this book
were designed by the author.

LIBRARY OF CONGRESS CATALOGUING-IN-PUBLICATION DATA

Steiner, James, 1925–
Hitler's Wehrmacht : German armed forces
in support of the Führer / by James Steiner.
p.   cm.
Includes bibliographical references and index.

ISBN-13: 978-0-7864-3045-1
illustrated case binding : 50# alkaline paper ∞

1. World War, 1939–1945 — Germany.   2. Germany — Armed
Forces — History — World War, 1939–1945.   3. Hitler, Adolf,
1889–1945 — Military leadership.   4. Germany — History,
Military — 20th century.   5. Germany — History —1933–1945.
I. Title.
D757.S85   2008   940.54'1343 — dc22   2007030873

British Library cataloguing data are available

Cover photograph: Adolf Hilter with his generals, 1941
(Ullstein bild/The Granger Collection)

Manufactured in the United States of America

*McFarland & Company, Inc., Publishers
Box 611, Jefferson, North Carolina 28640
www.mcfarlandpub.com*

To true patriots everywhere

Acknowledgments

The research that went into *Hitler's Wehrmacht* required time, a quality library, and input and support from observers of and participants in these events.

In the case of the latter, time had taken its toll. However, several men provided key direction and answers I sought to the basic question: What motivated the Wehrmacht to support Hitler? Toward the end of his career I was able to correspond with Telford Taylor, our chief prosecutor at Nuremberg; he had followed the illustrious and groundbreaking Justice Robert H. Jackson in that position. Secondly, Eric Weiss, a former Austrian attorney who had joined the British Army in the late 1930s, contributed significant insight into the motivations and incentives of the Wehrmacht leadership, based on his role as interrogator of key prisoners of war (POWs).

Solid research, key to any project like this, is based heavily on access to primary sources, and numerous booksellers helped me track down memoirs and other pertinent documents. The most significant contribution was the availability of the complete sets of International Military Tribunal volumes, both the translated wartime documents and the trial transcripts; here, one bookseller, Lois Gereghty, helped me to obtain these essential documents. Also, the British Public Record Office provided the full transcripts of the Kesselring Trial and other memorandas, both critical for ready access and study.

I am indebted to Elaine Steiner, whose 25 years as an English teacher and lifelong experience as a reader of fine literature came to the fore in critiquing and fine-tuning my writing style for clarity of message. Professor Gary Steiner provided invaluable support and consultation on the book overall, particularly with his translation of key material only available in German.

Lastly, photo materials, which provide an added dimension to the text, became available from remarkable collections in Germany maintained by ullstein Bild of Berlin/The Granger Collection, New York, the Bundesarchiv at Koblenz and the Bibliothek für Zeitgeschichte in Stuttgart.

Thanks to the resources above, this book, I hope, provides further insight into why those who supported Hitler did what they did. The author, of course, takes responsibility for the entire work.

Table of Contents

List of Maps and Figures

Preface

Most research on the topic of the Third Reich, particularly the Hitler regime and its politics and relationship with the Wehrmacht, chronicles and analyzes the events of that period, either from a historical, political, strategic or tactical position. My objective, however, has been to answer a simple but little studied question. *Why did the Wehrmacht support Hitler and his geopolitical ambitions?* Were they motivated by accolades, the idea of political success, or the spoils due a conqueror? Was it the ideology through which Nazism promised power? My research points to a spectrum of objectives, with *nationalism* and *patriotism* possibly at the core.

Many memoirs of leaders of the German forces exist and provide a solid foundation for answering these questions, but it is critical to read beyond the reoccurring narratives of innocence and legality. Memoirs can be used constructively when counterbalanced against historical fact, trial testimony and evidence, and peer writing and statements. I have used references such as the International Military Tribunal (IMT) volumes of testimony at Nuremberg, the Nazi Conspiracy and Aggression series of translated German documents and publications from the British Public Record Office. Contemporary participants and witnesses of these events have also provided abundant correlative information.

Such works as Wheeler-Bennett's *The Nemesis of Power*; Telford Taylor's *The Anatomy of the Nuremberg Trials* and his *Sword and Swastika*; B.H. Liddell Hart's *History of the Second World War* and *The German Generals Talk*; and Klaus-Jürgen Müller's *The Army, Politics, and Society in Germany, 1933–45* provide a significant knowledge base from which to work. Hans Rothel's *The German Opposition to Hitler* and Peter Hoffman's *The History of the German Resistance* don't delve into the question of what motivated cultured professional soldiers to support this regime. That is the issue here, and it is my intent to have filled this gap in the literature. All research is fully cited to facilitate any reader's desire to investigate further.

It is my belief that the conclusions from this study have applications for both present and future. Lessons learned from the significant events of the 1930s, as related herein, may provide help in resolving, or at least explaining, current developments.

Introduction

A Century of German Ambition

The German determination for continental, if not world, hegemony persisted from the mid-nineteenth century for a hundred years. Chancellor Bethmann Hollweg's "September Program,"[1] introduced shortly after the outbreak of World War I, characterized this objective in that it proposed the political ascendance of Germany over France and Belgium, the vasselization of much of Europe, and the removal of British influence from the continent.[2]

However, eventual defeat and the settlement terms of Versailles brought the direct antithesis of any German expansion, requiring massive economic reparations and prompting the loss of vital iron-ore possessions. The resultant deindustrialization and unemployment reduced the military to a rudimentary and inferior force.

World War II—The Reaction to Versailles

Hitler's ascension in the early 1930s promised a surcease of the serious travails of Versailles — high unemployment, loss of sovereignty, a fractured decimated military and second-class status in the political world; Germany was once again becoming a formidable political force. The expanding military meant promotions, improved status and career opportunities for soldiers. The Reichswehr (Army) formed a basic support structure whose commitment grew in fervor as Hitler's political and military ventures succeeded throughout the 1930s and into the mid-point of the war.

German defeat in Stalingrad in late 1942 through early 1943 was the first in a series of unsuccessful military actions, and the failure decreased moral support and ultimately turned the tide for the military leadership. As Hitler's aggressive agenda first became apparent through

5

his political and military actions in the late 1930s, several chiefs of the army general staff predicted that ultimate success was unlikely — Germany was taking on the world, facing overwhelming numbers.[3] What were the compelling factors that brought significant high-level military support for the program in spite of these odds?

What attitudes, motivations and personal agendas emerged within the military leadership during Hitler's ascension to power? How did key milestones and the increasing radicalization of Hitler's Third Reich, influence the leadership; how did the excesses and eventual military defeat affect the thinking and actions of the leaders of the Wehrmacht (the new armed forces)? Was Hitler's ideology a key factor for them, and how long did that dedication survive in the face of defeat? Were victory and its spoils the primary, if not the sole, incentive for most in the leadership? Did these men aspire European or world hegemony, or were they simply professional soldiers doing their jobs? We in the West search for the moral imperatives that were the underlying drives for the military: what were the convictions that became the motivating force for these soldiers — the leaders and the rank and file — in the Wehrmacht?

This work seeks the answers to these questions using a critical examination of memoirs, post-war trial testimony and evidence, peer analysis and commentary and the actions and recorded politics of the major Wehrmacht leadership. These individuals — the services' General Staff and Supreme Command leaders, the field generals and field marshals, and the many other top military leaders — were key to Hitler's successes and eventual failure.

The conclusions of this book are relevant in a far broader context than Germany in World War II. They provide a framework for understanding the range of motivations of military leaders, whether in an authoritarian or democratic regime. Further, the analysis aids in predicting and understanding the behavior of a military as it strives to fulfill the aggressive ventures designed by politicians in the pursuit of power. Perhaps the overview provided in this book will contribute to greater understanding of the politics and agendas of current aggressive forces.

1 The Interwar Years

Foundation of the Third Reich

No tanks, no submarines, no aircraft and virtually no army, navy or air corps comprised the residual left to a defeated Germany by the Versailles Treaty following World War I. For a land sometimes characterized as an army with a country rather than a country with an army, the extraction of its arms was particularly injurious. Add to this six million unemployed in an economy stripped of its economic engines by disastrous reparations, and a political-economic-social catastrophe was created. The military would be the essential support behind any resurgence in Germany's effort to regain sovereignty. With the coalescent efforts of the military and industry, the armed forces had prepared a foundation by the time Hitler entered the picture.[1]

A Truncated Military in Versailles' Aftermath

Versailles had broad negative impact on all aspects of German life, including the armed forces. Whereas the Germans had expected a reasonable peace based on American President Wilson's fourteen point plan, the actual Treaty of Versailles established those contentious points which would provide a fertile foundation for Hitler's National Socialists. Reparations were set far higher than Germany's ability to pay, especially considering the confiscation of Silesia, Alsace-Lorraine, the Saar and the Ruhr. In Alsace-Lorraine, which was deeded to France, 75% of Germany's iron-ore and 25% of her smelter furnaces were located.[2] Under these and similar extreme confiscations the weakly supported Weimar Government was unable to cope with financial straits, which by 1932 yielded some 6 million unemployed.

In retrospect World War I might be viewed as a first phase of an overall world war that would kill upward of 50 million people. Germany's loss of World War I put an end, at least temporarily, to a German army historically dedicated and bound by oath to "fatherland and monarchy" rather than to a constitution and its president. The Versailles Treaty was intended to eliminate German militarism and might succeed by prescribing limits on the new army's size to 100,000 professionals. This new army, the Reichswehr, was to continue the traditional apolitical or "unpolitical" officer corps, an approach reemphasized by its leader of the 1920s, Hans von Seeckt, who admonished that political strife within the army was incompatible with its objectives. Nevertheless, under his leadership the army came to represent a major political force in government.[3]

An extreme was represented by a few officers such as General Kurt von Schleicher, whose political intrigues were driven by objectives of personal power and position. Von Schleicher ascended briefly in 1932 to become chancellor; however, his political machinations and power-broker associations led to his demise at the hands of Hitler's SS (*Schutzstaffel*, or security force) troops during the Night of the Long Knives in 1934.[4]

The von Seeckt dictate was fine, however, with most career officers such as Gerd von Rundstedt, considered the army's senior soldier, whose inner convictions were to remain purely soldiers and let politics alone; the von Seeckt philosophy seems to have underlain and driven their conduct at least until the late 1930s, when Hitler intervened to radically alter the military organizational structure.[5]

Not all the military, though, were content to let the political sphere languish without their influence. The navy, army and air wings each involved themselves in active leadership in the effort to overcome the Versailles restrictions. Hitler and the National Socialist Party represented but one of the two arms of governmental support in this effort. Equally aggressive leaders emerged in each of the three military wings, where efforts were mounted that would be precursors to future major rearmament in Germany as soon as the political leadership had set the stage.

The Restrictive Covenant, the Navy's Challenge

Erich Raeder had emerged as the German Navy's chief architect well before Hitler's seizure of power in 1933. When he ascended to the role of chief of the admiralty in 1928, Raeder found that the Reichstag (parliament) and parts of the Admiralty were already well along in surreptitious efforts to resurrect the navy. American naval officer Alfred Thayer Mahan, himself a major influence on the World War I German Navy, had predicted a quarter of a century earlier such chicanery was to be expected in Germany's endeavors for hegemony and that she was not to be trusted.[6]

The Versailles Treaty restrictions had stripped Germany of territory vital to economic survival and had emasculated the country's military. By now a litmus test of international world ranking was the showing of a naval fleet. If sovereignty were to be regained, especially where Great Britain, the United States and Japan — the then-ranking naval powers — were concerned, Germany needed a credible naval force.[7]

Versailles was specific: Article 181 proscribed forces not to exceed "six battleships of the Deutschland or Lothringen type [10,000 tons each with 11-inch guns, compared with the Washington Naval Agreement of 1922 allowing the Allied powers 35,000 tons each with 16-

inch guns], six light cruisers, 12 destroyers, 12 torpedo boats ... No submarines are to be included ... All other warships ... must be placed in reserve or devoted to commercial purposes." Personnel were limited to 15,000. Under Article 191, "The construction or acquisition of any submarines, even for commercial purposes, shall be forbidden in Germany," and under Article 198 no naval air force was allowed.[8]

Notwithstanding U.S. President Wilson's fourteen-point representations to the Germans, who had thought as a result that an even-handed peace would follow the armistice and peace convention, the reality of Versailles was far different.[9] It inspired an entire generation in this most industrious center of Europe to recoup the country's self-respect by all possible means.

By the late 1920s the German government had become impatient; the government at the time was headed by President Paul von Hindenburg and Chancellor Hermann Müller, with a cabinet including, among others, Foreign Minister Gustav Stresemann and Defense Minister General Wilhelm Groener. Groener had placed rearmament in the hands of the Reichstag inasmuch as any such action would be contrary to the Versailles restrictions. Previous Weimar governments had refused to take any rearmament actions, but this administration was amenable to considering the issue.[10]

Accordingly, funding had been manipulated and redirected to support rearmament measures which were illegal under the Versailles Treaty. These included development of small motor torpedo boats and mine-sweepers and the design and construction of submarines abroad. In the case of submarines, a Dutch firm to serve as a front had been established at the Hague which was in actuality a confederation of German shipyards employing a number of former German submarine designers and engineers. As such, a valuable technical team was preserved and kept technologically up to date. A subsidiary activity built submarines in Finland according to plans provided by the Dutch design firm.[11]

When he became navy head, Raeder immediately selected the projects to be continued. Provided the government "legalized" them, selected projects were carried "under cover" with the approval of the defense minister. The Reichstag, through an executive committee, controlled the corresponding secret expenditures, which were given "a sort of legality" by inclusion in a secret budget which in every way complied with regular budget regulations.[12] The Dutch bureau initiated work on a 750 ton U-boat in Spain in 1927 which, when completed in 1931, carried out trials and diving exercises in the waters off Spain, trials supported by German officers, engineers and workers. This boat, subsequently purchased by Turkey, became the prototype for the German U-25 and U-26.[13]

By the time the von Papen government came to power in 1932, circumventions of the Versailles Treaty restrictions were well along. Raeder's plan for upgrading the naval fleet was approved by the defense minister, though U-boat final assembly and commissioning had to await results of the 1932–33 Geneva Disarmament Conference as well as the overall foreign situation.

Genesis of the Navy's Resurgence

The intensity of this naval resurgence in the post–World War I era finds its genesis in the Kaiser's pre–World War I concept of freedom of the seas; he saw it as a prime element in

Germany's expansionist needs and desires, which meant not only parity with the British, the preeminent sea power, but the ability to defeat the British at sea. Given Germany's impeded if not landlocked access to the North Sea and Atlantic Ocean, Kaiser Wilhelm's interest in *Weltmacht* (world power) depended on gaining the freedom of action such superiority would provide.[14] This had been a prime factor in exacerbating world tensions and a contributing cause of World War I.

In this pursuit the Kaiser was significantly influenced by the American naval officer Capt. Alfred Thayer Mahan, whose 1890 publication, *The Influence of Sea Power upon History— 1660–1783*, was the subject of an enthusiastic reception in Europe. Upon Mahan's arrival in Southampton in 1893 commanding the USS *Chicago*, he became the object of a continuing round of receptions and dinners. Most notable was an invitation to dinner with Queen Victoria and her grandson, the German Kaiser Wilhelm II. Once again the following year a second royal dinner invitation brought Mahan to the company of the two sovereigns; in fact, so enthusiastic was the Kaiser for Mahan's ideas that four days later the two would dine onboard the Kaiser's yacht *Hollenzollern* before both departed England.

So persuasive had Mahan's influence been on Wilhelm that by 1897 Mahan's book was on board all German naval vessels, and according to the Kaiser, was "constantly quoted by my captains and officers."[15]

Through the 1890s German naval large-ship construction tracked that of the British, ultimately, if not initially, in armament size as well as ship displacement. Under the Kaiser's influence, and with Admiral Tirpitz as state secretary for the navy, the German Navy by 1911 had overtaken the United States as the second largest navy in the world.[16]

Into this highly charged environment came then–Lt. Erich Raeder, newly appointed in 1910 as navigation officer on the Kaiser's yacht *Hollenzollern*. Raeder found life on the *Hollenzollern* informal and conducive to frank political and military discussions with the Kaiser. Two years hence Raeder departed the *Hollenzollern*, obviously impressed and indoctrinated with the Kaiser's politics, the legacy of which would impact the navy's growth under the future chief.[17]

If one searches for a reason the post-war Nuremberg Tribunal dealt with Raeder far more harshly than the other grand admiral, Karl Dönitz, it may be found in the legacy of naval *Weltmacht* impressed upon his former navigation officer by the Kaiser. U.S. Admiral Mahan, in turn, must take a large measure of credit for initially inspiring this thinking. Though Raeder had been replaced halfway through the war (1943) by Karl Dönitz, who had gone on to ascend the Reich's leadership, Raeder's impact on the reemergence of the navy was clear.[18]

A Tank Corps in Spite of Versailles

Faced with the Versailles restriction on tanks in the post–World War I period, innovation became imperative. Using crude mock-ups built around armored troop carriers which were on the approved-for-use list, concepts and tactics were developed for the eventual tanks that would be required. The army soon resorted to subterfuge to circumvent Versailles in a fashion similar to the navy's approach to submarine development[19]; by 1926 a testing station for German tanks had been established abroad, and contracts placed for a total of two each of five types of light and medium tanks. By 1932 a training tank had been developed which would eventually see battle.

Two preeminent tank experts emerged for Germany — Erwin Rommel and Heinz Guderian — who would, for a period, place the German Wehrmacht in the forefront of armor warfare during World War II. Both gained early recognition for their leadership in the rapid defeat of France in the campaign of May–June 1940. Guderian's panzer (armored) divisions formed the van of the attack through the Ardennes and on to Dunkirk; Field Marshal Erich von Manstein, author of the tactical plan for the attack, gives Guderian primary credit for its success.[20]

Rommel is better known than Guderian, probably due to the circumstance of his high-profile North African campaign, which yielded early victories, though it ultimately fell in defeat to superior Allied forces. Guderian, however, was assigned to the Eastern Campaign against Russia in the aftermath of the battle in France, and found lean success because of the Russian winters coupled with massive enemy resources.

Ironically, Guderian found his initial tactical armor background in books by the Englishmen Fuller, Martel and Liddell-Hart. The latter he credited with conceiving the armored division which combined Panzer and Panzer-infantry units, and to all three he credited the concept of the mobile tank as a primary weapon.[21]

Rommel entered active service in 1914 as a second lieutenant in the Reichswehr. He developed what have been considered sterling leadership qualities at Verdun, the Argonne, in campaigns in Belgium and Italy in World War I. Undoubtedly the pinnacle of his World War I experience, and precursor of the future, was the award of the Pour le Mérite for his lead in the storming of the Italian positions on Monte Matajur in 1917. Using typically Rommel tactics, when the German assault faltered, he launched the attack with his own company, on his own initiative and without orders.[22] In Rommel's words, success in leading troops demanded a philosophy of "vigorous command."[23] Though some have called him overly ambitious and brutal, once his confidence had been gained, he gave his staff and soldiers complete support.[24]

During the inter-war years in the Reichswehr, Rommel, an inveterate chronicler, lectured on these World War I experiences, drawing incisive and perceptive conclusions that would be his guide in World War II. By 1937 these lectures were published under the title *Infantry in the Attack* (*Attacks* in the U.S. edition).

Rommel's book played a decisive role in his future, bringing him to Hitler's attention. Having gained Hitler's recognition, and, as important for the future, his ear, Rommel went on to military command of Hitler's headquarters in the Austrian, Sudetenland and Czech occupations, and in the Polish campaign.

The Reichswehr in Politics

As the 1920s ended Adolf Hitler and his National Socialists were offering a panacea for relief from the shackles of Versailles: Germany would emerge from these shadows of illegitimacy to one of sovereignty by the restoration of German armed might and economic resurgence. Hitler promised this metamorphosis through his leadership.

Inevitably, as many had and would in the future, three army lieutenants of the 5th

Artillery Regiment based in Ulm, Germany, had bought the solution offered by Hitler. The three, Scheringer, Luden and Wendt, were arrested on the parade ground at Ulm on the 6th of March 1930. The three had despaired of "twelve years as subalterns ... A lost war, an impotent state, a hopeless system, ... a Reich at the brink of the abyss," as Scheringer put it. Their response had been a treasonable one, the promulgation of the National Socialist credo — propaganda — seeking to subvert army organization in the ranks of the Reichswehr officer corps, in open defiance of Hans von Seeckt's firm dictate calling for an apolitical Reichswehr.[25]

Eager to come to their defense, Hitler provided Scheringer with Nazi Party lawyer Hans Frank as his defense attorney. When called as a witness by Frank, Hitler was faced with a dilemma: whether to support his disciples, these purveyors of National Socialist doctrine, and thus earn the disdain and loss of support of the Reichswehr; or to separate himself from their disruptive actions, and plead his case of legitimacy and noninterference with Reichswehr functions. He chose the latter in an hour-long peroration to the court reminiscent of his plea from the dock in 1923 when, once before, he had salvaged disaster and converted it into a triumph. Hitler swore to a dubious trial judge that his National Socialist revolution would follow a constitutional road, but he did predict, "heads will roll" after his movement was victorious and a National Socialist court of justice was established.[26]

Hitler was extremely perceptive in assessing motivational needs of individuals and groups and the respective balance of power that was to be effected, and his determination was clearly that he was in need of the army's support, as they would need his in the future.

Caught up in the momentum generated by Hitler, the lieutenants' regimental commander, Colonel Ludwig Beck, a future Chief of the General Staff, had protested their arrest and had spoken at their trial in their defense. At stake was his reputation as regimental commander exercising adequate organizational control. But equally motivating was the fact that, like many of his associate officers, he had also heard and bought the National Socialist vision of a growing Reichswehr and the personal potential that offered, if not the equally sought goal of a reemerging and sovereign Germany.

As was Hitler's practice, he seldom forgot loyal supporters or those who crossed swords with him. Hitler had spoken for an independent Reichswehr and reaffirmed his intention of maintaining legality; by not choosing to cross the army by direct support of the three officers, he had extricated himself from the horns of a dilemma. Both he and Beck could be satisfied with the outcome, and Ludwig Beck's future would be impacted favorably in the near term; however, philosophically their paths would diverge fatefully as the 1930s wore on.

Sixteen years later Col.-General Alfred Jodl, OKW (Supreme Command) chief of operations, testifying at Nuremberg as a defendant, said that though previously skeptical, he had been assured by the positive broad impact of Hitler's speech in the Scheringer trial that he was opposed to any undermining of the Reichswehr.[27]

A Luftwaffe Emerges from the Veil

The Versailles Treaty forbade Germany the building or possession of military aircraft, similar to the restrictions on other motorized armaments and ships capable of potential military use. Accordingly, both overt and clandestine efforts emerged to counteract this handicap. For all to see and for wide utilization and training, glider clubs emerged in the inter-war years. The sport developed, however, in an atmosphere of national frustration, according to Adolf Galland, one of Germany's World War II aces. So intense was the resentment that a leader who could "one day throw off these fetters once and for all was assured of the fullest support from the enthusiastic aviators in the ranks of Germany's youth."[28] Glider technology proceeded vigorously with annual competitions, and in 1933 these clubs were formed into aero clubs, the first surreptitious elements of the as-yet unformed Luftwaffe (air force).[29]

On Hitler's ascension to power in 1933, Hermann Göring was appointed Reichskommissar (commissioner) for aviation with the mandate to organize civil aviation and a new air force. Heretofore German pilots had been secretly training in Soviet Russia; now with the liaison between Hitler and Mussolini, this training, still done in secrecy, was transferred to the Italian Air Force in 1933. Men from the aero clubs were candidates for this training, and when completed, were commissioned in the Reichswehr, and then discharged.[30]

These released pilots were then inducted into an air force barely in existence and sent to the Airline Pilots' School, which now became a fighter school for the new Luftwaffe, but kept under secrecy until rearmament was declared by Hitler in 1935.[31] The Luftwaffe had no formal structure before Göring's appointment, and accordingly, General Staff officers were transferred from the Reichswehr in 1933 to form the first General Staff of the new air force. Lt. General Walther Wever, the first Chief of the General Staff, was followed by Colonels Albrecht Kesselring and Hans-Juergen Stumpff; in addition Göring recruited Erhard Milch, retired from the Reichswehr in 1920 and current managing director of Lufthansa airline, and Ernst Udet and Hans Jeschonnek, World War I military pilots, to make up the basic structure of the new Luftwaffe.[32] It would grow from there.

Aircraft for the needs of civil, military and commercial aviation came under the jurisdiction of the Allied Air Control Commission, which was established in 1919; it monitored a ban on construction and import of planes and engines. Consequently, early German pioneer plane builders, like Ernst Heinkel, closed down in Germany and set up shop in Sweden. By 1922 the commission had amended the rules to allow low performance aircraft design and production. Heinkel and others returned but retained some off-shore work.[33] Customers for their efforts came from around the globe, including their own Reichswehr on a clandestine basis, Japan, America and the Soviets. The Soviets welcomed an arrangement with Germany in 1923–24 as they sought technical and organizational support for their industrialization program. An exchange of a Soviet airfield for such industrial support was negotiated so that pilots could be trained and new aircraft tested. For this exchange the Reichswehr Air Ministry made sure they would have a minimum of aircraft and pilots on a par with the technology of the period.[34]

The efforts did require a game of hide and seek with the Commission, according to aircraft manufacturers, so as to expand to meet the competitive technology, especially where military, racing and commercial requirements were concerned. By the early 1930s the industry was designing and building wind tunnels, catapults, streamlined racing and mail planes, a range of military planes and sports planes.[35]

During the inter-war years, civilian commercial transport in Germany was allowed but was in its early stages, and the few employment opportunities it offered were vastly oversubscribed. By the mid 1920s the first regular service was established in-country, though it grew by the end of the decade to include auxiliary carriers in South America, Spain and China. By the time Hitler took power Lufthansa also had routes established to Italy and the Soviet Union.[36] Erhard Milch's relationship with Hitler stems from the period before his ascension, when Milch, as managing director of Lufthansa, made it economically easy for Hitler to acquire aircraft for personal use. This would pay dividends in the future for Milch, who shared with Göring the major influence on the rise and fall of the Luftwaffe.[37]

A Country Prepares to Regain Sovereignty

Rather than accept the crippling restrictions dealt by Versailles, the Weimar government found the resources and will to innovate, however surreptitiously, to prepare for the point where it could regain its position in the world. The military and industry, which would become almost immobile if they failed to develop and expand extra-legally, made fundamental advances in military equipment by utilizing the facilities of other agreeable countries. When, by a combination of favorable circumstances, a leader equipped to respond to the vacuum that had been created appeared on the scene, the military, in concert with industry, was ready to accept any beneficial leadership he would offer. Hitler recognized this opportunity and used it to gain the eventual if not immediate support of the military.

2 Military Reaction to Hitler as Chancellor

Leadership Changes Produce a Reliable Team

Hitler, leading his National Socialist Party, the Nazis (NSDAP), arose to the German chancellorship in 1933 as a direct consequence of the economic and political hardship created by the Versailles Treaty. Territorial limitations, excessive reparations, trade restrictions and virtual elimination of a sovereign military with consequent damage to Germany's political relationships gave Hitler abundant ammunition for implementing the program he envisioned for Germany: rearmament and regaining of sovereignty despite Versailles.[1] To implement his program, however, he needed the full support of the military.

A Mixed Reaction from the Wehrmacht

Upon his seizure of power, Hitler faced army opposition at the very top. Shortly after he took power he removed the army chief, Freiherr von Hammerstein, a vocal opponent of the Nazis. This was followed by the bloody Roehm purge of 1934, also known as the Night of the Long Knives. The purge was orchestrated by Hitler, Himmler and Göring to wipe out all potential opposition. However, previously latent opposition intensified when Col.-General Werner Freiherr von Fritsch, Commander-in-Chief of the army, and Field Marshal Werner von Blomberg, minister of defense, were cashiered in early 1938.[2] These events (described later), further aggravated by societal strife stemming from Nazi pressure and the struggle against the church, caused the officer corps to assume positions ranging from latent opposition to outright enthusiastic support. This balance and its intensity shifted throughout the 1930s as Hitler pursued his agenda.

Reaction by the military to the National Socialist rise to power was based on some or all of the following points:

1. Acceptance based on the promise of remilitarization and the regaining of German sovereignty and all that implied,
2. Acceptance of the Nazis and Hitler as legally selected and the will of the people, conforming with Wehrmacht tradition in accord with von Seeckt's apolitical military,
3. Acceptance as the preferred alternative to communism,
4. Skepticism and/or disdain based on the radicalism Hitler and his NSDAP had exhibited on the way to power.

According to Admiral Erich Raeder, a consistent supporter once Hitler reached power, "National Socialism, conceivable only against such a background, harped upon the shackling treaty, and, with goals its party offered, struck a chord which resounded in the heart of every disappointed German of the day."[3]

Hitler's statement to Raeder in their first official meeting after the former became chancellor in 1933 was that it was his firm resolve for peace with England, Italy and Japan, and that he would like to reassure Britain that Germany would make no challenge to her supremacy of the seas. He intended to do this through negotiation of an Anglo-German agreement fixing relative naval strengths in Britain's favor.[4] In his post-war memoirs, Raeder says, "Hitler repeatedly reaffirmed his first statement to me that his strong desire was to live in peace with England, and I was convinced at the time this was his basic policy."[5]

The officer corps, and, indeed the bulk of the German public, applauded and supported Hitler's actions to counter the Versailles strictures, according to Field Marshal Werner von Blomberg, minister of defense up until 1938, a point corroborated by other military leaders in post-war testimony at Nuremberg.[6] Their concern centered on loss of Memel, the Polish Corridor and the Saar and Ruhr. A future war was regarded, they said in retrospect, as a necessity to rectify the consequent problems of the Corridor and rejoin East Prussia with Germany proper. During the years 1933–38, at least, "Hitler had led Germany out of its utmost misery, both politically in its foreign politics and economically," was the trial testimony of Col.-General Georg-Hans Reinhardt, pre-war chief of Germany's Army Training Section and later panzer group commander on the Eastern Front.[7]

Many top officers, like Gerd von Rundstedt, continually supported the Hitler regime. As he said later, though he, like so many of his comrades, opposed Nazi totalitarian ideas, as a soldier he could not "put up any resistance." He might entertain such ideas privately, but "a soldier cannot participate in political activities." Von Rundstedt's own adjutant, Salviati, proffered in mid–1941 just before the attack on Russia that the field marshal saw clearly almost everything that was wrong, "but that was as far as it went."[8] That is, he was not disposed to go against the legally installed leadership, however misdirected he perceived their actions. In his most positive stance against those actions of Hitler he judged doomed to failure, he offered his resignation or let himself be relieved of command.

In response to such loyalty, Hitler, for all his faults, was incisive in assessment of personal motivations and in taking full advantage; in von Rundstedt's case, for example, he would him at will, firing and rehiring him as the war situation demanded. In summary, Hitler relieved him first in the wake of Munich; then in 1941 as the German Army faltered in the first Russian winter; then in 1944 following the Allied invasion at Normandy; and finally as the last-gasp Ardennes Offensive was ground down in 1945. Driven by his mercurial approach to high-level army personnel, Hitler also hired von Rundstedt back repeatedly: first to lead the initial hot war campaign against Poland, followed by campaigns against France and Russia; then to take charge of the West as the Russian campaign faltered; and then finally to reemerge a second time as commander of Western Forces in late 1944, leading the final and futile Ardennes Offensive.

Throughout this entire period Adolf Hitler was building his following so that by 1933 his total of supporters in the Reichstag led to the chancellorship. The masses, von Rundstedt felt, had acclaimed Hitler as their leader. At the same time it was his opinion that had a democratic monarchy offering reasonable freedom been allowed to flourish, Hitler would not have come to power.[9]

By this point — 1933 — von Rundstedt had become Commander-in-Chief of Wehrkreis III, the Berlin Military District, a position he held until 1939. However, from 1933 on, von Rundstedt, a veteran of 40 years of army service, claims to have eagerly sought to resign from active duty. However, acquiescing to the various demands of President Paul von Hindenburg, Chief

Swearing the Oath of Allegiance to Hitler, August 2, 1934, upon Paul von Hindenburg's death; Hitler had rewritten the oath so it was now sworn to a man, as under the Constitution of 1871, instead of to a federal charter, the law since 1918 under the Weimar Constitution. Given without advance warning, this change was viewed as ominous by some who had accepted it precipitously. Bundesarchiv Photo no. 102 — 16107.

of the General Staff Ludwig Beck and Army Commander in Chief Col.-General Freiherr von Fritsch, he stayed on. His key objection during these years was Hitler's haste in conjuring up an army that von Rundstedt considered the antithesis of the well trained and united Reichswehr of pre–Hitler times. Additionally, it seemed this "new" army spawned an element of younger officers more in sympathy with Hitler's ideas, leading to a continuing contentiousness between "old" and "new."[10]

Karl Dönitz, like most German military men, had watched the emergence of the National Socialists during the inter-war years as they threw off the shackles of Versailles and rebuilt a sovereign Germany. In his mind it came down to the National Socialists or the Communists, and the latter, but for the Nazis, would probably have gained power by a bloody revolution; therefore, the reasoning went, the ascension of Hitler's party was the most desirable course for Germany. For these and obvious collateral reasons the armed forces welcomed the appointment of Hitler as German chancellor in 1933.

"At his party meetings Hitler demanded the end of class warfare, the liberation of the country from foreign political dependence and a concentration of all forces of the country on the tasks of eliminating unemployment and creating a well-ordered and healthy state," and these were aims to which all could subscribe given the dismal economic situation, the internal political dissension and still-existing Versailles foreign policy restrictions, he felt.

A cross-section of attitudes pervaded the officer corps. If some such as Blomberg and others felt unanimity existed among the corps, others disagree. Lt. General Hans Speidel, Rommel's last Chief of Staff (1944), and a post-war leader of the Federal Republic's new army, saw it differently. A significant number in the officer corps, principally general staff officers, disapproved of Hitler's pre-war policies both internally and externally.[11] Hitler, according to OKW Chief Wilhelm Keitel, recognized von Rundstedt's "hostile attitude towards National Socialist ideology" during this early period.[12] To the comments of Blomberg and others concerning an inevitable armed conflict with Poland over the Corridor, von Rundstedt testified at Nuremberg that he disagreed; only in the years immediately following World War I had he feared conflict with Poland, and it would be one that would arise by Poland's attack on Germany.[13]

Von Rundstedt agreed, however, with Blomberg, that Hitler did indeed have a majority of Germans behind him — 60% of the adult population and the entire youth. A few generals held Hitler's policy of hasty rearmament to be correct, though von Rundstedt, representative of the "old" army generals, who looked for a more systematic and rational approach, eschewed this revolutionary approach. They were concerned the world would see this as a challenge and one that could lead to war. At the same time, they recognized the younger officer corps welcomed the opportunities this presented to them without considering the implications for war.[14]

Hitler's appointment as Reich chancellor, though a surprise to then–Major Alfred Jodl, who was in charge of a group on the Army General Staff, was reassuring to Jodl on the basis of the appointment having been made by President Paul von Hindenburg with the obvious support of ex-chancellor Franz von Papen, Foreign Minister von Neurath and Finance Minister Schwerin von Korsigk. Jodl expected no excesses in view of Hindenburg's having "legalized this revolution."[15] Jodl was extremely skeptical and unconvinced by Hitler initially; however, Hitler's assurance that he was personally opposed to any undermining of the Reichswehr, which he had stated in the event of the Leipzig trial of 1930 (discussed in Chapter 1), impressed Jodl and assuaged many misgivings he had harbored earlier.[16]

Though Jodl would eventually rise to become one of Hitler's right-hand men in OKW, as a mid-level officer and by nature apolitical, Jodl never attended Hitler's meetings and knew only party members such as Ernst Roehm, retired Reichwehr officer and chief of Hitler's SA (Sturmabteilung, or storm troopers) and others in the military. At the time of Hitler's appointment Jodl assembled and addressed his staff: he explained that Hitler was called to head the Reich under the existing constitution and laws in force. He directed there was to be no criticism of the actions of the new chancellor as had been done in the past (referring to criticism of Hitler and his new measures), as such criticism would be inconsistent with the army's position. To one in that audience, Jodl's entire speech showed great worry and apprehension with regard to the coming developments; Jodl appeared to share the view of the then Army Commander-in-Chief General von Hammerstein, and was thoroughly opposed to Hitler and the party. That was the testimony given at Nuremberg in 1946 by one of his then-staff subordinates, General von Vormann.[17]

Allegiance to Man Versus Country

The second year of Hitler's reign brought two events which were harbingers of the future: the Night of the Long Knives of June 30, 1934, and the death of President Paul von Hindenburg. The first served to eliminate any and all of Hitler's perceived enemies or challengers, and the second caused the institution of a new and, to some, controversial oath.

Ludwig Beck's promotion to chief of the Army General Staff (Chef des Truppenamts in October of 1933, then Chef des Generalstabs des Heeres in July of 1935) was a logical move, sanctioned by the new chancellor, Adolf Hitler, then nine months into office. Beck's promotion can be attributed in part to his position in the Leipzig trial of 1930, which had provided Hitler a very supportive platform. However, Beck's thinking took a decidedly negative turn with these events of 1934.

Hitler owed his ascendance in no small part to the SA, his own private brownshirt army. By 1934, the SA, led by Captain Roehm, a former Reichswehr officer, had manifested a rivalry with the regular army which prompted Hitler himself to sense the threat to his own power. The Night of the Long Knives of June 30, 1934, conceived and executed by Hitler, Göring and Himmler, saw the murder of Roehm as well as all other recognizable and/or perceived potential threats to Hitler's eminence. The conservative army, typified by Gerd von Rundstedt, was also feeling a threat from Roehm and the SA and so supported the force and tactics Hitler had used.[18] The Reichswehr, of course, profited from the event as any SA challenge to their preeminent role of military primacy was removed.[19]

"This has been one of the most fateful moments of my life," was the way Beck described what happened next.[20] On August 2, 1934, one day following the death of President Paul von Hindenburg, the armed forces were asked to renew their oath. However, Hitler, who was assuming the dual role of the presidency and chancellorship, had revised the oath so that it now called for loyalty to him personally instead of to the Constitution and president as under the Weimar government. Well planned in advance by the party hierarchy with the collaboration of Minister of Defense von Blomberg, oath taking took place immediately at every garrison in the country.[21] Arms raised and with no advance warning of the new oath's fateful implications, the forces repeated as it was read to them, "I swear by God this holy oath, that I will render to Adolf Hitler, Leader of the German nation and people, Supreme Commander of the Armed Forces, unconditional obedience, and I am ready as a brave soldier to risk my life at any time for this oath."[22]

Beck could never rid himself from that day forward of the thought that he should not have given his oath, and considered it the blackest day of his life.[23] As the dedicated intellectual he was, Beck's vision was always to carry forward the century-old traditions of the General Staff, service and responsibility. He saw the ominous contravening implications of an oath that forgot allegiance to country and affirmed fealty to one individual.

The Constitution of 1871, article 64, required the armed forces to swear an oath to the monarch — the Kaiser. However, with Germany's defeat in World War I and the Kaiser's oneway trip to the Netherlands in November of 1918, Germany's centuries-long allegiance to a man as opposed to a federal charter seemed to have ended. The defeat of 1918 left Germany without the monarchy, but instead fraught with political and social strife. This vacuum was filled by the Weimar government, whose new, Western-oriented Weimar Constitution, article 176, asked its public officials and armed forces to pledge loyalty to the Constitution of the German Federation, a significant change.[24] Upon Hitler's seizure of power in 1933, Weimar and its constitution were never formally disbanded by the National Socialists. Hitler and his cabinet never even bothered to amend article 176 of the constitution until some three weeks after the oath taking.[25]

The Weimar government was heavily influenced by the victors of the Great War but without the enthusiastic support of a populace not yet ready for the personal independence and responsibility this absence of authoritarian leadership brought. Nevertheless the emancipating benefits were understood by many such as Beck, who had become accustomed to and understood the concept of state allegiance.

However, to the apolitical or non-skeptic the implications of the oath as now revised would be at the time inconsequential. Erich Raeder took his oath to Hitler "naturally" as did other key military leaders, since "the German people had repeatedly voiced their unanimous confidence in him ... no one would have suggested anyone better fitted for the Presidency." Raeder saw the navy, like the other services, giving unquestioned support to the succeeding German governments so long as they represented the will of the German people. Naval leadership considered their proper institutional position to be completely apolitical.[26]

There were many more in agreement with Raeder's position; Major Alfred Jodl had no qualms about taking the oath to Hitler. The full implications of the oath to man rather than state, rather than the reverse as under the Weimar Regime and most Western governments, escaped Jodl, as he felt soldiers were quite justified in taking the oath to Hitler because a higher law than the will of the people did not exist.[27]

The day would come, however, with military reverses and impending defeat, that the desire to end the war short of ultimate catastrophe would place the Wehrmacht on the horns of a dilemma. At least that is the post-war position taken by many in explaining their actions in supporting the regime to the end. For them their oath took precedence over intelligent and logical action that might be advisable in order to salvage the country's remnants and/or save lives in the dire straits of looming defeat.

Military Resurgence Begins

To many both in the military as well as civilian ranks, the decades-long violations of the Versailles Treaty stemmed only from Germany's desire for adequate defense. When the Führer came upon the scene, *his* intent was for Germany to reacquire a position as a world power; accordingly, this would of necessity require a dominant navy with free access to the oceans,[28] an army equipped with the latest advanced-technology mobile hardware and development of an air force. Fortunately for the regime, the ground work for these military elements had been laid throughout the inter-war period.

In the early years Erwin Rommel, like many of his peers, was preoccupied with the concerns of his profession, only much later developing a political insight as conditions demanded. His impressions of Hitler during the first years of National Socialist rule were negative; his reaction to the tactics used in the June 30, 1934, Roehm Purge[29] with the murder of Generals von Schleicher and von Bredow was that the regime should have been ousted at that point.

However, Rommel's opinion changed in 1935 when Hitler announced renunciation of the Versailles arms limitations, solved the unemployment problem and brought a reversal of the societal malaise which had become the legacy of Weimar. He began to see Hitler as a leader with peaceful aims who would forge a buffer between the West and the Bolshevik East. It was only after the Western Campaign of 1940 that he began to harbor doubts about the statesmanship and war leadership capabilities of the Hitler regime. In time Rommel's developing impressions of Hitler would become his determined convictions.[30]

Rommel, like many other senior commanders, felt he was in a position to take action with some degree of authority and even impunity, if the regime deviated from what he believed was a prudent and reasonable course. However, for him and most others these concerns did not become powerful enough to overcome support for the regime until the probability of Germany's defeat loomed some years hence.

Admiral Erich Raeder, more politically aware and proactive than many such as Rommel even before the accession to power of the Nazis, saw German plans and studies for naval warfare against England, drafted in 1938, simply as normal defensive contingency plans stemming from Hitler's long-range objectives, that is of "securing for the Reich its rightful position in the world."[31]

Raeder seems always to have attempted to position the navy in an aggressive posture, however. Naval development and, therefore, violation of the Versailles restrictions, accelerated coincident with Hitler's seizure of power in 1933. By 1935, in spite of Versailles, orders had been placed for two 27,000-ton battle cruisers, two heavy cruisers, a light cruiser (the *Nurnberg*), sixteen destroyers, twelve mine-sweepers, nine E-boats and thirty-six U-boats. Furthermore, total naval personnel had exceeded the 15,000-man limit, reaching 34,000.[32]

Clandestine development of the 250-ton U-boat prototype which had been initiated in Finland prior to 1933 facilitated the submarine program. The building and thorough trials of this prototype made it possible to obtain the parts for *U-1* through *U-24* starting in 1933 and continuing to 1935, long before final assembly of the vessels, with subassembly proceeding as far as possible within the bounds of secrecy. These major subassemblies were then hidden at Kiel and elsewhere until Hitler's declaration to rearm in 1935.[33]

Preparations for the army's future strategic and tactical requirements were similarly made by prescient individuals. Then-colonel Heinz Guderian, attempting to implement his earlier research on tank-type vehicles, sought Ludwig Beck's support in 1933 for three new panzer divisions. "No, no, I don't want to have anything to do with you people. You move too fast for me," he reports was Beck's response. In contrast, Guderian remembers Hitler's response to a panzer demonstration that same year by his platoon, when the Führer responded, "That's what I need, that's what I want to have."[34]

According to Guderian, the prime mover in Germany of the tank concept at the time, Beck, though a highly educated, perceptive and intellectual disciple of Moltke, appeared to him to have been, like so many, anachronistic in his approach to modern armaments, considering the proposed changes in armor warfare technically precipitous and too rapid in application. Guderian felt that Beck disapproved of the new armored panzer forces as independent organic elements, and, instead, insisted tanks be used primarily as infantry support weapons.[35]

Guderian may be misstating Beck's disposal toward the use of tanks, however, since Beck's writing indicates he was willing to raise as many tank battalions as possible, massed in brigades, and to then form them into divisions once they had proven themselves.[36] There is always the perception that generals, resistant to change and driven to what worked in the past, fight the last war, and there may have been at least an element of this in the more aggressive Guderian's perception. This, of course, was the period when de Gaulle and others promoted the concept of tank divisions, which would become pre-eminent before the end of the decade.

Positive Support from the New Air Wing

The politics of the new air force was destined to be fully supportive of the new regime when Hermann Göring, one of Hitler's closest associates from the early 1920s, was tasked to set it up. To jumpstart it, Hermann Göring used officers and men from the Reichswehr as the nuclei of the original cadre. With a dearth of capable aviators, the three who were recruited to head the most important Air Ministry departments — Albrecht Kesselring for administration, Walther Weaver for Air Staff and Hans-Juergen Stumpf for personnel — had no aviation background.[37]

Beyond this organizational structure, Göring, as Commander-in-Chief, surrounded himself with his early flying associates, many from the von Richthofen Squadron of World War I. These included Bruno Loerzer, Ernst Udet, Karl Bodenschatz, Paul Koerner and Erhard Milch, the latter one of the three founders of Lufthansa during the inter-war years.[38]

Because the new service was founded in this way and because Göring was so close to Hitler, the initial officer corps of the Luftwaffe was a group whose loyalty could be counted on. This lends credence to the oft-stated retrospective perception of the Wehrmacht that the Third Reich had an "Imperial Navy, a Republican Army and a National Socialist Air Force." The selection process for the future Luftwaffe was no chance endeavor. Whereas Hitler experienced political compatibility with the navy and a stormy relationship with the army, he recognized the new air force could be and was built on a positive political base from the ground up.

Once in office and with momentum to assuage the debilitating excesses Versailles had brought during the first half of the inter-war period, Hitler appeared to be moving toward his objective of reestablishing German political and military sovereignty as an integral part of the world. However, as the 1930s progressed Wehrmacht observers and participants developed misgivings.

3 An Emerging Wehrmacht Upsets Versailles

Promises of Restored Sovereignty Are Persuasive

By 1935 many Germans viewed with pride the significant changes for the better since Hitler's ascent to power. Many in the military were typified by then-naval Captain Karl Dönitz who felt the emphasis was on the dignity of labor and creating internal unity. Hitler took advantage of the positive response to make two major moves that would be the precursor of the future — he announced German rearmament and all that entailed, and he made the first armed transgression against Versailles, that of the Rhineland invasion. So far the Wehrmacht had followed his lead.

Germany Makes the Move to Regain Sovereignty

The National Socialists had led Germany from the depressed early 1930s with 6 million unemployed into an era of growth and relative prosperity. Only months after coming to power, Hitler presented a five-year plan for the Wehrmacht whereby naval chief Erich Raeder felt the services would be strengthened to the point that "he [Hitler] could place [it] in the balance as an instrument of political power."[1]

Growth of the military services was particularly influenced by the following major milestones of 1935, a pivotal year for the Wehrmacht:

- Renunciation of Versailles armament restrictions by Hitler on March 16
- Resumption of compulsory military training on March 16

24

- Conclusion of the Anglo-German Naval Treaty on June 18
- Establishment of a new submarine force

The declaration of regained sovereignty by this renunciation of the shackles of Versailles in 1935 was followed by the successful Saar Plebiscite and the remilitarization of the Rhineland in 1936.

Support at the Top for the Wehrmacht

What the Wehrmacht needed to assure the emergence of a new and strong Germany was support at the top. It found it in Hitler, whose desire to overturn Versailles and reassert German sovereignty and military equality, if not supremacy, began to have an impact from the start with his ascendance in 1933. Upon becoming chancellor Hitler appointed two individuals who favored modernizing the forces: General von Blomberg as war minister and General von Reichenau as ministerial chief. Hitler, himself, was interested in the problem of motorization and armor for the field forces. Consequently, when Guderian demonstrated his rudimentary experimental tank and anti-tank platoon, Hitler's positive prescient response had been immediate.[2]

With this encouragement, development of an armored force was given a significant boost. One of the results of Versailles was the inexperience of German industry in producing precision war materials. Consequently, labor training and material development became a major task. The rearmament that ensued was, in the view of many in the military, to achieve equality with Germany's thought-to-be highly armed neighbors, the victors of 1918. Any deficiencies in hardware and numbers they hoped to make up in organization, leadership and tactics.[3]

Germany looked forward to becoming a naval power as well, benefiting in the duality of the renunciation of the Versailles restrictions and the Anglo-German Naval Agreement. The British apparently welcomed the agreement, with Admiral of the Fleet Earl Beatty saying that it would preclude an armament race. The race, however, would take place, but in an unexpected way. The Germans would ultimately emphasize the submarine, not the large surface ships of the British Navy.[4]

At the beginning of 1935 — six months prior to signing this naval agreement — there were about six 250-ton U-boats ready for assembly, and six 275-ton and two 750-ton boats being prepared. Within *eleven days* after the June 18 treaty signing, which permitted U-boat construction, *the first U-boat was put in commission*. Some eleven years later, at the Nuremberg Trials, Raeder defended this activity on the basis that all preparations had been done exclusively abroad, and not in Germany.[5]

In July of 1935, following the Anglo-German Naval Agreement, Germany announced the commissioning of its new submarines and fleet construction plans for:

- two battleships, 26,000 tons each
- two cruisers, 10,000 tons each
- sixteen destroyers
- twenty submarines, 250 tons each
- six submarines, 500 tons each

- two submarines, 750 tons each
- additional battleships to be laid down in 1936 and subsequent years so as to expand the fleet to the agreed upon 35% of that of the British displacement (then 45%, and later going to 100% for submarines)

The British, in early 1935, had 12 battleships, 22 cruisers, 8 carriers, 150 destroyers and 54 submarines.[6]

With the signing of the Anglo-German Agreement in 1935, any naval limitations imposed by Versailles were superseded; the pact enabled Germany to adopt a 35:100 ratio in surface ships with an eventual 1:1 ratio in undersea craft relative to Great Britain. With this change and increase in U-boat complement, Navy Commander-in-Chief Admiral Raeder selected Karl Dönitz to head the new submarine arm of the German Navy.[7]

Dönitz felt that this voluntary acceptance of tonnage limitations lay in Hitler's desire to loosen the Versailles restrictions step by step; Hitler had issued a declaration on March 16, 1935, of Germany's resumption of her rights as a sovereign power and wanted Britain to dissociate herself from the opposition which he anticipated from the other Allied powers, which were intent on continued imposition of the Treaty on Germany. With this in mind he had already initiated negotiations for the naval agreement with Britain, which was signed on June 18. By the time the naval agreement was signed Germany had either already completed or had under construction 24 boats of three different types, all initiated surreptitiously, thereby circumventing Versailles.[8]

In November of 1936 Admiral Raeder deemed it urgent due to the military and political situation to speed up construction of boats *U-41* to *U-51* so as to meet the upper limits of the Anglo-German pact. This followed by some eight months the remilitarization of the Rhineland by German forces; as he said in retrospect, clouds on the horizon as result of the move into the Rhineland caused the armed forces to adopt a posture of the greatest caution.[9]

Raeder and his staff recognized the need for a naval air arm; however, Hermann Göring convinced Hitler of the desirability of a single all-powerful air force under central command. Therefore, the German Navy in World War II was to suffer the consequences of the lack of air reconnaissance and support since the Luftwaffe relegated the navy's needs to a tertiary position.[10]

In the period after the signing of the Anglo-German Naval Agreement and before Germany's eventual renouncing of that treaty in April of 1939, Germany had exceeded by some 20% the per-ship tonnage allowed by the agreement for the battleships *Scharnhorst, Gneisenau, Tirpitz* and *Bismark* and yet reported to the British that the treaty terms were being met. At his post-war trial in Nuremberg, responding to British prosecutor David Maxwell-Fyfe, Raeder could only explain the growth as a technical by-product of design and construction, and gave no reason for Germany's lack of candor in reporting to Britain as required by the agreement.[11]

Britain's acceptance of the terms of the agreement was based on the superiority in surface-ship tonnage mandated for her in the treaty. Since only surface ships and not submarines could provide the sea lane protection which for centuries had been the British Navy's strategic mission, they were willing to agree to an initial submarine parity of 45% and an eventual increase to equality. Further, the British — and even some in the German Navy — had doubts about the efficacy of the submarine; their own development of the Asdic submarine detection system had lulled the British into downgrading the underwater threat.[12]

Politics Stresses the Wehrmacht Internally

With the growth of the Wehrmacht it was inevitable that a cleavage which had political overtones would develop between those officers who had cut their eye teeth during the von Seeckt Reichswehr period of the 1920s and the newer, younger officers. Von Seeckt's philosophy of an apolitical armed force now yielded to increasing politicization of the Wehrmacht. This was easily accommodated in the new Luftwaffe and the smaller navy, but encountered opposing and/or ambivalent reaction in the tradition-bound army.

Werner von Blomberg, joined by generals such as von Reichenau and von Brauchitsch, was an enthusiastic supporter of Hitler, and deflected the efforts of von Seeckt purists such as Chief of the General Staff Ludwig Beck and Army Commander in Chief Freiherr von Fritsch, who attempted to curtail party intrusion and influence in the army. Hitler's momentum, propelled by his increasing foreign policy successes through the 1930s, decided the issue, however, and the services became increasingly politicized.

Organizationally these officers represented older conservatives who strove for a reinstitution of the classic World War I Great General Staff concept wherein the Army General Staff would assume overall supremacy over the three Wehrmacht services.[13] Beck, however, was after more than merely a highly organized Wehrmacht; his objective in trying to get control of the Wehrmacht in the army's hands was control and prevention of war, not its conduct, or at least not involvement in a losing encounter for specious objectives. With this mind he wrote, "Policy is governed by the capacity of the Army ... and the capacity of the Army determines the limits within which the aims of policy must be confined."[14]

Hitler would ultimately solve the issue in 1938 by establishment of a Supreme Command, OKW, over the three services, thereby relegating the Army Command, OKH, to a secondary, but equilateral, rank with the other two services.

A growing contempt, however, was inevitable on the part of many senior and/or conservative officers as they viewed the conduct of the Nazis through the 1930s. Old enough to be immune to radicalization of philosophy and having matured in a culture notable for deep personal and professional integrity, Beck and many of his peers recognized the anti-thesis of the National Socialist world to historic German culture.[15] Whether politically naïve or opportunistic, they had initially supported Hitler's ascension to power as leading to Germany's reemergence as an equal and sovereign member of the world community. The assumption that Hitler and the Nazis could be controlled and channeled to become a regime of laws was an error many fatefully made.[16]

Though a metamorphosis in their thinking developed, most persevered as the balance remained in the new regime's favor. Illustrative of this position is an address given by Army Chief Beck on October 18, 1935, at the reopening of the Kriegsakadamie (War Academy). The Kriegsakadamie, founded by Schornhorst in 1810 and closed by the Versailles Treaty following World War I, was reopened on this date exactly 125 years after its founding. The ceremony was attended by key retired as well as active duty army and Luftwaffe leaders. With

Hitler in the audience, Beck addressed the assemblage, extolling the glory of the "military minded nation" represented by Germany and calling on all to remember "the duty which they owe to the man who recreated and made strong again the German Wehrmacht."[17]

Beck's words reflected the tone of the characteristic military: as late as 1938, OKW would document, "war is still a law of nature ... it serves the survival of the race and state.... This high moral purpose gives war its ethical justification."[18]

Beck represents the enigma, if not anomaly, forced to develop among Wehrmacht officers as they attempted to support the developing economic and military advances of the regime while at the same time retaining a conservative political posture. Beck was a prime mover in building Hitler's army; in fact he had proposed 36 divisions in the initial plan, not the more conservative 21 planned by the government, whose objective had been to try to circumvent anticipated protests by the Allied powers in response to a larger figure. The strategy behind his plan was to eliminate repeated protests by the Allies by announcing the goal for growth in army size as one definitive number. Beck's plan had been for fully equipped combat-ready troops, not skeleton divisions as called for in the government's plan.[19] Events would eventually show that Beck was diverging from the radical politics of the National Socialists even as he gave aggressive support to their rearmament plans.

Trial Balloon for Future Aggression

A major inflection point for German politics emerged in 1936 with Hitler's plan to invade and remilitarize the Rhineland. "I must confess that we had the uneasy feeling of a gambler whose entire fortune was at stake," was Alfred Jodl's reaction to the plan as he expressed it at Nuremberg in 1946.[20]

To the world's most successful politico-psychologist of the moment, the Rhineland seemed an ideal and, to him, a safe excursion into the waters of aggression. After all, it was German territory and France and Britain would rationalize it away to stay on the safe side. The opportunity presented itself with the French-Soviet Mutual Assistance Pact of May 2, 1935. On that same date Hitler's minister of defense von Blomberg issued a secret "By Hand Only" memorandum for Operation SCHULUNG ("training," prophetic term) described as a "surprise blow at lightning speed" to be executed in the west on a date as yet indeterminate. Only a limited number of officers were to be privy in advance, and no mobilization preparations were to be made; if needed, East Prussian forces were to be transported west as reinforcements.[21]

Hitler took no overt action on the matter for the rest of the year — after all, 1935 had seen many audacious diplomatic moves on the part of Germany: the declaration of military sovereignty, the Anglo-German Naval Agreement and the reintroduction of conscription. Then in February of 1936 he announced by diplomatic communiqué that he considered the Locarno Treaty, which guaranteed Germany's western borders, incompatible with the French-Soviet Treaty and, therefore, null and void.

Few officers in OKH or OKW knew earlier than 2 to 3 weeks before the invasion of Hitler's specific intentions when Field Marshal von Blomberg issued his Rhineland occupation order on March 2, 1936. Planners in OKH and OKW were caught by surprise as Z day

Occupation of the Rhineland, 1936; photographed on March 7, 1936, are the first units of the German Army marching into the Rhineland over the Hohenzollern Bridge in Cologne into the zone designated as demilitarized by the Versailles Treaty of 1919. At the same time the German government revoked the Locarno Treaty of 1925. The General Staff officers assigned to prepare the plans — Alfred Jodl, Erich von Manstein, and Ludwig Beck, for example — expressed significant doubts as to the military viability of the reoccupation of the Rhineland in the face of apparently superior French forces watching; however, Hitler would not be dissuaded, and he won this venture, which was fraught with high political risk. Bundesarchiv photo no. S4233.

was then set for March 7. Erich von Manstein, Beck's *Oberquartiermeister I*, or chief of operations, had less than a day to draft orders for the occupation.[22]

The German forces consisted of 1 division, with only 3 battalions deploying west of the Rhine, 1 each to Achen, Saarbruecken and Trier. The generals in OKW felt the French covering army alone could have blown the German forces to bits. Ludwig Beck proposed to Hitler that Germany declare they would not fortify the area west of the Rhine, a proposal the Führer abruptly turned down. He also refused the request of the OKH generals made through von Blomberg that the three battalions be withdrawn provided the French withdrew four or five times as many men. Hitler would have none of this.[23]

All of this trepidation on the part of the generals reinforced the increasing distrust the former corporal harbored for them. In this instance he was right and they were wrong. The French Commander-in-Chief, General Gamelin, declared that if force were to be used, it would entail unpredictable risks and, therefore, could not be undertaken without general mobilization. The French would do no more than man their Maginot Line. In the House of Commons on March 9 the British foreign secretary confirmed his belief that Germany's action did not threaten hostilities.[24]

From now on — to Germany's ultimate peril — the Führer's "intuition" and "political insight" would threaten not only prospective adversaries but his own generals. This was not lost on the many, both military and civilians involved, who recognized increasingly the direction and future consequences of Hitler's actions.

Opportunities in an Expanding Military

But among officers rising in stature and rank in an expanding military, if these developments ever posed a dilemma, it was never sufficient to dissuade the ambitious militarist. Whether in the German military or as civilian leaders in the 1930s, most applauded the moves Hitler was taking to return Germany's sovereignty and economic status. They saw the remilitarization of the Rhineland in 1936 as a reparation for one of the Versailles injustices, and not the microcosm of a flexing of Germany's military and political muscle that would have serious consequences.[25]

If they took issue with Hitler's program in these early years, most Germans of any class saw a net positive coming from the Nazi regime. Many historians agree that had Hitler succumbed before the start of war in 1939, even after the Anschluss (the annexation of Austria), he would have inherited a legacy of singular greatness in German history. After all, he had rebuilt the economy, the military, and German sovereignty and thrown off the shackles of Versailles without firing a shot.

Many of the eventual top military leaders of the Third Reich's World War II campaigns assumed strategic organizational positions in the hierarchy during this period of rapid and aggressive expansion. Hermann Göring, in setting up the new Luftwaffe, had, as Commander-in-Chief, surrounded himself with his early flying associates. These were individuals whose loyalty both he and Hitler felt was assured.[26] A litmus test to be passed by the cadre was political accommodation and support of an increasingly radical and, at times passed, despotic leadership. For most of those recruited for key Luftwaffe spots, apolitical accommodation of the regime's leadership, beginning as it had for most of them in the inter-war von Seeckt Reichswehr, was not a precipitous issue. It was gradual and proportionate to the demands of the period.

One of the key selectees from the old Reichswehr for Göring's Luftwaffe was Albrecht Kesselring, who would rise to top air and army commands. If political conflict entered Kesselring's thinking, it would have been in the picture primarily in the last few years of his military career — 1943–45. Otherwise Kesselring, typical of many officers and the ranks in the rapidly expanding Wehrmacht, appears to have encountered an upwardly mobile, compatible and supportive environment under the Hitler regime. Kesselring, as one of Göring's key officers in the new Reichs Air Ministry, agreed with Göring that the new Luftwaffe they configured and designed was to be used as an offensive weapon which would force political solutions because an air force, they agreed, could not be otherwise configured.[27]

An Ideologic Chameleon

Military leaders such as Beck, Rommel, von Rundstedt and many of their peers gave continued support to the regime even though they were on the horns of a dilemma because their personal stances were in many cases compromised by the radical nature of National Socialist politics. Others such as Dönitz, Kesselring and Raeder seem not to have been perturbed, but accepted and went along as if the politics of the matter were irrelevant — and perhaps they were for many as long as upward mobility continued. The Army Chief of Staff at the time of Hitler's ascension, Kurt von Hammerstein, was an ardent anti–Nazi from the outset, and retired a year after Hitler took power. He was recalled with the outbreak of war, and would have participated in anti–Hitler action with the conspirators if his troops and assignment had allowed, which it did not.[28] Some early Hitler associates such as Erich Ludendorff, World War I Chief of Staff to Paul von Hindenburg, had left the party and severed association with the Führer because, in Ludendorff's case, he had lost confidence in and was critical of Hitler's veracity by the time he had taken power.[29]

The naval leadership, as noted above, seems to have been solidly in Hitler's camp, however. The impression Hitler made on Erich Raeder in the early period was that of an extraordinary man born to lead, with great charm, cordiality and "incredible sixth sense in determining how far he could go ... with others."[30] In those early days Raeder was convinced that attacks on the church or some reported Nazi brutality were not ordered by Hitler, a perception he based on Hitler's bearing, his words and the general impression Hitler made.

Similarly, if such rising officers as Karl Dönitz and Albrecht Kesselring saw any negatives in the regime they rationalized them as they rose in their careers. For then-captain Dönitz personal success in the pivotal year of 1935 overwhelmed any serious misgivings concerning Hitler's party. In fact, this continued for both men throughout their careers.

Alternatively, the regime was viewed critically from the sidelines as "that pack of presumptuous vulgarians" in the diary entry of Italy's foreign minister, Count Galeazzo Ciano.[31] From the inside, Hjalmar Schacht, once Hitler's minister of economics and earlier Reichsbank president, observed retrospectively, "under Hitler we meet with nothing but gaping boredom and emptiness in all intellectual, scholarly and artistic spheres."[32] So those who no longer profited from the association with the regime and could suffer no retribution could produce enlightening, but not surprising, critical assessment.

This early period in Hitler's Third Reich elicited polarized responses from his military leadership. However, by the mid–1930s any negatives seemed to have been outweighed by the overt successes and advances made — employment was up, the West was accepting the reversal of Versailles, the military was expanding, even with acquiescence if not endorsement of the Allies. A small incipient movement of disagreement within the Wehrmacht with Hitler's policies did find its genesis in this period and would slowly grow despite his successes and because of his failure to recognize and/or act on warnings of a future debacle.

4 Conspiracy to Make War
Hitler Overcomes Officer Corps Opposition

Hitler's long-espoused objective of *Lebensraum* ("living space") in the East for the German people at the expense of those European neighbors affected was greatly enhanced by his success in gaining control of the Wehrmacht structure, and particularly the recalcitrant army. The army fatefully declined to accede to efforts within its officer corps to stop his potential warmaking. He had convinced them the rewards outweighed the danger to the country of any threat of war.

The Initial Conspiracy

Late in the afternoon of November 5, 1937, Hitler assembled his commanders in chief and presented them with a plan for aggression, one that the victors of World War II would consider a key element in the original conspiracy to wage aggressive war, Count One of the Nuremberg Indictment.

Hitler spoke endlessly, as was his custom, in this conference known as the Hossbach Meeting, and he said some damning things. Germany needed more living space — the question to be solved was where to get it at the lowest possible cost. Force was the only way, he said, and "it must be our first aim [therefore] to conquer Czechoslovakia and Austria."[1]

Von Blomberg, von Fritsch and Constantin von Neurath all objected to his plans, to their subsequent peril, whereas Hermann Göring and Erich Raeder raised no objections. Though secrecy was called for by Hitler, Colonel Hossbach, who had transcribed the meeting, showed its contents to Army Chief Ludwig Beck, as did Foreign Minister von Neurath.[2] Beck agreed that von Fritsch, army Commander-in-Chief, should attempt to reclaim the situation and pull the Führer back from the brink of war in view of the serious military consequences to Germany. Pragmatist as always, and further, as a military professional, Beck was, according to associates, strongly opposed to aggressive war; he felt the army must be a strong defensive force, making an attack on Germany unlikely.[3]

The Year of Incipient Cataclysm Begins

Apparently action as opposed to cerebration characterized the National Socialists. Too, Hitler could not tolerate members of his leadership circle who did not wholeheartedly support his program. Accordingly, the three who had raised objections to Hitler's Hossbach plans — von Neurath, von Fritsch and von Blomberg — were destined to be cashiered as soon as a propitious situation developed.

Col. General Ludwig Beck, Chief of the Army General Staff; sharply critical of Hitler's plans to control Europe, he was forced into retirement in 1938, and met his death in the aftermath of the 1944 attempt on Hitler's life. Ullstein bild/The Granger Collection, New York.

Intrigue on the part of Göring and Himmler was the genesis of the cases of both von Fritsch and von Blomberg. Given the circumstances in each of these cases Hitler was provided the foundation for reorganizing the command structure of the Wehrmacht, and particularly the army, along lines that would afford him maximum control. Von Blomberg was removed as the result of his marriage to a woman from the lower social strata, who ultimately was found to have a police record and a questionable past. Particularly damaging was the fact that Hitler and Göring had been present at his wedding, and prior to that Göring had endorsed the marriage. Once rumors spread, the dossier became known and the lady had to go. Beck, ever mindful of General Staff honor, concurred that divorce or removal from the officer list was demanded; as he said, "One cannot permit the highest ranking officer to marry a whore."[4]

With that development Hitler assumed von Blomberg's position as minister of defense, thereby becoming supreme commander of the Wehrmacht. At the same time (on February 4, 1938), he appointed Wilhelm Keitel as

Hitler in March of 1940 with then-Army Commander-in-Chief Col. General Walter von Brau-chitsch, later field marshal; designated by the Führer as army chief in the 1938 organizational upheaval, von Brauchitsch was near the end of his tenure. Bundesarchiv photo no. 183/ 2001/0706/501— AV 58448.

chief of OKW, an appointment that would be half of a duality designed to facilitate his control over the services from OKW.[5]

Von Fritsch, army Commander-in-Chief, was framed by Heinrich Himmler and his deputy Reinhardt Heydrich using trumped-up charges of homosexuality, charges that were ultimately, but belatedly, proven untrue. However, time was of the essence to Hitler, who wanted to make a clean sweep of the army high command, and von Fritsch was dismissed before any fair trial was held.

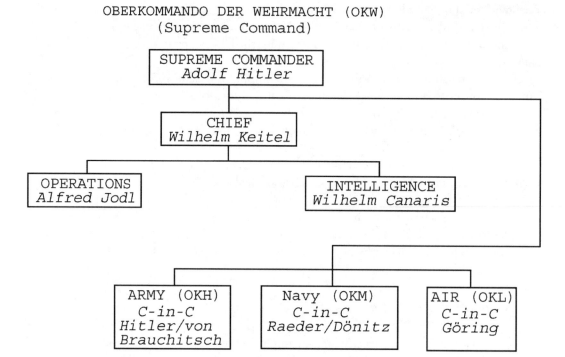

OBERKOMMANDO DER WEHRMACHT (OKW)
(Supreme Command)

SUPREME COMMANDER
Adolf Hitler

CHIEF
Wilhelm Keitel

OPERATIONS
Alfred Jodl

INTELLIGENCE
Wilhelm Canaris

ARMY (OKH)
C-in-C
Hitler/von
Brauchitsch

Navy (OKM)
C-in-C
Raeder/Dönitz

AIR (OKL)
C-in-C
Göring

German Military Organization, 1938–45

Whereas Gerd von Rundstedt had endorsed Hitler's earlier move against the SA in the Night of the Long Knives affair in 1934, which supported the army, he saw the prestige of the army compromised in the dismissal of von Fritsch. The honor of the highly regarded von Fritsch was important to army leaders, and accordingly, von Rundstedt and Beck went together to Hitler on January 31, 1938, to plead for a Court of Honor for von Fritsch. Hitler reluctantly agreed. Von Rundstedt further urged Hitler to reappoint von Fritsch to his old position as army Commander-in-Chief once he had cleared himself, but Hitler refused. Instead, after some negotiation, he suggested Walther von Brauchitsch, which von Rundstedt accepted; to the army this was a better alternative than Hitler's actual favored selection, von Reichenau, who was considered by the army a political radical.[6]

Wilhelm Keitel, whom Hitler had elevated to chief of OKW concurrent with cashiering von Blomberg and assuming the role of Supreme Commander, had been afforded high visibility in his prior jobs by both von Blomberg and von Fritsch. Von Fritsch had recommended Keitel as chief of the Armed Forces Office and von Blomberg had maintained a close relationship with Keitel.[7] This had placed Keitel in a prominent and visible position by the time Hitler reorganized the command structure of the Wehrmacht in 1938, and he was a logical selection by Hitler as chief of OKW. In that position Keitel would play a key, if not totally dominant, role in Hitler's running of the future war.

Now the army staff and other responsible army generals began to hound von Brauchitsch day and night demanding he support his predecessor's immediate rehabilitation and reinstatement, and that von Fritsch further be promoted to field marshal. Hitler was not about to accede: he could not admit he had been a victim of deceit in von Fritsch's case, and, anyway, he now had a hand-picked Commander-in-Chief he considered more amenable to his dictates. The army had now finally passed a major watershed, losing prestige and yielding dominance to the Führer.[8]

But General Beck was not through with attempting to reclaim von Fritsch's honor. He convinced von Fritsch to challenge Himmler to a duel for his deplorable role in the affair. The challenge was signed by von Fritsch and given to von Rundstedt for delivery. The latter could not see his way clear to encourage this bloodletting, and, in time, convinced von Fritsch to let the matter drop.[9]

Though von Fritsch had been cleared by the court, his replacement by von Brauchitsch was not rescinded nor was his status restored, and he died as an honorary colonel on the Eastern Front. Many in the army — Guderian is representative — felt this was a black day for the army. In fact, the lack of trust represented by von Fritsch's fate permeated Hitler's deteriorating relationship with the army to the end.[10] Nevertheless, it took the turning of the tide from victory to looming defeat for the generals to eventually act on this cleavage.

One General Takes Action

Following the Blomberg-Fritsch affair, Army Chief of Staff Beck was consumed by the irresponsible attitude the German hierarchy under Hitler took toward a possible war and their casual belief that any conflict would be short-lived.[11]

Beck elected as a consequence to attempt to remove from Hitler his warmaking means — the generals. During the months of May, June and July of 1938 he drafted three significant memorandums addressing the catastrophic military-political prospects that any implementation of the Hossbach Meeting Plan of November 5, 1937, would promise Germany. He laid each on his superior, Commander in Chief von Brauchitsch, asking him to take action, as was the Commander-in-Chief's prerogative, in influencing the senior generals.

In Beck's first memorandum, dated May 5, 1938, and which he gave to von Brauchitsch on May 7, he wrote in essence:

> The potential power balance in Europe, should a war develop, would align France and England against Germany; in fact, they are already aligning themselves, as in 1914, politically and militarily, and as in the earlier conflagration, they would draw on America as supplier of military needs. Russia surely, and possibly Italy, would align themselves against Germany in any eventual war. The rest of Europe would be subject in its alignment to forces brought to bear by the potential combatants.
>
> Though England has sought up to now to avoid war and France continues to abhor a conflict, they are commencing to rearm. Sentiment against Germany is especially negative among the English intelligentsia. France sees significance in the Anschluss as a precursor of events to come and may feel honor bound to support the Czechs should they be threatened. England would follow France into such a fray, would ultimately lead, and, though the Czech cause might be lost in the early stages, the Western Powers, with America's help, would prevail over Germany and Germany's allies in a protracted war.
>
> The military balance pits Germany against unacceptable odds — all the Western Powers enhanced by Russia and the small powers. In the long war the adversary envisions and will conduct Germany will not be successful.[12]

37

Hitler's first field marshal, Werner von Blomberg, defense minister, with Col. General Freiherr Werner von Fritsch, Commander-in-Chief of the army, and Admiral Erich Raeder, Commander-in-Chief of the navy, in 1936. The first two men lost their jobs in 1938 by disagreeing with Hitler's plans for taking over Europe, as laid out in the Hossbach meeting of November 1937. Ullstein bild/The Granger Collection, New York.

Von Brauchitsch may well have had the fortitude to leak the contents of this first memorandum to Hitler or at least to Field Marshal Keitel, now OKW chief, and/or Col.-General Alfred Jodl, next in line in OKW. These were the two officers that functioned for the rest of the Third Reich's existence as Hitler's dual messengers, sometimes called toadies. He used them to facilitate his control of the Wehrmacht. Not coincidentally, Hitler convened the senior leaders of state and party on May 28 and essentially countered and negated the general points made in Beck's memorandum.[13]

Beck, who was present, then drafted his second memorandum and presented it to von Brauchitsch on May 30; in it he first discusses points of agreement with Hitler, then his points of disagreement, and finally, presents a sharp critique of Hitler's plans for war against Czechoslovakia:

> It is correct that Germany needs more *lebensraum* and that Czechoslovakia as constituted by the Versailles Treaty "is intolerable for Germany" and this must be rectified even if by violence. However, France and England stand as an impediment to any such expansion of power by Germany, and, indeed, are responsible for "Czechoslovakia's [current] militarily provocative

Hitler with his adjutant, Col. Friedrich Hossbach (to his right) in September of 1937 at maneuvers in Mecklenburg. Hossbach is notable for his having transcribed Hitler's November 5, 1937, conference with his five commanders in chief, where he laid out his plans to take over Europe. Three that disagreed — Neurath, Blomberg and Fritsch — were shortly replaced. Ullstein bild/The Granger Collection, New York.

attitude." Under these circumstances it behooves Germany to line up support of Hungary, Poland and Yugoslavia.

Though the national and ideological unity of Germany of the late 1930s provides strength, this is overbalanced by multiple weaknesses and personal resources in terms of war space, finance and the foe's material and personnel resources. The great political successes of 1933–38 are no guarantee of the future, and, in fact, have themselves caused the alignment of the West against Germany. If the German populace could be caused to favor war, and that is doubtful, should such a war to solve the Czech question draw in France and England, "the campaign against Czechoslovakia can run its course successfully, but Germany will lose the war."

The current command structure whereby the Commander-in-Chief of the Wehrmacht [Beck refers here to Hitler, but not by name] proceeds without constant expert professional military advice on questions of warfare is untenable. The impractical but intensified work on the Siegfried Line — the West Wall — and the resort to surprise attack as the primary rationale around which an entire plan of operations revolves as opposed to sober reflection are but two examples of this *modus operandi*. Unless this changes, the fate of German Armed Forces as well as Germany itself in a future war can be viewed "in only the blackest of colors."[14]

Beck was only in error by one in terms of Hitler's confrontations — no one aided the Czechs so few shots were fired, but Poland, the second, would be the fuse igniting World War II and Germany's ultimate demise, as he had predicted.

That same day, May 30, 1938, Hitler signed *Fall Gruen* (Case GREEN), plans for the war on Czechoslovakia,[15] in which he said, in part, "It is my unalterable decision to smash Czechoslovakia by military action in the near future."[16]

Alfred Jodl of OKW records a note of caution in his war diary on that same date, May 30, saying, "The whole contrast becomes acute once more between the Führer's intuition that we *must* do it this year and the opinion of the army that we cannot do it as yet, as most certainly the Western Powers will interfere and we are not as yet equal to them."[17]

Beck, despairing of von Brauchitsch's lack of personal adversarial initiative where the Führer was concerned, now drafted a third significant memorandum, which he presented to von Brauchitsch on July 16 together with a proposal for concerted action on the part of the generals.

In this latter proposal he recommended that the generals be convened and the critical issue of war or peace and consequent destruction or salvation for Germany depended on their influence and leadership. "Their soldierly obedience has a limit where their knowledge, their conscience and their responsibility forbid the carrying out of an order. If their advice and warnings find no audience ... then they have the right and obligation to resign from their offices.... If they all act with one united will, then ... [war] will be impossible." Beck went on to point out that absent "the intoxication of ideology," it can only be concluded that Germany was not capable of war either from an economic, military or political basis, and that if their effort to avert war succeeded, the radical side would incite "considerable internal political tensions" and the army would need to defend itself against accusations of having scuttled the Führer's plans.[18]

Beck's third memorandum, that of July 16, reiterated that:

> Based on all current information, France and England will inevitably come to Czechoslovakia's aid if Germany attacks: French Premier Daladier, in his speech of July 12, has made France's position clear, saying, "The French ... [position regarding] Czechoslovakia ... [is] ineluctable and sacred for us." Therefore, Germany is facing a European if not a world war, which, for Germany, will "end not only in a military catastrophe but in a general one for Germany."
>
> The German people hold their military leader responsible to not undertake anything militarily that does not have an adequate prospect of success. Both the people and the army leadership feel instinctively that such prospects do not exist. The Czechs are now in a defensive posture so that surprise is no longer an option. Therefore, a quick victory cannot be seen as an inhibitor to action on the part of France or England. Consequently, the matter devolves into "a war over life and death for Germany" as opposed to simply intervention on behalf of Czechoslovakia.
>
> Help through alliances with prospective allies — Poland, Hungary and Italy — is unsure. Under these conditions Germany now enters a two-front war with the army initially preoccupied in the Southeast [Czechoslovakia] campaign, while deferring a Western [French Front] deployment with attendant damage on that front. A diversion of German forces from East Prussia not only promises delay in rectifying the Western Front, but opens Germany to Polish mischief.
>
> [Although Beck's first draft of the following conclusion tendered his resignation should the course not be altered, he reconsidered and withdrew that threat.] In conclusion, "I consider myself obligated ... [in view of my position] to request *that the highest Commander-in-Chief of the Armed Forces [Hitler] suspend the war preparations that he has ordered.*" The military conditions for Germany are hopeless, and this view is shared by all the *Oberquartiermeistern* [Deputy Chiefs of the General Staff] and department heads of the General Staff.
>
> A discussion between the army Commander-in-Chief and the commanding generals should be conducted so that a clear and unified position can be presented to the Führer in a subsequent meeting with him. Further, the army Commander-in-Chief should attempt to effect unity on this issue with the other commanders in chief, Raeder and Göring.[19]

Responding to Beck's urging and/or, as he said in testimony as a witness at Nuremberg, because he believed Beck's argument to be "absolutely fundamental," von Brauchitsch finally convened the generals in early August, even as *Fall Gruen* preparations proceeded. Beck had gone so far as to prepare a speech to be given by von Brauchitsch in presenting the Beck memorandum. But no call for action came from von Brauchitsch, a man who was never able to stand against Hitler. Rationalizing the majority of Germans supported Hitler, von Brauchitsch had persuaded himself to go along, according to post-war statements he made while a POW of the British at Bridgend, Wales.[20]

Von Brauchitsch did, however — based on unanimous approval of the generals — present Beck's memorandum to Hitler. A heated argument ensued culminating in Hitler's telling von Brauchitsch that "he [Hitler] alone knew quite what he had to do." Hitler further forbade "once and for all" any interference in his policy by the generals and demanded "unconditional obedience."[21]

Hitler's formal response came in the form of a meeting convened on August 10 of the chiefs of staff — except for Beck who was not invited — at the Berghof. When General Weitersheim raised the question — and this was the last such meeting where questions were entertained — of inadequate German military strength to hold the western fortifications for more that three weeks, Hitler exploded with, "I assure you, General, the position will not only be held for three weeks, but for three years." And the generals? They retreated en masse: no protest, no démarche.[22]

Beck's persistence opened the widening cleavage between von Brauchitsch and himself; it finally confirmed his absolute rejection of Hitler's policies, leading to Beck's retirement on August 21. However, Hitler, as was his practice, insisted on an absence of notoriety. Franz Halder replaced Beck immediately, though Beck's retirement was announced quietly on October 31 so as not to adversely affect the Führer's persona.

The Last Conservative Influence

> [T]he German High Command from 1938 on is one ... in which military judgment was increasingly subordinated to Hitler's personal dictates ... 1938 ... [saw] the removal of von Blomberg, von Fritsch, and Beck, and of the last conservative influence on German foreign policy.

So reported the Chief of Staff of the U.S. Army in his report of June 1945 to the U.S. secretary of war.[23]

Germany's political direction since Hitler's accession had been typified by the cashiering and replacement of independent-minded leaders with subordinates Hitler could control. This latest reorganization of the military lent the coup de grace to Reichswehr tradition and influence. Under such oppressive leadership prescient observers saw the reemergence of a virulent form of German militarism with concomitant disaster.[24]

5 The Anschluss/Czech Transition

The Pan-German Era Brings Expanded Military Opportunity

Hitler, now supreme commander, was ready to embark on his long-time plan of Eastward expansion for Lebensraum. The military applauded the Austrian Anschluss, and then the peaceful settlement of relations with the Czechs through the Munich Agreement. If the seizure of Prague, which broke that agreement, represented a move to armed conflict, most of the military still felt Hitler would solve inter-country issues peacefully in the end. Meanwhile, the more politically attuned navy saw reason to anticipate and prepare for a broadened threat, that of Great Britain.

The Politics of "Cold War" Aggression

Hitler's chosen army and Supreme Command leaders were now in place; accordingly, his European plans escalated, especially intended, as Hjalmar Schacht, his former economics minister, points out, to create a fog around the furor created by the Blomberg-Fritsch affair. Keitel received a call from Hitler on February 12, 1938, asking that Keitel be present at the Berghof (Berchtesgaden, Hitler's primary residence) within the hour as Hitler was expecting a visit from the Austrian Chancellor Schuschnigg. There was to be a serious discussion of problems between Germany and Austria, Hitler told Keitel, and he wanted Keitel and Generals Sperrle and Reichenau present "so that Schuschnigg would see a few uniforms around [and] the significance would not be lost on their guest."[1]

Keitel was much impressed by this new experience, which when the details were relayed to Alfred Jodl, chief of OKW operations, caused the latter to pen in his diary, "Schuschnigg signs under the strongest political and military pressure."[2]

By the following month Hitler had moved events to the point of armed intervention in Austria. On March 11 Hitler issued, and Keitel and Jodl initialed (as would be their standard procedure for the duration of the Third Reich), Hitler's directive, Operation OTTO in this instance, which was the forced union of Austria and Germany. Point One of the Operation OTTO memorandum sets forth the ostensible objective of the action with the words, "I intend to invade Austria with armed forces to establish constitutional conditions and to prevent further outrages against the pro–German population."[3]

Keitel, in his role as chief of OKW, acquiesced completely so that when both the Army General Staff and army Commander-in-Chief asked Keitel to persuade Hitler to call off the operation, he made no attempt to intercede with the Führer. In due time, however, he called the army chiefs back to advise that Hitler had rejected both protests.[4]

Most German generals approved of and applauded Hitler's political successes of the mid- to late 1930s, which started in early 1938 with the Anschluss, the peaceful invasion of and union with Austria. To Heinz Guderian the Anschluss was an occasion for "rejoicing" for both countries; the Germans seemed to be welcomed by the populace, who apparently felt a pan–German affinity, and, of course, the spirit of the military procession pervaded the crowds. Following meetings witht the Austrian generals, Guderian set out on a tour of units of the Austrian Army to assess how best to incorporate them into the German army.[5]

With this union, which violated the Versailles restrictions, the German military leaders sensed apprehension in the West. Though the German Army was not yet ready for war, it could have made short shrift of the outdated Western armies, in the view of the German military leadership. The Western generals were considerably more skeptical than their politicians as to their ability to confront the Germans if that were required; they saw no way to build up the needed strength given the political climate of the day. Guderian, reflecting what the majority of generals in any army feel prior to the start of war, felt that differences could, hopefully, be resolved peacefully, and that was the feeling of most, though not all, in the inter-war Reichswehr.[6]

The Anschluss had been bloodless, though attended by significant international and internal stresses. It represented an amplification of the Prague invasion as well as one more implicit warning to prescient observers of future events. This trend had been what Ludwig Beck's memorandums had been intended to mitigate when he attempted to marshal the generals against Hitler's plans for aggression. The generals, however, had been persuaded against action, and Beck's proposition went for naught against the Führer's determination and their own obvious lack thereof and/or latent support.[7] Typical of their thinking was Albrecht Kesselring, who wrote retrospectively that he "rejoiced at the reincorporation of Austria into the German Reich" through the Anschluss. The years of National Socialist intrigue that culminated in this forced union and the events it could portend were not an issue with this seemingly apolitical commander and many of his peers.[8]

German Intrigue Shifts Europe's Power Structure

Much strategic-political intrigue on the part of the Germans followed the Anschluss. The late March 1938 entry in Jodl's diary reveals the anatomy of the plans: "After the annexation of Austria, the Führer mentions that there is no hurry to solve the Czech question because Austria has to be digested first. Nevertheless, preparations for Case GREEN [*Fall Gruen*, the plan against Czechoslovakia] will have to be carried out energetically ... [because] of the changed strategic position ... [following] the annexation of Austria."[9]

Jodl retrospectively, in his June 6, 1946, testimony at Nuremberg and earlier in a speech given on November 7, 1943, referred to Czechoslovakia's position following the Austrian Anschluss as being enclosed in a pincers with a strategic position so unfavorable she would fall victim to any vigorous attack (see map, "German Acquisitions, 1935 through Mid-1939"; page 45).[10]

The strategic position of Czechoslovakia blocked pan–German expansion eastward, Hitler's long-time ambition; politically, Hitler wished to absorb the 3–4 million ethnic Germans in the Sudetenland, and their territory, and, thereby solve the multifaceted geopolitical issue confronting and impeding his plans.

Czechoslovakia was high on Hitler's agenda, and in late April of 1938 he ordered preliminary General Staff studies for a conflict with that country. The Czech problem, Hitler said to Keitel, would have to be solved sometime, because of the way in which the Czech government was oppressing the German population living there but also because of the strategically impossible situation if the time came for the reckoning with the East, that is Lebensraum. Hitler meant not just the Poles but particularly the Bolsheviks. However, he said he had no intention of unleashing a war on the Czechs, but that politics might take over! His key words were, "for the time being it is not my intention." Keitel in no way got the impression from all this that provocation would be employed, or so he said in his testimony at Nuremberg.[11]

Yet notes on Keitel's meetings and discussions on the subject with Hitler in April of 1938 imply Hitler's desire to move against Czechoslovakia, but only on some diplomatic or other provocation so as to avoid hostile world opinion. By May 30 *Fall Gruen*, the action against Czechoslovakia, had been issued as Most Secret. It noted Germany's "unalterable decision to smash Czechoslovakia by military action in the near future."[12]

Jodl writes in his diary that by May 30, 1938, "The Führer signs directive GREEN, where he states his final decision to destroy Czechoslovakia soon and thereby initiates military preparation all along the line." Further, Hitler felt this must be done this year of 1938, whereas the army felt Germany was not ready, given the possible interference of the Western Powers.[13] The army was still apprehensive in view of the defense alliance of France with the Czechs, despite Hitler's implied threat and his attempt to discourage their honoring of the alliance by erection of fortifications between France and Germany. This defensive line was known as the "West Wall" or Siegfried Line. The army's negativity grew out of concern for tactical deficiencies of the West Wall fortifications if France reacted negatively.[14] For Jodl, the army was unenthusiastic because they did not, in the final analysis, "believe in the genius of the Führer." Though this schism between Hitler and his generals was common talk, Jodl was sure Hitler could overcome consequent morale problems "when the right moment comes."[15]

One of the few remaining opportunities to avoid further armed intervention on Germany's

German Acquisitions, 1935 through Mid–1939

part had been presented by Ludwig Beck through his memorandums; his prescient warning, which could have upset all of Hitler's plans and aspirations, was deflected by the army's inaction. There are an obvious multitude of rationales for their inaction, but clearly Hitler's success thus far in leading Germany out of the Versailles morass both economically and socially, but particularly in the rearmament of Germany, were strong inducements against action by the military leaders.[16]

Keitel was occupied during the same period, the summer of 1938, with large-scale "maneuvers" in Silesia, Saxony and Bavaria in preparation for the attack on Czechoslovakia. Every imaginable camouflage was used to conceal the operation; Hitler himself suggested many of the ideas. General Jodl had prepared the timetable so that Hitler had only to fix the date for D-day.[17] Hitler, of course, had been responsible for the overall strategic ideas, and his two OKW seconds, Jodl and Keitel, knew their roles by this point.

In fact Keitel had found by now that Hitler was difficult to deal with, not just for him personally, but for everyone. "If he got an idea into his head, no man on earth could ever shake him out of it; he always had his way, whether it was approved or disapproved by his advisors." When, for example, Halder and von Brauchitsch differed with him on the combining of armored formations in Czechoslovakia, Hitler tolerated nothing but obedience to his strict orders. Note that Generals Guderian and von Manstein, who were of stiffer timber, would later suffer the loss of their commands during the 1941–44 Russian Campaign for having the fortitude to speak up to Hitler.[18]

Prior to the Czech crisis in late 1938, but as an aspect of his plans for that country, Hitler succeeded in dissuading the French from honoring their existing defense alliance with Czechoslovakia. He did this, in part, by authorizing Dr. Todt, the inspector-general of road building, to begin construction of over 5000 small bunkers as a "West Wall" along the sector between Karlsruhe and Aix-la-Chapelle (see map of German acquisitions page 45).[19] Keitel felt this was a major factor in influencing the French when the question of ceding the Sudetenland resulted in the 1938 Munich "Peace in Our Time" meetings. By this point the French attitude on the Sudetenland question was expressed by French President Daladier, when he said, "We won't tolerate war over this, the Czechs will just have to give way. We will simply have to force them to accept the cession."[20] As to the British response at Munich, politics aside, they were in an early stage of rearmament and in no position to counter Hitler regardless of internal politics in England.[21]

By May 21 of 1938 the Prague government, alarmed by reports of German troop concentrations in Saxony and Silesia and aware of the German-fomented unrest in the Sudetenland, initiated strategic troop concentrations within Czechoslovakia. Hitler, now afraid of loss of prestige, according to Alfred Jodl, signed Operation GREEN, and the die was cast.[22]

Hitler's subsequent directive of June 18, 1938, initialed by both Keitel and Jodl, called for solution of the Czech problem by a deadline of October 1, but he would take action only if "as in the case of the occupation of the demilitarized zone [Rhineland, 1936] and the entry into Austria [Anschluss of March 12, 1938] ... I [Hitler] am firmly convinced ... that France will not march and therefore England will not intervene."[23]

In Jodl's view, the Führer's basis for any military action was to be a surprise attack, and four days' advance notice would be required for the army to assemble in battle position. An "incident" would either have to present itself, or, according to Jodl, they might have to help it along a bit by exploiting one of the minor incidents that occurred continually on the frontier.

Accordingly, Jodl, with Hitler's endorsement, issued a memorandum of August 24, 1938, which records the first steps in the seizure of Czechoslovakia as follows, "Operation GRUEN will be set in motion by means of an 'incident' in Czechoslovakia, which will give Germany provocation for military intervention."[24]

The genesis of the "incident" lay in Hitler's exacerbation of normal irredentist tensions among Czechoslovakia's citizens of German heritage living predominately in the Sudetenland. One of them, Konrad Henlein, was selected by the German National Socialists to assume political leadership of the Sudeten Germans, and he was subsidized from 1935 on by the party. So important was this liaison to German plans that Henlein started meeting with Hitler soon after the Austrian Anschluss. By mid–September of 1938 OKW had assigned a German officer,

Lt. Colonel Koechling, as advisor to Henlein.[25] The "incident" involved the demands of the Sudeten Germans for autonomy, as well as instigation of similar demands through Henlein on the part of the Slovaks. The harassed Czech government was also subjected to threatening diplomatic tactics intended to increase tension.

The "incident" was catalyzed by Hitler's Nuremberg National Party Day (Reichsparteitag) closing address of September 12, when he accused Czech president Benes of torturing and planning the extermination of Sudeten Germans. Supplementing this, Henlein's Free Corps was tasked to maintain disturbances and clashes in the Sudetenland. In response, the Czechs mobilized their armed forces partially on September 14 and fully on the 23rd, which Hitler then seized on as the "incident."[26]

Hitler's provocative speech at the National Party Day reflected the growing tension between Germany and Czechoslovakia.[27] To the Czechs as well as Germans the future began to look ominous. Germans in the Sudetenland felt the impending wrath of the Czechs and were ready to pack on short notice. Czechs on both sides of the border were in the same position relative to the Germans, afraid of impending political moves by either side. In late September the army began to prepare for the march into the Sudetenland. The generals felt the refusal of the Czechs to agree to any concessions had increased the possibility of war.[28]

September of 1938 brought a series of conferences between the concerned parties, most important of which were negotiations between Britain's Neville Chamberlain and Hitler. However, while the meetings were taking place Hitler was setting the stage for the result he desired: Jodl's diary of September 16 recorded the preparation notes: "The order is given ... to line up ... [troops] along the Czech border ... [and for] the railways to empty rolling stock in readiness clandestinely ... so ... [the army] can be transported starting 28 September."[29]

On September 26 Hitler gave a speech in Berlin saying of his discussions with Chamberlain, "I assured him ... when this problem is solved there will be no more territorial problems for Germany in Europe.... When Czechoslovakia solves its other problems ... with their other minorities ... I will no longer be interested in the Czech State ... I will guarantee it. We don't want any Czechs."[30]

However, by the end of September the Munich Agreement had cleared the way for a peaceful solution, and without bloodshed for the immediate future. This was the feeling among military leadership, as reflected in Alfred Jodl's diary entry for September 29, 1938. "The pact of Munich is signed. Czechoslovakia as a power is out.... The genius of the Führer and his determination not to shun even a World War have again won the victory without the use of force. The hope remains that the incredulous, the weak and the doubtful people have been converted and will remain that way."[31]

Jodl's diary entry followed the fateful meeting in Munich where "peace in our time" was sealed by Europe's leaders, France's Daladier, Mussolini from Italy, Chamberlain and their host, Hitler. The German public greeted the visitors enthusiastically, filling the streets. Following three weeks of tenuous meetings between Chamberlain and Hitler, the pact was signed by the parties on September 30 without much further discussion giving over the Sudetenland of Czechoslovakia to the Third Reich.

Then-Czech President Eduard Benes marked this as Europe's final escalation down the slippery slope of appeasement; the initial move in this direction had begun in 1935 with

France's Pierre Laval and Britain's Sir Samuel Hoare giving Italy's Duce the OK for his aggression against Abyssinia.[32]

Eight years later Jodl, on trial at Nuremberg for his part in war crimes, was questioned by British Prosecutor Geoffrey Roberts: had war not been averted by the Munich Pact, would Germany have used the "incident" as the reason for going to war? "No," Jodl replied, the world would have been told the truth "that three and one half million Germans cannot be used as slaves by another people permanently. That was the issue."[33]

Reality on this point, for former chancellor Kurt von Schuschnigg of Austria, who was deposed and imprisoned by Hitler at the time of the Anschluss in 1938, was that all the tightly compacted countries of Europe hosted "irredentists," foreigners within respective borders who may to some extent have felt unfairly treated by the host government. In fact, Schuschnigg estimated some 27 million such people lived in countries such as Yugoslavia, Hungary, Czechoslovakia, Poland, Rumania and Italy. However, they were there for — to them as well as local industry — beneficial economic reasons, a situation that has always persisted. *What Hitler did was to exacerbate incipient pressures to support his rearrangment of European power.*[34]

Germany's Peaceful Conquests Heat Up

By the close of 1938 the army looked forward to peaceful assimilation of the newly acquired territories. The military applauded the acquisition of the Sudetenland and the positive effect it was to have on the Sudeten Germans. However, their greatest satisfaction was that the political situation had taken a peaceful turn, or so it appeared.[35] Heinz Guderian felt Hitler's great achievements in foreign policy had dissipated any negative feelings among the German military due to National Socialist tactics internally.

To some in the leadership, such as Karl Dönitz, the Anschluss of 1938, a key element of Hitler's early series of political successes followed by the acquisition of the Sudetenland through the Munich Agreement, was a chronology of political and economic success all patriotic Germans could applaud. As to the obverse side of National Socialism, Dönitz claims he knew practically nothing up to late 1938: "We officers most firmly disassociated ourselves from the excesses" that began to appear, that is they disapproved of these actions of the party and the regime. Dönitz requested his commanding officer, Admiral Boehm, as did others, to so advise the navy Commander-in-Chief, Admiral Raeder, of his disagreement with the excesses he had observed, he claims. His assumption was that Raeder would in turn pursue the issue with Hitler, surely a vain hope given the abject support the former gave Hitler.[36]

However, not all German leaders were so disposed. Chief of the General Staff Beck had resigned in September of 1938 because, Guderian recognized, Beck could not subscribe to Hitler's foreign policy, considering it dangerous. Guderian, returning from the Sudetenland in late 1938, had looked forward to a "long period of peace." In his view it was, therefore, regrettable that Commander in Chief von Brauchitsch failed to actively support Beck's call for the generals to make a unanimous declaration for peace and thereby thwart Hitler's war plans. What represented a historic and critical point in history was thereby forfeited and Guderian's "long period of peace" was not to be.[37] This position is believable even though it is part of Guderian's post-war retrospective. After all, with peace, the military had expanded and would continue to do so, the economy was vastly improved and promotions for top officers were abundant under Hitler. Once a hot war had started officers such as Guderian had but one option if they wished to continue to prosper, and that was an obvious one. The key question focuses on their persistence in that pursuit, and when and why they may have deviated and for what reasons. That test was about to start.

Munich Becomes History

Three weeks after Munich Hitler conveyed to Keitel his concerns about Czechoslovakian ties to Soviet Russia, a liaison which would ultimately threaten Germany, he felt. It became obvious to Keitel there was little prospect of winning over Czechoslovakia by peaceful means; accordingly plans were initiated to remove the Czech threat by force as early as possible. When on March 14, 1939, President Hacha of Czechoslovakia was to meet with Hitler, Keitel asked Hitler whether he should postpone the invasion orders given two days earlier; Hitler firmly rejected that approach and explained that come what may he was still planning to march into Czechoslovakia next day — whatever the outcome of the talks with the Czech president might be.[38]

By March of 1939 the Czechs had been incorporated into the Reich as what was described as a "protectorate," leading to a major impact on the international situation, one that Hitler had caused, according to Guderian. He also felt that by May of 1939 there was no lack of political warnings, but Hitler and Ribbentrop had persuaded themselves that the Western Powers would never risk war with Germany, and they assumed they had a free hand in Eastern Europe.[39]

What should have been another early warning of Hitler's overall intentions was his order in early November, 1938, instructing the High Command to draw up General Staff studies on the reoccupation of Danzig and Memel; the return of Danzig to the Reich was one of Hitler's unshakeable objectives as part of his plans to overturn the Versailles restrictions. Since he recognized moves over Danzig might escalate into a conflict with Poland, he focused his attention on the relative border strengths.

To ensure the necessary balance in Germany's favor, at least psychologically, the Germans once again employed intimidation of the prospective enemy. Germany initiated East Wall fortification work on the Oder Front from Breslau down to Frankfort-on-Oder (see map of German acquisitions, page 44), which was clearly visible to the Poles from a distance. Keitel considered the intensified work at this time on the fortifications provided a safety net and would avert war with the Poles. Fighting was not a prospect unless they attacked Germany.[40]

By April, 1939, Hitler felt he would have to solve what he believed was the unacceptable geo-political position for Germany whereby East Prussia was geographically cut off from the rest of the Reich; he believed he could not delay action on this. Though Polish foreign secretary Beck was counting on Britain's help, Hitler was sure they would pull back the "outstretched hand" once Germany's resolve to erase the inequities of Versailles was seen. Hitler, with his usual persuasive powers with the generals, convinced Keitel that he neither planned nor desired war with Poland; politics would resolve the contentious areas. It would be necessary, though, Hitler told him, to resort to threats of military or other sanctions.[41]

Hitler's aggressive political stance inevitably permeated the entire military, the leadership of the major services recognizing the end-game. As German land and sea forces grew in strength throughout 1939, the naval leadership recognized that "the steady growth of German power must, notwithstanding the Naval Agreement, inevitably provoke an attitude of hostility with Britain ... I believed, therefore, that war with Britain would soon be upon us and I pressed ... for acceleration of the German submarine program," wrote Karl Dönitz after war's end describing his feelings at the time as then–Captain Dönitz.

The Navy Sees a Broader War

It inevitably followed that Hitler confirmed to Admiral Raeder in late May of 1938 that Britain must be added to the list of possible future adversaries and, as a result, subsequently approved a long-term naval building program, the Z Plan. Completion was scheduled for 1945, a date, in Raeder's estimation that was out of sync with Hitler's political program, though obviously based on realistic projections of Germany's ability to produce this large fleet; it involved 6 battleships, 12 cruisers, 4 carriers and 233 U-boats. Dönitz felt this date was too late and had projected a need for 300 U-boats to be available when an effective war against England was to be mounted.[42] That would have meant 1940.

Dönitz felt not only that the date set for the Z Plan was too late, but also that too little emphasis was placed on U-boats; he had projected a need for 300 boats so that 100 could be operational at any one time, this number based on war games held in 1938–39. Admiral Raeder, then Commander-in-Chief, conceded in his post-war memoirs that if Hitler had envisioned an early war against England, then the Z Plan should never have been adopted, and, instead, the total emphasis should have been devoted to submarines.[43]

Whatever the schedule for war, Dönitz questioned the priority given battleships at the time. German Navy surface ships were at a disadvantage given Germany's particular geography and consequent land-sea limitations. The British Isles block German vessels from the North Sea, while the southern route through the English Channel is impassable in war. The only other exit from the North Sea is via the narrows between the Shetlands and Norway. On their way to the Atlantic, German forces can from the outset be detected and from that point on are exposed to air and sea forces. Only under exceptionally favorable conditions can surface naval forces slip through unobserved to the Atlantic. However, for the U-boat these strategic disadvantages are of much less importance.[44] (See map, "The German Ocean Access Problem," page 51.)

True to his standard modus operandi, Hitler repudiated the 1935 Anglo-German Naval Agreement on April 26, 1939, a move which to all prescient observers meant actual hostilities were certain if not imminent. However, on July 22, 1939, Hitler communicated to the officers of the U-boat arm "that under no circumstances would war with Britain come about. For that would mean Finis Germaniae. The officers of the U-boat arm had no cause to worry."[45] However, following the Sudetenland, events began to arouse misgivings; the "allegedly unavoidable attack on Poland and ... war ... [were] a bitter blow," according to

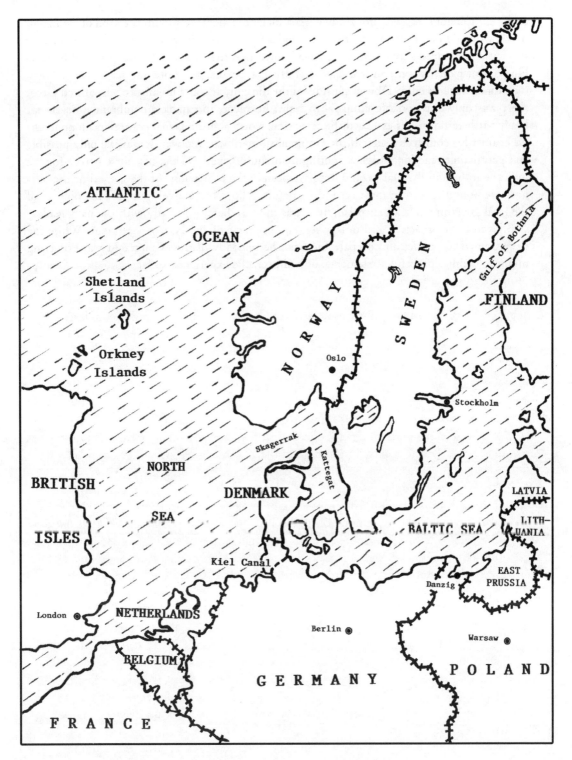

The German Ocean Access Problem

Dönitz.[46] Obviously he was not ready with sufficient U-boats to mount the kind of campaign he knew would be needed to overwhelm England if the Polish attack led to the obvious. By now even convinced supporters must have known that the balance of Europe would be running out of patience with and/or fearful of Hitler's expansionary plans.

Once war had come Dönitz considered the die cast, and as a member of the armed forces there was only one possible course — to fight; however, to expect a commander to accept heavy battle responsibilities and at the same time worry about internal politics let alone struggle against his country's leadership was unrealistic; "to win the war ... was the only possible and permissible reaction which a fighting man could have."[47] This, of course is true for the military or these individuals would not have been in the profession. At the same time the military are bound to and in most cases do espouse, follow and actively support the politics of the legal government. Not surprisingly it was the case here, especially with the navy leadership given their proactive and outspoken endorsement of the Nazi government. While the navy seemed to project and prepare for war, the majority of the Wehrmacht was expecting minimal-conflict peaceful settlements, as had been the experience so far.

6 The Inevitable Hot War

Poland's Rapid Defeat Leads to Wehrmacht Hubris

Though the German Army claims never to have considered war as a solution to political problems, once Hitler had altered the momentum by initiating war on Poland, the generals found considerable satisfaction, if not glory, in the results. The same developments produced enough reality so that efforts involving the military grew to head off enlargement of the Polish conflict following its victorious conclusion. With victory in hand, why face the acknowledged most powerful European army?

Environment for Conflict in the East

For Germans — especially those in the army, who were closely affected by its impact — Versailles produced many onerous problems. The severance of East Prussia from the Reich proper by virtue of the establishment of the corridor and the loss of Danzig was equally if not more rancorous than the other territorial cessions. The German Army never considered war as a solution, according to von Manstein, though they felt the Poles would not consider a negotiated solution, and, in fact, might try to encroach on the frontier at some future time. "General Staff policy in the years 1918–39 ... was not to wage a war of aggression or revenge but to safeguard the security of the Reich."[1] Should Germany force the issue, the nemesis of the old "two-front" war would be confronted.

Many Germans agreed with Col.-General Hans von Seeckt, chief of the Post–World War I Reichswehr, in his approach to resolving the issue, when he said,

Poland's existence is intolerable and incompatible with Germany's essential needs. It must disappear and will disappear through its own inner weakness and through Russia with our help. For Russia Poland is even less tolerable than it is for us: no Russia will come into accord with Poland. Poland can never offer any advantage to Germany economically for it is incapable of development and it cannot offer any advantage politically because it is the vassal of France.[2]

Von Manstein, however, was representative of the group that saw Poland as being a necessary buffer between Russia and Germany. The German Army was reticent to resort to an aggressive armed solution, at least in the pre–World War II years, and post–World War I feeling in the army was that the "union of East Prussia with the Reich ... could well have been harmonized with Poland's desire for a seaport of her own" instead of armed conflict.[3] Of course this would have taken a reciprocal agreement affording both Poles and Germans free passage through the corridor as well as joint governance, something not amenable to prevailing politics at that time.

With Hitler's appearance on the scene, however, speculation would turn to action. On August 22, 1939, eight days before Germany's attack on Poland, when Hitler addressed his generals at the Obersalzberg, he said in effect that conflict with Poland was inevitable and was to be Germany's primary objective.[4] He said, in part,

It was clear to me that a conflict with Poland had to come sooner than later. I had already made this decision in the spring, but I thought I would first turn against the West in a few years, and only afterwards against the East ... I wanted to establish an acceptable relationship with Poland in order to fight first against the West. But this plan, which was agreeable to me, could not be executed since essential points have changed [failed negotiations]. A beginning has been made for the destruction of England's hegemony.[5]

In his second speech of that day to his commanders, Hitler continued on the subject of Poland, saying, in part,

the destruction of Poland shall be the primary objective. I shall give a propagandist cause for starting the war — never mind whether it be plausible or not. The victor shall not be asked later whether we told the truth or not. In starting and making a war, not the Right is what matters, but Victory.... The start will be ordered by Saturday [August 26, 1939].[6]

The generals were split as to whether war was inevitable. For von Rundstedt, representing one group, war was not inevitable, and he gives two reasons: first, the collaboration of the Russians, which Hitler contemporaneously announced, rendered the Polish position untenable; and, second, the group considered this a replay of Munich: Hitler was simply employing the final squeeze through this high-profile commanders' conference. This latter point was further emphasized by Hitler's erratic, conflicting orders immediately preceding the actual attack order of September 1, 1939.[7]

Von Manstein's impression on the other hand was that Hitler was determined to resolve the German-Polish question, even if it meant war. If the Poles wished peace on a compatible basis, that was agreeable to Hitler; if war did come, Hitler's view was that the Western Powers would not enter into the issue in view of their lack of preparedness and the blood sacrifice involved. Their biggest surprise, though, was Hitler's revelation to them of his intention to conclude a non-aggression pact with Stalin.[8]

Hitler resolved the question with Fall Weiss (Operation WHITE), Führer War Directive No. 1, the war on Poland, which commenced on September 1, 1939. The Wehrmacht was provided its first opportunity to apply the blitzkrieg war tactics in preparation through the 1930s, and which utilized unorthodox self-sufficient tank formations supported by a superior air force. Poland's position proved hopeless in the face of von Rundstedt's Army Group South, von Bock's Army Group North and the Russian Army. Within six weeks the two German army groups had captured 690,000 Poles, and Hitler had already redirected his sights on the West, withdrawing and diverting available troops to the Rhine area. Poland had been decimated, and, in the view of many German generals, the troops had been "blooded."[9]

Many in the Wehrmacht went through a seeming metamorphosis in thinking on the subject of war with Poland and war in general. Far from reticence on war, under Hitler's influence and the flush of success many in the leadership, such as von Manstein, who had served as Chief of Staff to then-col.-general Gerd von Rundstedt, Commander-in-Chief of Army Group South, now declared that the new Wehrmacht had passed its *first* test with flying colors.[10]

Equally jubilant was Alfred Jodl, newly appointed as OKW chief of the Operations Staff, when, on October 28, 1939, he wrote the Police president of Bruenn, Moravia, telling of Germany's satisfaction with the Polish Campaign and asking him to make sure to keep the Czechs quiescent and prevent any uprising while the conflict lasted. "This wonderful campaign in Poland was a grand opening for this hard decisive struggle ... the sanctimonious British will not succeed in throttling our economy, and militarily we are without worry ... [I am confident] ... that you ... will ... [keep] the Czechs at it and ... not ... [let] them perk up."[11]

The Polish attack gave Heinz Guderian, as commanding general of the 19th Corps, the first opportunity to battle-test his panzer concept, with the result that the new concept of war, Blitzkrieg ("lightning war"), descended on the world out of the six-week campaign. Like other commanders he applauded the results, feeling that the panzer troops had shown their mettle, and the early work and planning that had gone into the armored corps had paid off.[12]

Guderian's initial reaction to Hitler's pre-attack announcement at Obersalzberg had been negative, and he felt this reflected that of the army in general. If war with the Poles were to expand, and it could since the British had guaranteed Poland's sovereignty, most of the generals who had been through the first world war knew full well what was in store for the army, and viewed it gravely. On the plus side was the existence of the Russian Pact, which offered some support for Germany's position; however, they recognized the frailty off such a pact, and they felt a second front in the East might well result.[13]

Beyond Poland

Guderian told Hitler at the close of the Polish Campaign that the army had reacted to the news of the Russian Pact with a sigh of relief since it appeared to preclude the two-front war which had contributed to Germany's defeat in World War I. One can also conclude this was a factor in Hitler's thinking as he sought to psych up his army for the attack on Poland, the first engagement of what we know he envisioned as a long, protracted war.

This answer unsettled Hitler, Guderian thought, as the former had expected to hear an expression of surprise with the announcement of a National Socialist pact with the Communists. After all, for over twenty years Hitler had been touting the clash between the two ideologies and must have been looking for confirmation of the impact of his ideologic message. On the other hand, the German Reichswehr of the inter-war period, under Hans von Seeckt, had grown accustomed to friendly, cooperative relations with the Russian military, sharing reciprocal visits and developing personal relationships; all this had facilitated officer training and ordnance development and testing outside the scrutiny of Versailles. Nevertheless, by late 1940–early 1941 it became obvious to German military observers reflecting on the results of Russian Foreign Commissar Molotov's visit to Berlin that Hitler was secretly planning the future attack on this new ally who, in reality, he continued to hold in great contempt.[14]

The relative inaction of the Western Powers in fulfilling their guarantee to Poland implied there was no threat to Germany's future actions. At the same time, many Germans felt, like von Manstein, that Britain's entry into the war on September 3, 1939, in support of Poland, was to ensure Germany's defeat on the Continent. To the German mind, Britain could not tolerate a too-powerful Germany. Instead, von Manstein, adopting the line long espoused and promulgated by the National Socialists, felt Britain should have addressed the more important issue of promoting a world balance of power to prevent the Soviet Union's success in its dedication to world revolution.[15]

This thinking reflected the dichotomous extremes in Germany in the 1930s brought on by the failure of the Weimar government. As presented to the German public by the Nazis, the choice was either Communism or Nazism — the Germans had been encouraged in the aftermath of the dire economic straits left by Versailles to see no middle or third option such as democracy. They also failed to recognize Britain's primary need, that of maintaining a balance among the major powers in Europe so as to prevent the threat of Nazi aggression from overwhelming Europe.

In retrospect Albrecht Kesselring, then-chief of Airfleet 1, claims in his memoirs to have decried the breaking of the Munich Agreement and the subsequent attack on Poland, laying the blame on von Ribbentrop and his irresponsible advice to Hitler. Göring, he states, was like-minded.[16]

Nevertheless, Kesselring, in a somewhat anomalous position, characterized the Luftwaffe forces he commanded and had developed as specifically "offensive" in nature, because, as he said, air warfare is inconceivable as other than an offensive activity.[17] They had played such a role, of course, in Poland, an experience Kesselring then used in preparing his Luftwaffe forces for what he termed "a more powerful enemy."[18] So it is clear a metamorphosis in his thinking may possibly have occurred as a result of the Polish action, not unlike that of many of Hitler's other commanders as they contemplated the future.

Faith that Hitler would continue his non-violent political successes had convinced Admiral Raeder, naval chief at the time, that in his opinion at that time, even on the eve of the attack on Poland, Hitler did not want war. Notwithstanding Hitler's saber-rattling speeches to his commanders after Prague[19] and before the Polish attack,[20] Raeder persisted in believing these problems would be solved without bloodshed.[21]

As Raeder said in his post-war comments at Nuremberg, though his judgment ultimately turned out to be faulty, at the time he still had confidence in Hitler's political ability, even considering the 1939 pact with Russia.[22]

Aid from Aggressive Military Leadership

Raising some question as to the complete veracity of these statements was Raeder's approach to preparations for and conduct of the war itself, which was single-minded and dedicated. The legacy left by the Kaiser's pre–World War I dreadnaught construction competition with Great Britain seems to have had its influence on Raeder. The Kaiser's one-time navigation officer seems to have been propelled in his own like endeavors well before Hitler's seizure of power.

And further, once the attack on Poland had commenced, Raeder, in October of 1939, pursued with Hitler the issue of possible British occupation of Norway. Then, by March 26, 1940, he had reached the point of advising Hitler to take action by the next moon, April 7, though a British landing was not yet considered imminent.[23] A severe interpretation of Raeder's modus operandi, thinking and discrete actions falls close to that behind the verdict rendered in his post-war Nuremberg trial.

Two further controversial issues developed on Raeder's watch which contributed to the Nuremberg Tribunal's judgment against him: the sinking of the *Athenia*, a British ship, on September 3, 1939, and the decision to wage unrestricted submarine warfare. In the case of the *Athenia*, this unarmed passenger vessel, outward bound for America, was sunk by the German U-boat *U-30*. The German government charged the British with the sinking and persisted in this charge despite later determining that the commander of the *U-30*, Oberleutnant Lemp, was guilty of the sinking. To compound matters, the log of the *U-30* was found to have been altered to deflect judgment. Raeder, in testimony at Nuremberg, claimed to have been uninvolved in the entire affair; however, he had been "extremely embarrassed" by charges printed in the October 23, 1939, issue of Joseph Goebbels' party paper, the *Voelkischer Boebacter,* that the British first lord of the admiralty, Winston Churchill, had deliberately sent British and American subjects to their deaths. However, Hitler refused Raeder's request that the German government admit the truth to the world once *U-30* had returned from sea and the true facts were known. Raeder could do nothing, he said.[24]

The Germans recognized Britain's lifeline was ocean transport and accordingly set about determining how far to go in destruction of that commerce. Raeder, after extensive dialogue with the Foreign Office, issued on October 15, 1939, a memorandum setting forth submarine warfare guidelines. In sum, it called for attacking British sea communications "with the greatest ruthlessness; ... try to consider the interest of neutrals, insofar as this is possible without detriment to military requirements."

The German Navy under Raeder, and later under Karl Dönitz's leadership, carried out unrestricted submarine warfare, sinking unarmed neutral ships and practicing non-rescue and machine-gunning of survivors, contrary to the London Protocol of 1936, to which Germany was party.[25]

A Persistent Minority Wages a Futile Battle

The desperate situation of the German people was responsible in large part for their overwhelming support of Hitler and his National Socialists; however, the tenets of Nazism —

Admirals Raeder (L) and Dönitz with Hitler following the return of U29 (Lt. Commander Otto Schuhart) after sinking the 22,450 ton carrier, HMS *Courageous*, on September 19, 1939. This was far west of British coastal waters, and after two attacks on carriers in two days Britain withdrew these valuable assets, thus easing the threat to German U-boats. Bibliothek für Zeitgeschichte, Stuttgart.

terror, despotism, and extreme ideological racism — never convinced a prescient, perceptive and/or courageous minority of Germans. Despite the post-war pronouncements that internal resistance alone was futile once the regime was in power, various resistance movements grew through the 1930s.

Within the army, reaction to the National Socialists had been significantly amplified by the Blomberg-Fritsch affair and Hitler's interference and intrusion into direction of the armed forces. The genesis of plans for Hitler's removal by the military found its foundation here as the first plan for a coup attempt emerged in 1938 amid this crisis. It involved key civilians — Karl Goerdeler, former mayor of Leipzig, Hjalmar Schacht, former Reichsbank president and minister of economics — and the key and necessary military element, including Col.-General (later Field Marshal) Erwin von Witzleben; former Chief of the General Staff Ludwig Beck; current (1938) holder of that office, General Franz Halder; Admiral Wilhelm Canaris, head of Abwehr, the OKW intelligence arm; and others.

The conspirators endeavored to enlist broad support, particularly within the armed forces. When Schacht approached von Rundstedt, however, he was coldly received. The Berlin commander haughtily replied he would know what to do when and if he chose to act. This first plan, which was so dangerous for the conspirators, came to naught in late 1938 when the

Munich Agreement defused the threat of war and resulted in the overwhelming support for the Hitler regime by the German people.[26]

According to key resistance worker Hans Gisevius in testimony at Nuremberg, he and others such as Canaris and General Georg Thomas had discussed this first and subsequent coup attempts with upward of a dozen generals, but few ever seriously declared their intention of helping to overthrow the system. Among the few that agreed initially — including von Rundstedt — Erwin von Witzleben "was the only one that stuck to his word ... when everything was ready, [the others] ... would not start."[27]

Witzleben, in command of troops in Berlin, was to implement the plan through his commanders; Halder's role was to fix the date and then convince his superior, General von Brauchitsch, to assume the temporary position of chief of state. He would subsequently be replaced by a civilian, once an orderly transition had occurred.[28]

The conspirators were convinced that Hitler must be removed. Goerdeler had left government in protest against the National Socialists to devote himself to resistance efforts in Germany and abroad. Schacht, one of those influential civilian leaders responsible for Hitler's original ascension to power, saw Hitler by the late 1930s as bent on war. He describes himself as one of the collaborators, and corroborates Halder's version of events. The veracity of Schacht's claim is confirmed by Hans Gisevius, former German vice-consul in Zurich who covertly worked against the Nazis under cover of the Abwehr, the German counterintelligence service.[29]

However, a funny thing happened on the way to consummation. Halder never really "talked expressly to Brauchitsch about [his role in] this. But he knew my attitude and had a notion of what was going on," said Halder in his post-war interrogation at Nuremberg. In fact, Halder went on to say that it was common practice to talk around a subject so that one could not be easily betrayed to the Führer or his agents.[30]

Halder had set three conditions for a coup to be successful:

- first, a clear and resolute leadership was required
- second, the masses must be motivated to follow the revolution, and
- third, the timing must be right

All were in place and properly aligned, "But now came Mr. Chamberlain, and with a stroke the danger of war was avoided. Hitler returned from Munich as an unbloody victor" and the German people were overjoyed with the peace he had delivered, so reported Halder when interrogated at the Nuremberg trials.[31]

The critical hour for force was lost, and the conspirators would, according to Halder, wait and watch for a next opportunity. However, he notes, "extreme importance must be attributed to this Munich Agreement, not only because of the impression it made on the population, but also upon the Wehrmacht. From this time on, you could always hear the saying, 'Well the Führer will do it somehow; he did it at Munich.'"[32]

Why did Halder's three conditions not reassert themselves before the attack on Poland? Halder claims that Hitler, in his August 22, 1939, briefing to his commanders, maintained that Polish-German negotiations were proceeding, leading Halder, as well as many other generals in attendance — von Rundstedt and von Manstein are typical — to believe a rerun of Munich was afoot.[33]

However, in his two speeches delivered to his commanders that day Hitler stated clearly that conflict with Poland "had to come sooner or later," and "the destruction of Poland shall be the primary objective." The moment, Hitler said, was more favorable now than it would be in two or three years.[34] As Halder had implied, overriding the literal message was the perhaps wishful thought that war would be averted just as Hitler "did it at Munich." In his postwar retrospective, however, he blamed Hitler's mastery of camouflage and deception for the generals' false conclusions following the August 22 speeches.[35]

Halder's three conditions became subject to a fourth impediment: however satisfied these conditions might be, the Germans now had "a fully armed enemy in front ... the French and British had deployed their troops and they were ready to fight."[36] An internal revolution in the face of this threat could now have led to dire circumstances for Germany. And further complicating this picture, now that war had started, was, for Halder, duty as a soldier, where a plot against the State carried with it the term "treason." "I was in ... [an] awful dilemma."[37]

Overriding the issue of whatever the generals had concluded about the reality of Hitler's war plans are the concrete facts that by now they all knew of his Hossbach plans for encroaching on the countries of Europe; and, second, they had seen his demonstrated relentless abuse of the Munich Agreement and the broaching of Austrian sovereignty with the Anschluss. These were intelligent, calculating men who must have weighed the probabilities in each option, especially the major shift after the Polish Campaign. There appears more than a little obfuscation on Halder's part here in his explanation of their inability to assess Hitler's intentions along the way.

One step further removed from supporting the conspirators was von Rundstedt. Though von Rundstedt had spurned the entreaties of the conspirators, he appears to have been on the horns of a dilemma in view of his dubious opinion as to the prospects of success for Hitler's aggressive ventures. Nevertheless the prime driver for him, according to his longtime Chief of Staff, General Blumentritt, was the credo that "once high politics had [been] decided, ... nothing remained ... but to comply loyally and correctly," and he would demonstrate this until his final dismissal by Hitler in early 1945. Whether it was age — he was close to 60 by late 1938, before the major incursions began — or skepticism of the successful outcome which drove him, he was allowed to retire in November of 1938 after leading the Second Army in the seizing of the Czech Sudetenland.[38] He was actively engaged again by Hitler for the Polish Campaign and would continue to play an intermittent role for the balance of the war, despite his own dubious assessments for the outcome of most campaigns he was involved with subsequently: Barbarrosa, Normandy and the Ardennes.

7 Phony War and Attack on France

Rapid Victory Keeps the Military Interested

Despite the defensive attitude and proposed attack plan of the Army High Command, Hitler's field generals developed an effective plan for use against France. Using an element of surprise, the German armies had pushed the Allied Forces back to Dunkirk in slightly over two weeks' time. Whether by Hitler's misjudgment, Luftwaffe failure or failure on the part of army leaders, the Germans allowed the British to rescue their army and enabled them to come back to fight another day.

Internecine Warfare over the Attack Plan

After Hitler struck Poland on September 1, 1939, the soldiers were not told of conditions which would have prevented full-scale war. Responding to Britain and France's declaration of war on Germany, in accord with their alliance with Poland, "We were fobbed off" by Hitler, writes Keitel, maintaining that the declaration of war by the two powers was unwarranted meddling in issues between Germany and Poland which they needed to resolve themselves. None of their European interests was being injured in any way. The military would see their fears for the Western Front were of little basis. Hitler further maintained to his key OKW staff that neither Britain nor France was in position to intervene with sea or land forces, anyway.[1]

The Führer's view on September 27, 1939, with Poland in ruins, was that if peaceful overtures toward the West — England and France — failed, a direct assault, launched sooner than later and using ruthless methods, was called for. Though the West lacked adequate attack weapons, the passage of time, he feared, would alter that in Germany's disfavor. Hitler was anxious to attack France which represented to him no more difficult an adversary than Poland. The French people, he felt, were of less value than the Poles and represented a weak link for France; Hitler's immediate goal was destruction of the French Army.[2]

However, this proved impossible in the face of adverse autumn weather, where heavy rain, snow and sharp frost made the use of tanks and aircraft inadvisable if not impossible. A further impediment to an autumn attack was the divergence of opinion for an attack plan. By the end of the victorious Polish Campaign, a schism had appeared between OKW, the Supreme Command, and OKH, the Army High Command, and between the army groups and OKH. It would soon develop as well between the Führer and each of these entities.[3]

The OKH War Office under von Brauchitsch and Halder felt any attack in the west would only kill chances of peace talks; Hitler, in opposition, felt a rapid response against France after the Polish Campaign was critical to success in the West. Learning of Keitel's having met with the two generals in October of 1939 at Zossen to discuss the matter, Hitler violently accused Keitel of diverting his plans and conspiring with his generals against them; he insisted that Keitel accept and identify himself with his war plans and represent them without reservation to the War Office. He insulted and bullied Keitel, accusing him of fostering an opposition group among his generals. Keitel's consequent resignation was refused.[4]

Chief of the General Staff Col. General Franz Halder (to Hitler's left) at the map table with (L–R) Field Marshal Wilhelm Keitel, OKW chief; Field Marshal Walter von Brauchitsch, Commander-In-Chief Army until late 1941; and the Supreme Commander, Adolf Hitler. Ullstein bild/The Granger Collection, New York.

Hitler and, from left, General Officers Friedrich Paulus, Wilhelm Keitel, Franz Halder, Walter von Brauchitsch and Adolf Heusinger discuss plans at OKH headquarters, near Angerburg, East Prussia, in 1941. Ullstein bild/The Granger Collection, New York.

Western Attack Plan Success Despite Internecine Warfare

Germany's plan for attacking France was originally designed in 1905 by Chief of the General Staff Count Alfred von Schlieffen to provide victory in the West and was modified by his World War I successor, General Helmuth von Moltke.[5] Schlieffen's plan called for minimal forces on the left, with the major force attacking through Belgium. Von Moltke reversed Schlieffen, employing almost half the force strength for an attack in the South. Responding then to Hitler's direction, OKH had proposed an attack plan much like the old Schlieffen Plan of 1905: a concentration of forces north of the Liege area and a wheel about Antwerp for a sweep south (see map, "German Western Attack Plans," page 64). In fact, the Army High Command wanted the attack in the West to be more defensive than aggressive.[6]

Von Manstein admits his first reaction to the OKH plan was negative because Hitler had recommended it; he also realized the OKH plan did not expect to achieve decisive results over the French Army in a first move, but in achieving territorial gains from which to launch further attacks. The old Schlieffen Plan, had envisioned a single-stroke victory through defeat

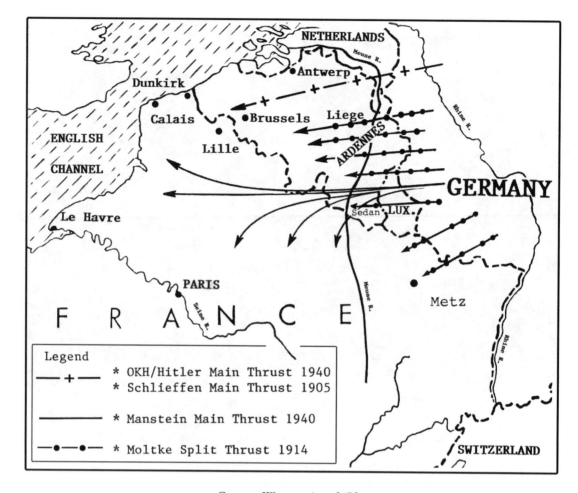

German Western Attack Plans

of the northern forces, a quick move to the west of Paris, and a wheel pushing French forces to a line between Metz and the Swiss border.

In the mind of Erich von Manstein, then–Chief of Staff to von Rundstedt's Army Group A, the French and British forces would expect a replay of the Schlieffen Plan and a battle of attrition could result. Instead, von Manstein, in consultation with Heinz Guderian (considered Germany's leading tactical tank expert), conceived and proposed a plan whose baseline would be "surprise." Von Manstein felt the Schlieffen Plan could be improved by a surprise move through the heavily wooded and hilly Ardennes country of Belgian Luxembourg, as shown on the map ("German Western Campaign, 1940," see page 66) and then a second move south to defeat the balance of French forces. A force of three or four armies would attack through the heavily wooded Ardennes area of Belgium. Guderian was confident he could breach the Meuse on day 5 or 6 and race ahead of the infantry, driving a wedge sufficiently wide that the enemy could not attack the flanks.[7]

OKH — Halder and Commander in Chief Walther von Brauchitsch — called this approach "senseless" and "impossible." At the war games of February 7, 1940, held at Army

Hitler with Generals von Kluge and Rommel (first row, L–R), then Adjutant Schaub and General Alfred Jodl (second row, L–R), in January of 1940, preparing for the French Campaign. Rommel, noted first for his success in the 1940 advance, then in the African Campaign, was later assigned to Italy, then to a major role in the defense of France in the Allied invasion. He met his demise when he was implicated in the 1944 attempt on Hitler's life. Ullstein bild/The Granger Collection, New York.

Group A headquarters in Koblenz to validate von Manstein's proposed plan, Halder held that the armor should wait for the infantry, that "a concerted attack across the Meuse would be impossible before the ninth or tenth day of the offensive."[8] Again on February 14 in war games at 12th Army Headquarters a similar confrontation developed between Guderian and Halder.

However, three days later von Manstein had an opportunity to personally brief Hitler. Despite von Manstein's repeated memorandums via OKH channels, Hitler had never been briefed on the Manstein Plan. Now with this briefing by the plan's author, Hitler was induced to support the proposed Ardennes attack. Once he had convinced Hitler of the advantages of this approach and OKH was obliged to go along, he credited General Heinz Guderian for the success of the plan in his rapid thrusting of German armor to the channel.[9]

The rest is history — Guderian's performance earned him a panzer group for the next and final phase of the French Campaign. However, nowhere in Franz Halder's diary does he mention von Manstein's contribution of the Ardennes-Sedan attack plan, which Hitler and OKW accepted as the baseline. In fact, some expression of ill feeling is evidenced in Halder's

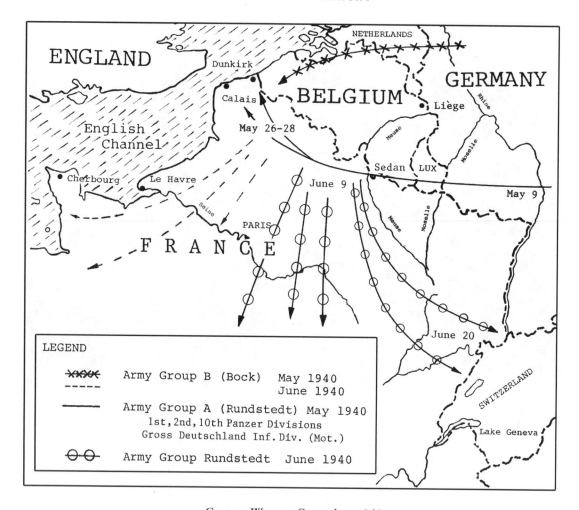

German Western Campaign, 1940

May 18 diary entry, implying that OKW, Hitler's Supreme Command, was given the impression that the Ardennes Manstein Plan was conceived by OKH, the Army High Command. Internecine warfare appears at play here, but the competitive elements it spawned may have contributed to the dramatic success on this second campaign of the war.[10]

The consensus is in accord with Hitler's estimate: Erich von Manstein is regarded as one of the top military tacticians of the World War II German military. Hitler had allowed von Manstein just hours to prepare the orders for both the action to remilitarize the Rhineland in 1936, and, two years later, the Austrian Anschluss. In contrast, his most challenging and substantive task had been the conceiving of the western attack plan of 1940 whereby France would be quickly defeated. For his superlative performance, however, the forces of internecine warfare in the Army High Command caused von Manstein's removal from the center of action as Chief of Staff in von Rundstedt's Army Group A; instead, he was sent to cold storage as Commander of 38th Corps, where he would see little action in the French Campaign.[11]

General Heinz Guderian after the battle of Langres, France, in June of 1940; he had been a leader in the rapid panzer attack through the Ardennes. Key to the development of Germany's tank technology in the inter-war years, Guderian also functioned as Inspector General of Armored Troops. In 1944 he became Chief of the General Staff, replacing Kurt Zeitzler. He was never charged in the post-war period, possibly to avoid increasing East-West political cleavage. Ullstein bild/The Granger Collection, New York.

Command Interference at the Top

One of Hitler's apparent talents was the ability to prepare solid arguments even on the home fields of the generals — at least that is what is repeatedly reported. Alternatively, it is quite possible they let him win for a multitude of obvious reasons, at least as long as victories were promising.

Though Hitler had not interfered in military operations up to and including the Polish Campaign — Austria and the Sudetenland/Czechoslovakian efforts being primarily political — the campaign in the west was to be quite different. The basis for this metamorphosis lay in the period of positional eclipse the army High Command had entered relative to Hitler and the Supreme Command, OKW, characterized and fostered by the Blomberg-Fritsch affair of 1938.[12]

Following the Wehrmacht's dramatic success in Poland, Hitler used OKW, on October 9, 1939, to unilaterally advise the commanders in chief of all three services of his intention to proceed with the Western Campaign, and thereby violate the neutralities of Holland, Belgium and Luxembourg. Given the tactical need to avoid the Maginot fortifications, attack through Belgium, the Netherlands and Luxembourg was mandated and necessarily violated the neutrality of those countries. Whereas Hitler had guaranteed the neutrality of these three countries on October 6, 1939, he abrogated that promise just three days later by his decision to adopt the Manstein Plan for invasion of the West. That plan called for transit through these countries for the attack on France. In Jodl's testimony at Nuremberg on June 6, 1946, he justified this violation on the basis that "this neutrality was not kept, for British flyers flew over this area by day and by night." France and England shared the blame for forcing them to forfeit their neutrality, was the rationale for him.[13] Even retrospectively Hitler commanded obedience and adherence to his proscribed agenda from some of his more devoted lackeys despite the lessons so dramatically projected by the war. Their behavior and approach to issues, even in the post-war period, seems to have mirrored his, which was not unexpected given the atmosphere in which they worked for so long.

At this juncture, before the attack on France, von Manstein saw two General Staffs, one in OKH and one in OKW, though only the latter had authority. This development he attributed to Hitler's "insatiable thirst for power and his excessive self-esteem ... engendered by undeniable successes and encouraged by ... party bosses and ... his retinue.... Moreover, he had a genius for suddenly confronting his military collaborators with political and economic arguments ... they could not immediately refute."[14]

Hitler had reached the point of not only ordering military offensive measures, but deciding on the *timing* and *method* to be used and *how* the operation should be conducted. Hitler's lust for power caused him to usurp the role of supreme commander as well as head of state. His unilateral decision making would shortly yield a strategically important negative effect in the final stage of part one of the Western Campaign.

Bluff Diplomacy Ends, Hitler Attacks

The start of the French campaign met continued delay after the Polish victory for reasons of weather, the strategic controversy discussed above, and Hitler's interest in attempting peace feelers with Britain. Von Rundstedt, Commander-in-Chief of Army Group A for the Western Campaign, was fortunate in the early stages of the planning to have Erich von Manstein as his Chief of Staff. Von Manstein, with Heinz Guderian's support, led von Rundstedt into endorsing Manstein's plan which relied heavily on the efficacy of massed tanks. Von Rundstedt, according to Guderian, had initially failed to appreciate the potential of tanks and had opted for a more cautious approach in the attack on the west.[15]

In the late 1930s and even into the Polish Campaign France had the strongest land army in western Europe and the numerically strongest tank force. However, the French had spent all of their money on the static Maginot Line instead of modernizing their mobile forces as de Gaulle and others had proposed. The Manstein-Guderian approach was diametrically opposed to the static theories of World War I that France adhered to, a strategy recognized by the Germans at the outset. Though they knew and respected the French soldier from World War I experiences, the inaction of France during 1939–40 implied to the Germans France's limited enthusiasm for the war.[16]

By May of 1940, when Germany launched its attack on France, the German Army had 2800 armored vehicles, including reconnaissance cars, as opposed to 4000 of the Anglo-French forces. The French tanks at the time were superior both in gun caliber and armor, but inferior in control facilities and speed. However, the French preoccupation with firepower and position, as in the Maginot Line (rather than mobile warfare as de Gaulle had espoused), a concept rooted in their World War I experiences, would render them ineffectual against the German onslaught. The rapid French capitulation in June of 1940 convinced Hitler of the efficacy of tanks, and he gave orders to elevate tank production to 1000 per month, about 12 times the existing production rate.

Guderian's 1st, 2nd and 10th Panzer Divisions and Gross-Deutschland Infantry Regiment formed the van of the attack on the west (see map, German Western Campaign, 1940, page 66). Von Manstein, who conceived the successful World War II version of the Schlieffen Plan of 1905 for Germany's classic attack on the west,[17] in giving Guderian credit for the success of his plan, says, "Apart from the energetic leadership of Col.-General von Rundstedt, this success is, I feel, primarily due to the tremendous verve with which General Guderian translated the Army Group's operational principles into action."[18]

Heinz Guderian and Erwin Rommel emerged from the war with the distinction of having been the German Army's two tank generals — Guderian in Russia, Rommel in Africa and both in the earlier French Campaign of 1940. Rommel had asked Hitler before the French action for a field command and was given the Seventh Panzer Division with its 218 tanks in February of 1940. An infantryman by experience and training, Rommel recognized and quickly learned the new tank techniques developed in the 1930s by Guderian and further perfected in the Polish Campaign.[19]

The Seventh Panzer Division was part of Hermann Hoth's 15th Panzer Corps under Gerd von Rundstedt in Army Group A. Again, Rommel distinguished himself in the drive to the sea, this time capturing the British Highland Division and 40,000 prisoners on June 12, 1940.[20]

A Blunder at Calais

As the Western Campaign hurled forward into France, Guderian advanced to Calais, much farther than authorized, and with the intent of pursuing the Allies to Dunkirk. It had taken his tanks some two weeks to reach the Channel Coast from the start of operations on May 9, 1940. As the German armies approached Dunkirk Hitler gave his controversial halt command of May 24. Guderian says, "[without an explanation given] it was forbidden to cross the stream [the Aa River] ... the orders contained the words: 'Dunkirk is to be left to the Luftwaffe.' ... Fierce [Allied] air activity [then] met little opposition from our air force."[21]

Despite the varying attributions of fault, persuasive evidence exists that von Rundstedt, possibly concerned with exposure of his southern flank, persuaded Hitler, when the latter visited his headquarters (HQ) the evening of May 24, to issue the stop order. Von Rundstedt maintains the stop order was Hitler's idea alone and that he immediately protested. In any event, the two-day delay that ensued enabled the British Army to escape to the homeland, to fight another day. Alternatively, Hitler reportedly expressed the view that eliminating the entire British Army at Dunkirk would diminish the possibility of a negotiated peace with Britain, and so gave them an opportunity to save face by escaping.[22]

According to Keitel, who claims to have been present at the briefing in the War Office when the decision on this question was demanded of Hitler by the Army General Staff and its Commander-in-Chief, Hitler has been unfairly charged with this decision. The memory of the low-lying Flanders plains that had flooded in 1914, plus reports from commanders in the field that this was poor tank country with innumerable trenches and canals, caused the generals to pass the decision to Hitler. While the "Führer's order was ... wrong," Hitler was "unjustly credited ... with the responsibility for making the wrong decision," as the generals should have had the guts to make the decision themselves and not have passed it to Hitler.[23] Yet, as discussed earlier, if Hitler was injecting himself to the extent he apparently did, he did relieve the generals of the final prerogative, though the more aggressive ones might well have objected had they been present.

According to von Rundstedt and his Chief of Staff (1942–44), General Guenther Blumentritt, Hitler issued this order on the mistaken belief that marshy ground around Dunkirk was unsuitable for tanks and that the number of operational tanks had been reduced to an unacceptable level.[24]

If Hitler had actually been so advised, he may have given the responsibility to the Luftwaffe for delivering the coup de grace to Allied forces on that basis. Luftwaffe intelligence chief Lt. General Josef Schmid claims to have heard Reichsmarschall (Reich Marshal) Hermann Göring propose, and Hitler accept, that the Luftwaffe be given that role. In fact, the air bases were too remote and air operations were restricted by fog over northern France on May 29–31 so that air was destined to be ineffective. The air attacks that were made were directed at the city and harbor, and did nothing to interfere with the rescue operations between May 26 to June 4 of some 338,000 British soldiers.[25]

This decision which resulted in the successful Dunkirk evacuation by the British is considered by von Manstein as one of Hitler's most decisive errors. Whether Hitler was led to believe the area represented bad tank country or that the Luftwaffe could best finish the task, both theories were wrong militarily. Notwithstanding Hitler's desire to facilitate an understanding with Britain, it was a prime error and was to have serious future repercussions. It hampered him in his subsequent plan to invade Britain (Operation SEALION), and enabled the British to fight on in North Africa and Italy.[26]

To von Manstein the French capitulation on June 22, 1940, marked the peak of Hitler's career. Though the British had been beaten off the Continent, both they and the Soviets represented a latent threat.[27] However, others such as Erich Raeder found the defeat of France to be the basis for future expansion, saying, "The successful summer campaign in 1940 and the surrender of France had given us invaluable seaports in the channel."[28] Raeder, like Rommel, encouraged Hitler to reach a rapprochement with the French. As the result of his discussions with Admiral Darlan, Commander-in-Chief of the Vichy French Navy in 1942, the Vichy French would have looked favorably on an arrangement; such an accord would have been a safeguard against the Allied attack through French North Africa as well as taking advantage of whatever French antipathy existed toward England. However, Hitler could not be persuaded.

Perhaps Erich Raeder never outlived his early navy days as the navigation officer on the Kaiser's yacht and the consequent political indoctrination. His view of Germany's destiny on the continent and justifiable tactics to gain that hegemony is reasserted in his attitude on the question of violation of the neutrality of Holland and Belgium at the time of the attack on France. Hitler's rationale had been, "[It] is unimportant.... No one will question that when we have won." Raeder, when asked at Nuremberg, six years later, said, "It is not exactly my opinion, but I had no cause to raise any objection ... [to Hitler's strategy] at that moment."[29] Again, Raeder demonstrated his singular energetic and proactive support of the regime's aspirations, a role the Tribunal would recognize in its assessment and decision regarding him.

8 Interlude After France Falls

The Führer Seeks
Additional Victories—But Where?

A great day in the history of the German Army. German troops have been marching into Paris since 0900.

— Franz Halder's War Diary, June 14, 1940[1]

France's conquest was a resounding victory, one that shocked the world. Despite Foreign Minister Joachim von Ribbentrop's advice to the Führer to the contrary, France and
Great Britain had declared war on Germany two days after Germany's September 1, 1939,
attack on Poland. Now Britain's inflexible resolve to fight to the end was further underscored
with France's rapid defeat, and peace proposals from Germany would now be clearly unacceptable to the British, in the minds of Germany's military leadership.[2] "The Führer is greatly
puzzled by Britain's unwillingness to make peace" was Halder's diary entry of July 13, 1940.[3]

Out of the precipitous defeat of France, and seemingly in the vacuum of the absence of
a follow-on war plan, Operation SEALION (Seeloewe) emerged. SEALION was a stillbirth, however, for two reasons. First, the preparations took so long that the operation could not have
proceeded until late September, past an acceptable weather window; and, secondly, the
Luftwaffe had not reached the point of requisite air supremacy. Von Manstein believed that
a successful invasion required the existence of a long-range war plan predating the Polish
Campaign; and, secondly, such a war plan would need to have included detailed plans for an
invasion. Neither existed, however. If such had existed and if the plan had been seriously considered, it would have been unthinkable to have allowed the British Expeditionary Force to
have escaped at Dunkirk. Had a rigorous and serious plan existed, the Luftwaffe would have
had to coordinate its air campaign against Britain in 1940. Instead the German Air Force

simply diminished its resources by embarking on an air war without coordinating with those invasion plans that did exist, however minimal they were.

With the obvious demand for follow-on action, OKH Chief Franz Halder's meeting with Hitler on July 13, 1940, was devoted to plans for SEALION. Hitler, in fact, did not approach such a move with enthusiasm because the defeat of Britain, should an invasion succeed, meant the disintegration of the British Empire. This Hitler saw as being of no benefit to Germany. German blood would be shed for something which would primarily benefit Japan, the United States and others, he believed.[4]

"Britain's position is hopeless. The war is won by us. A reversal in the prospects of success is impossible," was Hitler's view on July 22 when he met with von Brauchitsch. The latter, who functioned as OKH's main interface with the Führer, passed this on to Halder. In this meeting, Hitler, in an unusually prescient observation, also considered a cross–Channel invasion very hazardous, a move to be taken only if no other way was left to bring Britain to terms.[5]

In this atmosphere OKH proceeded with plans for SEALION. Since "Britain must be reduced by the middle of September," according to the word Brauchitsch brought to Halder from Hitler, we are reminded once again of the vacuum that existed in terms of an overall war plan.[6] Von Manstein, a great one for plans, wondered if any such thing as a war plan existed. No one had been authorized to draft such a plan; the effect in practice, he felt, was that "every one left things to 'the Führer's intuition.'"[7]

Halder and von Brauchitsch, as the leadership of OKH, appear to have been driven by Hitler's demands and/or their own overoptimism born out of an effort to please him. Their planning actions for SEALION were the direct antithesis of what had always typified German General Staff planning. Schlieffen's plan for attacking France dated from 1905 and was subjected to multiple modifications before its derivative was considered for the 1940 campaign. Further, it was a land campaign, familiar to OKH. So the acceptance of a short, two- to three-month planning period by Halder and von Brauchitsch for such a monumental task as a seaborne invasion, which was completely foreign to them, can only be considered naïve and perilous. At the same time it is also testament to the Führer's persuasive ability as well as whatever other pressure he brought to the situation.

The numbers and consequent problems for an ocean invasion were daunting. Landing craft to transport 100,000 men could not be constructed by September, so 2000 river barges were being converted for the crossing. However, barges were considered poorly suited for the task in view of ocean currents, and their diversion would drastically reduce intra-country transit. Further, a viable location and means of embarkation also presented a problem. The barges would in any event be lost on the first crossing and so would be unavailable for a second trip.[8]

Navy Commander-in-Chief Raeder was lukewarm on SEALION and proposed its delay until spring of 1941. Halder noted on August 6, 1940, "the navy is full of misgivings, and the air force is reluctant to tackle [the] mission; and OKW ... just plays dead." OKH, said Halder, was the sole proponent, a position which seems out of context with the obvious political winds his diary implies normally existed.[9]

Ultimately, the navy under Raeder advised against the operation on the basis of the German Navy's inability to support such an invasion against the British fleet. Rommel felt it was wrong not to risk the landing in England in the period following Dunkirk, which he saw as a window of opportunity; he felt victory over Britain required the invasion. Kesselring proposed to Göring that gliders and parachutists would provide a successful invasion approach. He felt sufficient glider planes and parachutists could have been made available to swamp the defenses on the coastal front and seize airfields on which airborne divisions could then have been landed.[10]

In the final analysis, the supreme commander, who seems to have been ambivalent towards conquering Great Britain, ultimately called off SEALION. Planning was so late and inadequate that postponement until May of 1941 seemed a necessary option, but then the German military initiative would be reduced, with Britain only growing stronger. Further, the air war over Britain had not been coordinated with SEALION, a basic requirement for a successful invasion. Also lacking were the necessary amphibious assets, and the navy was distinctly negative in view of the overwhelming size disparity of the German Navy, which was only 15% of the size of the British Navy.[11]

Hitler's cancellation of SEALION, according to Keitel, is attributable to his awareness of the enormous risks and, "... above all ... [it would mean] ... loss of his last chance of settling the war with Britain by diplomatic means..."[12]

Kesselring, who had been enthusiastic when SEALION was postulated, felt Germany had made a grave mistake in shelving the invasion plans. As he reportedly confided in his son, Germany was fighting a poor man's war and needed a quick victory before the wealthier but temporarily disadvantaged foe recovered to crush her.[13] Kesselring must have encountered a metamorphosis in his thinking, since, according to his memoirs, he had objected to Hitler's breaking the Munich Agreement[14] and the subsequent attack on Poland.[15] If this was his position at the time of these events, then Hitler had won him over to his aggressive aspirations, and, like the other generals, once the war had commenced successfully, he was caught up in the sense of future victories and what they might mean.

Another element in SEALION's cancellation was the failure of the air war against Britain. Kesselring lays the blame on Hermann Göring and the Luftwaffe Command for inept planning. In fact, Kesselring was partially responsible for failure of the 1940 air war, which would have had to succeed in order to precede a successful invasion; it was Kesselring, as chief of the air staff, who had recommended against production of 4-engine bombers in 1937. The Germans were left with aircraft of inadequate range, capacity and tactical characteristics for the over–Channel task. According to Ernst Heinkel, one of the major aircraft suppliers to Germany in both wars, the Heinkel 4-engine HE 177 could and should have been mass-produced for the air war against England, but for political and/or technically deficient reasoning which mandated dive-bombing as a required capability for all bombers, it was discarded.[16]

That SEALION could emerge and die for the above reasons was for von Manstein the fault of one person in Supreme Command — the politician Hitler. In fact Hitler simply did not want to land in Britain. A failure of this magnitude — and the risks were great — would have gravely damaged Hitler's prestige, both in Germany and the world as well. The *Lebensraum* he felt obliged to find for the German people was only to be found in the East, where his real aims lay.[17]

Whether disingenuous or realistic in his post-war observations, von Manstein comments

Chief of the General Staff Col. General Franz Halder (L) with Commander in Chief Army Col. General Walter von Brauchitsch in 1939, shortly after Hitler's recasting of the army to suit his geo-political plans had catapulted them into leadership roles. Ullstein bild/The Granger Collection, New York.

Reichsmarshal Göring and Field Marshal Kesselring watch the take-off for the first major attack on London in 1940. Kesselring, chief of the 2nd Air Fleet during the French Campaign, was promoted to field marshal in mid–1940, just before the Battle of Britain air war commenced; subsequent commands included Commander-in-Chief of the Italy-Africa theater, then almost at war's end reassignment as Commander-in-Chief West. He was tried and convicted of war crimes by the British after the war for his actions against Italian partisans while retreating from Italy in 1944. Bundesarchiv photo no. 26 – bl.33/3/0.VI.

on the momentum for peace he felt existed with the German people at this juncture. The German public demonstrated their enthusiasm for peace in their response to British prime minister Chamberlain's visit to Munich for the Munich Agreement in 1938. Some 20 months later, following the French capitulation, the German people would have welcomed a peace, and were not desirous of annexing Polish territory or dominating Europe; the Master Race idea, he claims, was only taken seriously by a few party fanatics. All Hitler had to do was "whistle his pack of propaganda enthusiasts to heel and the general approval for a reasonable peace would have been free to express itself." However, he doubted Hitler could have accepted a peace based on "reason and justice" as he was then drunk on the belief of his own infallibility.[18] The momentum generated by the regime and Hitler's personal agenda, as expressed in the earlier Hossbach meeting, certainly precluded any pursuit of peace, especially in the East. Certainly, the military as well as the people had been indoctrinated at this point to expect great conquests ahead, and turning back would have been a tenuous action politically.

Under the circumstances Hitler's mind now turned eastward; in his conference with Halder on July 31, 1941, he advised that "To all intents and purposes the war is won.... Britain's [only] hope lies in Russia and the United States ... with Russia smashed, Britain's last hope would be shattered. [This would make] Germany ... master of Europe and the Balkans."

Russia's collapse would induce Britain to give in, he maintained, and with this in mind he had set the Russian ally's destruction for spring of 1941.[19] In reality, Hitler gave up the risk of invading Britain for the equally if not greater risk of a second front in the East with his attack on Russia on June 22, 1941.[20]

9 The Russian Quagmire

Wehrmacht Doubts Grow as the Leadership Sees the Apogee

Hitler had ridden to power using the Bolsheviks as his prime antagonist — he would, he said, save Germany and the world from their hordes. Too, students of *Mein Kampf* and Hitler's early writings will recognize his preoccupation with expanding eastward to provide *Lebensraum* for the German people. So when France fell, the time was ripe. However, Hitler was at his acme where confidence and support by his officer corps resided so when BARBAROSSA, the attack and campaign in Russia, became a quagmire with serious reverses, support began to deteriorate in the Wehrmacht.

The Easy, Quick Victory

Once France had fallen and SEALION had been discarded, Hitler diverted his armies to the East, saying he had not created this powerful army only to have it rot for the rest of the war and that he had never lost sight of the inevitable clash of the world's two most diametrically opposed ideologies. It was better for him to shoulder this grave burden now, in addition to others, than to bequeath it to his successor.

In the face of this von Rundstedt and the other senior commanders attempted unsuccessfully to head off Hitler's plans to attack Russia, warning him against this massive undertaking as they contemplated a two-front war, involving Germany's nemesis, World War I. However, like Napoleon I, Hitler and his OKW staff were underrating the vast Russian potential and, furthermore, disregarding the lessons of World War I. Hitler was not to be deflected; his most positive response was to agree that the Russian Campaign, BARBAROSSA, must be decided west of the River Dnieper.[1]

The generals, according to Guderian, saw the problems ahead clearly. All of them had studied the campaigns of Charles XII of Sweden and Napoleon I and could envision the vast difficulties of the threat that BARBAROSSA represented. They also recognized that adequate preparations for so overwhelming an undertaking were lacking. At the top, hubris had set in at the Supreme Commands of OKH and OKW based on the recent victories, and they were now blind to the realities of the impending campaign.[2]

Hitler himself had criticized German World War I policy leaders for precisely this strategic blunder. So optimistic were OKW and OKH that they anticipated defeating the Russians in eight or ten weeks.[3]

Keitel responded to the impending plans for attack by presenting Hitler with a memorandum suggesting the dire results such a war with Russia could produce. The response was less discussion than a one-sided critical lecture. Hitler lectured him that Stalin never had any intention of abiding by their pact and simply wanted a share of the spoils in Poland as well as to spur the German attack on the West, in the belief that Germany would bleed to death in that campaign. Further, all of the military and strategic considerations put forward in the memorandum were erroneous as far as Hitler was concerned. In the end, Keitel's resignation was refused.[4]

Rationale for the Attack

Hitler laid the political groundwork for BARBAROSSA by spreading propaganda that the Russians intended to attack not only Germany but the whole of Europe. Only days after the Germans crossed the demarcation line it was clear that the Russians had not been planning an attack and that the German attack had, in fact, taken them by surprise, said von Rundstedt in 1948. He was more defensive of German moves two years earlier, though, when he testified at Nuremberg in 1946 that, based on Russian installations and captured maps, Hitler must have been right, that their ally had intended to attack Germany.[5]

"The sooner Russia is crushed the better" was Hitler's dictum in mid–1940, even before he invited Russian foreign minister Molotov to Berlin late that year. A quick victory consuming no more than five months would beat the threat of winter: first Kiev, then the Baltic States and a drive on Moscow followed by a drive on the Baku oil fields. The supreme commander viewed the Russian soldier as inferior, and in an army lacking leadership; equipment such as tanks, he claimed, was no match for the Wehrmacht and was mostly obsolete.[6]

Both Russia and Germany had made moves the other regarded as in conflict with their pact of August 1939. Consequently, Russian foreign minister Molotov visited Berlin in November of 1940 for conferences with Hitler. From the outcome of these meetings, Keitel was unconvinced that Hitler had turned every stone in an effort to prevent the war with Russia. The possible rationale in Keitel's mind, however, for a German preemptive attack was the presence of significant Russian forces on the Eastern Front, which the Germans, Hitler in particular, interpreted as preparations for an attack.[7]

Erich Raeder never really expected the alliance with Russia to last and was not surprised when he learned of Hitler's eastern attack plan. However, Raeder, in trying to dissuade Hitler from embarking on BARBAROSSA, pointed out the decisive importance for the war's outcome of controlling the Mediterranean so as to wrest control of the entrance to the Mideast and North Africa. He was especially concerned about any diversion from what he termed the "main danger," England.[8]

Behind his rationale and decision to mount BARBAROSSA, Keitel concluded in his memoirs that Hitler had become obsessed with the idea that his mission was to destroy Communism. If he knew what a war on two fronts would mean, he opted to go ahead because he and his advisors had wrongly assessed the reserves of Bolshevism and the Stalin state. Thus he was instrumental in bringing about the ruin of himself and the Third Reich he had created, Keitel felt.[9]

The mission of BARBAROSSA as described by Halder in early 1941 was to "crush Russia in a rapid campaign," to destroy the Russian Army without pause in an area no more than 500 to 1000 kilometers into Russia; the River Dnieper was the easternmost invasion point so as to prevent the Russians from retreating to safe enclaves, with the concomitant overextension of German supply lines.[10]

Fully supporting Hitler's expansionist plans, and, in fact, having been fully involved in their implementation, Halder addressed the chiefs of staff on June 4, 1941. He told them Operation BARBAROSSA was based on the need to "build a Europe finally without Britain ... [and give Germany] a free hand."[11]

Heinz Guderian could scarcely believe the news from the Chief of the General Staff when he was briefed on Operation BARBAROSSA. Not only was a second front, the nemesis of World War I, to be undertaken, but Halder was estimating in late 1940 that Russia's defeat would require just "eight to ten weeks."[12]

Planning the Attack

The forecast of a matter of weeks for victory emanated from OKH and OKW prior to the attack on Russia. However, von Manstein, assigned his first of key Eastern Front commands, 56 Panzer Corps, in early 1941, says two errors on Hitler's part caused the eventual failure of the campaign: the underrating of the Soviet Union's resources and the fighting qualities of the Red Army, and, second, failure to achieve a uniform strategic policy at the summit, that is, between Hitler and the Army High Command.

Halder, however, in a post-war retrospective describes the army's position in early 1941 regarding the upcoming Eastern Campaign as apprehensive and negative. The Army High Command, OKH, met with Hitler and OKW on February 3, 1941, and warned Hitler of Russia's overwhelming strength in manpower; their huge tank count, estimated at 10,000 units; and that the length of the front would double, far beyond the adequacy of German forces to cover. Hitler, Halder says, had countered all army objections.[13]

The transcription of that February 3, 1941, meeting survived to tell a far different tale when presented at the Nuremberg Trials, however. Halder, leading the meeting, stressed equivalent troop strengths, with the Germans being "far superior in quality." Only one general, Timoshenko, was said to be of any quality. Russian tank and artillery quality was given by Halder as inferior, though of greater quantity. Hitler entered into the discussion throughout the meeting. Mutual cooperation and resolution of any apparent impediments set the tone of the meeting as opposed to the confrontation implied by Halder's report, described above. In the final analysis the Führer on the whole was in agreement and reminded the group that the main aim was "to gain possession of the Baltic States and Leningrad."[14]

Halder's diary entry of December 5, 1940, recounting his meeting with Hitler on that date, attests to his heavy involvement in BARBAROSSA planning; his diary records much of the basic material he presented in the February meeting. His discussion with Hitler reviewed plans for the annihilation of major industrial centers in the Ukraine, in Moscow and in Leningrad, and the destruction of Russian forces.[15]

Further, Halder had previously tasked his deputy, General Paulus, in September of 1940, to study all elements of an attack plan on the Soviet Union; then in January of 1941 he was a key observer and participant in military exercises at von Rundstedt's headquarters in St. Germain, near Paris, the object being to review the forthcoming attack on Russia by von Rundstedt's Army Group South.[16]

Hitler saw Moscow as the center of Russia's political power but the Ukraine as the critical breadbasket, the Donetz Basin the center of heavy industry and the Caucasus the source of oil. He had been persuaded the war would only be successful if all of the latter three areas were seized, so that his and OKW's military strategy and tactics were constructed accordingly. Von Rundstedt's purely military solution was to attack Leningrad in the north and cutoff Russia from the Baltic and then move south-east to Moscow followed by a continued move southeasterly. If reverses developed, Rundstedt's view was to employ a defensive withdrawal to the west, a tactic regarded as anathema by Hitler. Von Rundstedt predicted a war with Russia lasting a period of years, whereas OKH and Hitler's entourage were predicting a matter of weeks to bringing the Russians to their knees.[17] (See map, "Eastern Europe, the Fatal Second Front," page 82.)

Despite his personal misgivings, however, once the political decision had been made nothing remained for von Rundstedt but to comply loyally and correctly.[18] This was to become vintage Rundstedt as the war progressed. The factors responsible for his attitude represent the paradigm separating Hitler's generals in varying degrees, a most important enigma emerging from World War II Germany. That is, some, such as von Rundstedt, repeatedly saw impending failure, but continued as long as Hitler would have them, at the other extreme were those whose philosophy drove them to act against him before reverses were evident. The great middle group of his military leaders, though, gave full support as long as victory lay ahead, but support would erode in varying degrees to war's end as defeat began to present itself. The first major reverses began in Russia in the first BARBAROSSA winter, 1941–42. This encouraged anti–Hitler attitudes including an attempt by army officers to assassinate him in early 1943, a failure attributed to a faulty bomb mechanism.[19]

Erich Raeder also had a predilection against BARBAROSSA, but for different reasons: he felt the war should have been pursued in the Mediterranean, as discussed above. Nevertheless once the decision had been made he moved ahead aggressively to initiate action even before the commencement of BARBAROSSA. The Naval Command requested OKW approval on June 15 of the navy's plan to attack and destroy non–German submarines entering the Baltic Sea before B-day. The reason given was to preclude Russian submarines from carrying out mining operations or lying in wait to be used as torpedo platforms in the event either side started hostilities. The "hostilities" Raeder referred to were those that occurred as a result

Eastern Europe, the Fatal Second Front

of Germany's planned but still secret attack on Russia, which commenced on June 22. OKW chief Keitel responded to Naval Command's request in the affirmative and directed that the ostensible reason to be given for attacks prior to B-day, June 22, was that German Naval Forces had believed they were dealing with penetrating British submarines.[20]

Sir David Maxwell-Fyfe, British prosecutor at Nuremberg, asked Raeder during testimony on May 20, 1946, whether he endorsed this deception six days before the attack on the Soviet Union. Raeder responded, "I consider ... [it] right ... because it is always important to get in before one's opponent ... [and secondly it] was ordered by the Führer."[21] Raeder exhibited one of the more aggressive and proactive postures of Hitler's military leaders; that being the case, it is difficult to accept and/or believe his excuse that his had been a military and not a political mission, as he told the court in his final plea at Nuremberg.[22]

B-Day, the Attack

Following the launching of Germany's "preventive attack" on June 22, 1941, a stereotypical Keitel, unlike the more independent von Rundstedt, felt obliged to concede that Hitler had been right about the imminence of a Russian invasion of Germany. However, because of his having observed the Red Army's 1931 maneuvers and having seen the country's vast resources, his view of Russia's war capacity differed significantly from that of Hitler who had not been privy to these events, but relied on second-hand inputs from his entourage.[23]

However, the Germans, particularly OKH in the person of Franz Halder, would demonstrate a poor record of extrapolating Russian materiel and manpower, which then yielded an unreliable military timetable. Just eleven days after B-day, the attack on Russia, Halder's War Diary of July 3 records, "It is thus probably no overstatement to say that the Russian Campaign has been won in the space of two weeks."[24] This is a repetition of Halder's earlier unrealistic July 11, 1940, acceptance of the German Air Force's estimate of 14 to 28 days to smash the British air assets, a tendency that would wreak havoc with BARBAROSSA's prospects for success and would yield sizable losses in equipment and manpower.[25]

Problems would now compound themselves. Misled by the summer victories of 1941, Hitler, now calling the shots through OKW, misread the military possibilities as winter approached. He ordered von Rundstedt, Commander-in-Chief of Army Group South, to split his forces and attack Kursk to the north, Poltava to the northeast and Rostov to the south. Strong Russian counterattacks in the Rostov area dictated a tactical defensive retreat behind the River Mius so at to prevent German forces from being isolated and cut off. After repeated unanswered requests to OKW for approval of this retreat, von Rundstedt added his request that if Hitler differed on the withdrawal, he must find another commander as replacement.[26]

"The Führer went up in smoke over this," according to Field Marshal Keitel in OKW; Hitler was well aware that he himself had been responsible for the looming debacle, but his rage was based on his feeling that von Rundstedt had turned against him. He immediately replaced von Rundstedt with the pro–Nazi Field Marshal von Reichenau. Ironically, within days Hitler, after personal investigation at the front, acquiesced, allowing von Reichenau to order the withdrawal.[27]

Guderian, commanding Panzer Group 2 in von Bock's Army Group Center, had other but not dissimilar command problems. He found strategic objectives continually changed: first the objective of OKH and the Supreme Commander was to be Moscow via Smolensk; but, by August 23, Guderian was ordered to attack south, away from Moscow and toward Kiev, targeting the Ukraine. By October Moscow was again the target, but by now, with two months wasted, winter had arrived to provide a greater foe than the Russians. By December 5–6, 1941, the attack ground to a halt, short of Moscow.[28]

Driving to 24 Panzer headquarters in this bitterly cold winter of 1941, precursor of things to come, Guderian recalled with a serve of déjà vu the futile campaigns of Napoleon over a century earlier and Charles XII of Sweden in the 1700s.[29] "Only he who saw the endless expanse of Russian snow during this winter of our misery and felt the icy wind that blew across it, burying in snow every object in its path: who drove for hour after hour through that no-man's land only at last to find too thin shelter with insufficiently clothed , half-starved men: and who also saw by contrast the well-fed, warmly clad and fresh Siberians, fully equipped for winter fighting: only a man who knew all that can truly judge the events which now occurred."[30]

The German onslaught found itself in a quagmire compounded by lack of preparation and adaptability of men and machines to the devastating Russian winters. No provision had been made for winter clothing such as snow shirts, boot grease, underclothes and woolen trousers. Each regiment had lost some 500 men to frostbite; as a result of the cold the machine guns were no longer able to fire, and with the 37mm anti-tank gun no longer effective against the T-34 Russian tank, panic was setting in.

The Germans, normally characteristically methodical and thorough, had misjudged their Russian foe in both manpower and armor as well as the fighting environment. However, neither armor nor numerical superiority should have been a surprise to the Germans. When Germany attacked her ally, German tank strength was some 3200 tanks.[31] In 1933 Guderian had visited a single Russian tank factory which was producing 22 tanks a day. Further, as far back as 1937, German intelligence figures estimated as many as 17,000 tanks in the Russian inventory. Guderian estimated a conservative 10,000 in his 1937 publication *Achtung! Panzer!* though he found printing that figure proved difficult politically given the Third Reich's propensity for propaganda hyperbole.[32]

Prescient German officers in the Ordnance Office and their suppliers, the manufacturers, had concluded before the start of BARBAROSSA in June of 1941 that the Russians probably possessed superior and heavier tanks. Hitler, anxious to awe and intimidate his soon-to-be foe, had encouraged the visit of a Russian tank commission in the spring of 1941 to inspect German tank factories and schools. During the visit the Russians refused to accept that the Panzer IV was Germany's heaviest tank; they felt the Germans must be hiding the newest models as they had been advised by their government they would be shown everything.[33] The actual comparison of World War II tanks, shown in the table "Major World War II Tanks," indicates the significant disparity in tank strength between the two countries.

Within months after the attack on Russia was launched the riddle was solved when the Russian T-34 appeared on the front. The attack by the Russians on the 4th Panzer Division south of Mzensk on October of 1941 was the first occasion in which the "vast superiority of the Russian T-34" to German tanks became plainly apparent. At the time, defensive weapons against the T-34 were only successful when conditions were unusually favorable. The Germans found the short-barreled 75mm gun of the 4th Panzer was only effective if the T-34 were attacked from the rear; even then a hit had to be scored on the grating above the engine to knock it out, taking great skill in maneuvering into position.[34]

German Tank Capability Wanes

In late 1941 as conflicting orders arrived from OKH and OKW redirecting the original Moscow attack plan, Guderian attempted to reclaim the situation with Hitler so as to direct forces to Moscow in a timely fashion relative to the weather. General Guenther Blumentritt, then Chief of Staff to Field Marshal von Kluge in 4th Army, considered Moscow could have been captured if Guderian's plan had been followed, but Hitler had his way and it was not.[35] In a second meeting Guderian sought permission for a defensive pull-back and advised Hitler that many of the problems of equipment, supply and tactical direction could be reduced if general officers who had actual front-line experience traded places with OKH and OKW headquarters personnel. This "stirred up a hornets nest," and led, on December 26, 1941, to Guderian's removal from command and placement in the reserve pool; his participation in the Russian Campaign had ended for the ensuing 14 months.[36]

Major World War II Tanks

Country	Tank	Total Produced	Weight (tons)	Production Period
Germany	Panzer IA/B	1,500*	5.4–5.8	1934–39
	Panzer II A/B	1,000*	9.34	1934–42
	Panzer IIIA–N	5,664	15–21.9	1939–45
	Panzer IV A–J	9,000*	17.3–24.6	1940–44
	Panther D	600	45.5	1942–45
	Tiger	1,335	55	1942–44
	King Tiger	500*	69.7	1944–45
Russia	T34/76/85	40,000	26.3–31.5	1940 on
	T40/60	8,000	6.2–5.71	1941–43
France	Renault 35	1,600	10	1935–40
	Char B1-bis	365	32	1935–40
Britain	Churchill Mk I–VIII		39–40	1940–45
	Mk 6 A15	5,300	19	1940–43
	Mk II A12	3,000	11	1938–43
Italy	M13/40		14	1940–43*
USA	M3/Grant/Lee	6,258	26.78	1941–42
	M4 Sherman	40,000	29.6	1942–46
	M3/M5 Stuart		12.3/15	1941 on

*estimate[37]

As the campaign wore on a proliferation of tank concepts and configurations emerged. So many variations and types were designed that field repair and logistics became a quagmire. To combat the superior T-34 the 60 ton Tiger tank under development was augmented by a light tank, the 35–45 ton Panther. By May of 1943 monthly production of these tanks had reached 285 and 250, respectively. Hitler ordered reequipping of older Panzer IIIs with new 75mm cannon and the use of Panzer II and Czech T-38 chassis as assault platforms.[38]

Changes and modifications continued in an attempt to confront ongoing tactical problems. By mid–1943 production of the Panzer III was discontinued in favor of assault guns. It was hoped that a Hitler fantasy, the gigantic 100 ton Mouse, would be in production by the end of 1943. Armor plating was to be added to the Panzer IV and Panther tanks to defend against Russian anti-tank weapons. The end result was simply creation of countless variations of the original, each requiring its own unique spare parts, and thus representing a complex repair and logistics problem.[39]

Meanwhile the Russians continued to mass-produce their outstanding T-34. As was found in World War I the essence of successful tank warfare lies in the mass commitment of armor. The Russians had been able to do this by concentrating on a single tank model; the Germans had debilitated their ability to do so by their multiple programs.[40]

Finally recognizing the morass being created, the General Staff convinced Hitler to abandon all but the Tiger and Panther production. But abandonment of the Panzer IV, in Guderian's view, unless countermanded, would lead to rapid defeat of German forces by the foe even without any aid from the other Western Allies.[41]

In view of the critical armor problem, insightful officers prevailed on Hitler to consult with Guderian to find a solution before the impending collapse. Guderian forged an agreement whereby he was rehired and appointed inspector-general of armored troops reporting directly to Hitler. Reorganization of tank programs and their fielding ensued under his direction; this continued through 1944, though in the face of internecine warfare involving OKW, OKH and interference of the mercurial Supreme Commander.[42]

The third problem confronting the Wehrmacht was the vast and seemingly endless resource of Russian manpower. As an old Czarist general said of the German assault, "We were just beginning to get on our feet and now you arrive and throw us back twenty years. ... we are fighting for Russia. ... we are all united."[43]

Sixth Army's Debacle, Precursor of the Future

In September of 1941 von Manstein's performance as commander of 56 Corps in a dash from East Prussia to Lake Ilmen led to his promotion to command of Eleventh Army. Eleventh Army was engaged in the Crimean Campaign during this first Russian winter and under von Manstein conquered the Crimea and defeated the Russian landings at Kerch (see map, Eastern Europe, the Fatal Second Front, page 82). With the fall of Sevastopol Hitler promoted von Manstein to Field Marshal.

By late 1942 von Manstein was given command of the Don Army Group consisting of Sixth Army, Fourth Panzer Army and the Third Romanian Army. Sixth Army, under General Friedrich von Paulus, was charged with capturing and holding Stalingrad. However, in late December of 1942 Sixth Army's position at Stalingrad had deteriorated such that it was imperative the army break out in a southwesterly direction. Hitler agreed but insisted it hold its encirclement on the north, east and western fronts of the cauldron, which it could not do in addition to breaking out. Von Manstein, as commander of the Don Army Group, ordered Sixth Army to make the break out without holding its positions, however, General Paulus reported insufficient fuel to follow the army group orders and so by default maintained his

Field Marshal Erich von Manstein with troops in Sevastopol in 1942; Manstein conceived the successful Western Attack Plan of 1940, a variation on the older Schlieffen and von Moltke plans. Commander of the Don Army Group late in BARBAROSSA, he was active in the attempt to save Sixth Army at Stalingrad. He was considered one of the best brains in the German Army. Ullstein bild/The Granger Collection, New York.

Stalingrad position, and avoided running counter to Hitler's orders. Even had Paulus elected to break out in accord with group orders, that move could have had catastrophic consequences given possible adverse circumstances of fuel, weather and enemy attacks.[44]

Göring and Hitler had promised that adequate airborne supplies would be provided to Sixth Army, but that never occurred. Finally, by January 22, 1943, Paulus sought Hitler's permission to capitulate, this time doing so with von Manstein's approval. Despite this Hitler ordered Sixth Army to fight to the end with the result that 90,000 German troops were taken prisoner by the Russians.[45]

The rationale for von Manstein's giving Paulus an order contrary to Hitler's order lies in his belief that "no general can vindicate his loss of a battle by claiming that he was compelled — against his better judgement — to execute an order that led to defeat." The only course open is that of disobedience; success or failure will decide whether he has chosen correctly, he writes in his memoirs and so testified at Nuremberg.[46]

On February 6, 1943, in a meeting with von Manstein, Hitler admitted his exclusive responsibility for the loss of Sixth Army. Initially von Manstein had the impression Hitler was deeply depressed in view of the fate of the soldiers; yet later he wondered if Hitler "did not regard all of them — from field marshal down to private soldier — as mere tools of his war aims."[47]

Von Manstein was finally relieved of command at the end of March of 1944 with the reason given that the large scale operations for which von Manstein had been needed were now a thing of the past. Hitler said his plan now was to hold stubbornly to what the Germans now occupied. Von Manstein felt that though Hitler pretended continued confidence in him, that now only applied to superior military expertise, but not to the ability to pursue a Russian victory. More to the point Hitler had a difficult time getting his way with von Manstein; his pragmatism apparently had engendered a fatal reputation as a defeatist among the Hitler clique, including Goebbels, Himmler and Göring, and it would be easier to work with a more pliant commander.[48]

In von Manstein's view Hitler had reached the peak of his success with the conquest of France in mid–1940; for von Rundstedt, if not the invasion of Russia, then certainly Stalingrad, three years later, signaled the loss of the war. Field Marshal Wilhelm von Leeb, Army Group North commander in the invasion of Russia, saw Hitler's zenith in 1942 on his way to the Stalingrad debacle.[49] Pursuant to Hitler's tendency for precipitous action, von Leeb was put on the retired list in 1942 after his failure to take Leningrad, and von Manstein was retired in 1944 after the loss at Stalingrad.

Chivalry and the Rules of War — Dispense with Them!

In March of 1941, before the start of BARBAROSSA, Hitler had addressed his senior commanders earmarked for the Eastern Front at the Reich Chancellery in Berlin; he advised them that with the aggressive intentions of the Western Powers, Britain and America, and based on his thesis that war with the Soviet Union had become inevitable, to sit back and wait would tilt the balance against the Reich. He further admonished them to dispense with the outdated ideas about chivalry and the accepted rules of war. He directed execution of Soviet political commissars out-of-hand on capture, which was to become the notorious Commissar Order, and he outlined the BARBAROSSA Order which called for ruthless treatment of people in conquered areas and leniency toward German soldiers accused of excesses against the population.[50]

As Hitler said in his meeting of June 1941 just before the attack on the Russian ally, treating the civilian population too leniently had been interpreted as weakness in the Balkans; the Russians would be far more troublesome, and, accordingly, "the mailed fist would ultimately be the kindest way; one could only smash terror with counter-terror.... It was not with law books that he himself had smashed the German Communist Party's tactics, but with the brute force of his SA [brownshirts] movement."[51]

The verdicts handed down in late 1946 by the Nuremberg Trial judges in the cases of Alfred Jodl and Wilhelm Keitel were heavily influenced by authorship of and/or being signatory to the long series of orders regarded by many Germans as shameful; these orders promulgated Hitler's commands to the services directing their treatment of both civilian and military adversaries. Most notorious were the BARBAROSSA, Commissar, anti-populace measures and Commando Orders (execution of commandos upon capture), the first three being directed at the campaign against Russia.

Jodl stated in testimony at Nuremberg that BARBAROSSA was a shameful order all soldiers would oppose. BARBAROSSA, signed by Keitel, Jodl's superior in OKW, and issued on May 13, 1941, was comprised of two parts: Part One, "Treatment of Offenses Committed by Enemy Civilians," dispensed with courts and called for ruthless treatment using extreme methods. Part Two, "Treatment of Offenses against Enemy Civilians" by members of the Wehrmacht, made prosecution of German soldiers non-obligatory, and in rendering judgments it was to be borne in mind that Bolsheviks had accounted for the blood of many Germans in the fight against National Socialism. A subsequent order was issued on July 27, 1941, which called for the destruction of all copies of BARBAROSSA, but retained its validity. Jodl testified he did not remember this order.[52]

Jodl drafted another order, which was issued on July 23, 1941, which charged the occupation forces with "spreading such terror ... as is alone appropriate to eradicate every inclination to resist" and ordered that instead of requesting more troops for maintenance of peace in occupied areas they were to apply "draconian measures." Quixotically, Jodl felt this was an entirely proper order, not terrible as the Nuremberg prosecutor suggested, and was clearly within the bounds of international law which he said required that "inhabitants of occupied territory must follow orders ... of the occupying power. ... any resistance ... is forbidden."[53]

BARBAROSSA was only one of numerous directives drafted and/or signed by Keitel. Representative of these were the Nacht und Nebel (Night and Fog) Orders issued in an attempt to control and prosecute offenses against German forces in occupied areas. One signed by Keitel on December 12, 1941, says, in part,

> "The Führer is of the following opinion. If these offenses are punished with imprisonment, even with hard labor for life, this will be looked upon as a sign of weakness. Efficient and enduring intimidation can only be achieved either by capital punishment or by measures by which the population do not know the fate of the criminal. This aim is achieved when the criminal is transferred to Germany."[54]

The essence of the *Nacht und Nebel* concept is embodied in the order of February 2, 1942, which says,

> (a) the prisoners will vanish without leaving a trace,
> (b) no information may be given as to their whereabouts or their fate.[55]

Responding to British Prosecutor Sir Maxwell-Fyfe during his Nuremberg Trial, Keitel said the *Nacht und Nebel* decrees weighed most heavily on his mind of all the orders he had signed and/or issued.[56]

One other onerous order issued, this by the Army Commander in Chief von Brauchitsch, was the Commissar Order of June 6, 1941. This order, originating in the Supreme Command but promulgated through the army, called for all Russian political officers captured with their troops to be summarily executed. In his memoirs and testimony at Nuremberg, von Manstein said he informed his superiors that this order, which he considered unsoldierly, would not be implemented; his attitude, he claims, was endorsed by his higher command. Though the order was never rescinded, he never implemented it.[57] However, evidence at Nuremberg showed differently, finding that Eleventh Army under von Manstein had indeed conducted executions under this order, as discussed in Chapter 16.[58]

Jodl reviewed the Commissar Order (execution out-of-hand of Soviet political officers upon capture), but did not draft it; he suggested to Keitel, and thus to Hitler, it be redrawn as a reprisal order. Drafted and signed by his deputy, General Walter Warlimont, the draft, dated May 12, 1941, a month before the attack on Russia, carried a postscript by Jodl, "We must reckon with possible reprisals against German airmen. It would, therefore, be better to consider all these measures in the nature of reprisals."[59]

Evidence presented at Nuremberg shows the Commissar Order to have been in violation of the Hague Conventions, which Jodl must have known. Jodl claims to have offered the reprisal recommendation in order to defer activation of the order until its use was clearly justified.[60]

When questioned by Prosecutor Roberts, Jodl admitted his preparation of the Commando Order (execution of commandos upon capture), which he and his staff prepared in conjunction with the chief of the Armed Forces Legal Department. He said he opposed the order almost to the last moment since it could be used arbitrarily against uniformed soldiers engaged in actions within the bounds of international law. He did not completely agree with the order but relied on the highest legal authority at the time. "It was one of the few — or the only — order" Jodl received from Hitler that in his mind he completely rejected, he told the court. He maintained the field commanders supported this thinking, interpreting the order in the mildest way, and that few incidents occurred and those that did were justified.

As a final explanation of his acquiescence to Hitler in promulgating the Commando Order, Jodl asked the court to empathize with his five and one-half years under the Führer, which, not unlike his then-current POW status, was a sort of forced servitude. The actions of the British Commandos "put the Führer into a rage against which I was powerless," he said.[61]

As the result of the shooting of 50 English Royal Air Force officers at Sagan in March of 1944, when they were recaptured after escaping, Jodl claims to have finally reached a point where he felt Hitler was "disavowing all humane conceptions of right." Up to this point Hitler's actions could have been justified under international law as reprisals — but "This act was not a reprisal." Jodl claimed not to have served with unabated loyalty from that point forward. He said informally at Nuremberg that he knew that Keitel would not stand up against Hitler on such issues, so that he, Jodl, took it upon himself to buck Hitler at every turn on such matters which he felt could never be justified. In the end, he recognized that Hitler was without conception of honor and with no feeling for human beings except as masses and pawns in his ambitious schemes.[62] Jodl's professions at this point need to be qualified by the fact that he had been under continuous questioning by the prosecution, and under this influence might have begun to either empathize with Allied attitudes or thought he ought to appear to, and/or perhaps he began to reflect on the reality of Hitler's conduct for the first time.

Keitel or Jodl were the conduits for these orders to the field commands, a necessary element to Hitler's modus operandi. Keitel facilitated the Commando Order, which was issued by OKW but not signed by him; "according to my inner convictions I did not consider it right, but after it had been given I did not oppose it or take a stand against it in any way," he said in 1946.[63] Another order, of September 16, 1941, signed by him and intended to control and suppress communist insurrectionary movement in the occupied territories, said, in part,

In order to nip in the bud any conspiracy, the strongest measures should be taken. ... one must bear in mind that in the countries affected human life has absolutely no value and that a deterrent effect can be achieved only through the application of extraordinarily harsh measures.[64]

In his memoirs Keitel relates that, with Hitler dead, these orders he had ordered Keitel to prepare and forward to the field commands were used against him by the tribunal prosecution. Then in Nuremberg testimony, whether faced with no realistic alternative or seeking the mercy of the court, Keitel accepted full responsibility for the orders he signed as well as the results.[65]

Why did Keitel sign these onerous orders then? Testifying in further explanation in his defense, he attempted to answer, "[T]he fulfillment of urgent tasks assigned by Hitler ... demanded complete self-abnegation.... [Many of these] questions which conflicted with my conscience and my convictions ... [were] a blow to my most intimate personal principles."[66]

One further rationalizing point was found by Keitel when he pointed to the words in many such orders signed by him, "It is the will of the Führer after long consideration." He claims in his testimony that he felt the recipient military commander in the field would immediately recognize from this rhetoric that this was an order OKW neither approved of nor considered right. In his OKW position it was his lot to place his signature on a vast number of orders, many of which he had little or no familiarity with nor responsibility for.[67] Yet he is grasping at straws here; as Hermann Göring said of "yes men," he did not know too many "no men" working for the Führer. At the same time Keitel did what he had to do to keep his rank, his job, and his position in the hierarchy, and not to cross Hitler.

General Franz Halder, Chief of the General Staff from 1938 until his dismissal in 1942, gave his opinion of the reason for Keitel's unlimited allegiance to Hitler as Keitel's "lack of talent and his feeble character." This opinion is significant in that Halder's position in OKH had been parallel to that of Keitel's in OKW. That Halder was dismissed would indicate Hitler found him less than willing to render the uninhibited support found in Keitel and Jodl. More pertinent to Halder's dismissal was probably his continued incorrect estimates of men and materials on the Russian Front. In Keitel's case, Hitler could only tolerate a "Keitel" as a facilitator.[68]

Reflecting the post-war court assessment of these three men, Keitel and Jodl were hanged at Nuremberg while Halder ended his post-war career working as a historian for the U.S. Army.

BARBAROSSA *Falls to Major Miscalculations*

Of the three major German miscalculations — manpower, equipment and weather, combined with the vastness of Russian geography — the first, manpower, grew to haunt Franz Halder. While he had estimated Russian strength as 50 to 75 divisions, his estimates had risen steadily to some 200 by April of 1941; then by early August, a month into the two-year Russian adventure, OKH had identified 360 Russian divisions.[69]

Using a yardstick of two divisions for every million of population, Halder originally stated that the number of divisions which had confronted the German Army by that point was the maximum the Russians could raise, saying, "we need not anticipate further large-scale activations."[70] Reality was far more staggering, however. By 1942 the Germans were estimating that Stalin could still raise another one and one-half to two million men (about 150 divisions).[71]

In a second serious error, the capability of Russian tanks, both in quality and quantity, had been vastly underrated by the Germans. General Heinz Guderian, probably their leading tank expert, describes the first encounter with the "vast superiority of the Russian T-34," that of the Russian attack on the First Panzer Division on October 6, 1941. The division suffered grievous casualties in the encounter. German defensive weapons were found to be only successful against the T-34 where conditions were extremely favorable, as noted above, on a rear attack, requiring great maneuvering skill.[72]

According to Halder after the war, Hitler completely rejected the Army High Command's reliable 1942 intelligence report that Russian output of first line tanks amounted to at least 1200 per month, calling it, "idiotic twaddle."[73]

The German General Staff Fades into Irrelevance

In the words of a Führer Directive of August 21, 1941:

> The proposals of OKH for the continuance of the operations in the East, dated 18 August, do not conform with my intentions. I order herewith: ... not the capture of Moscow, but rather ... occupation of the Crimea ... isolation of the Russian oil regions in the Caucasus and ... the encirclement of Leningrad.[74]

To further insult the Army High Command, Hitler formally reproached the Commander-in-Chief, von Brauchitsch, in a memorandum of August 24, 1941, for failure to conduct operations along the lines he desired. Halder now regarded the Führer's pervasive interference as "unendurable for OKH" and proposed to von Brauchitsch they both tender their resignations. They took no action.[75]

Their summary conclusion regarding the memorandum and the August 21 Directive was that the former was filled with contradictions and that Hitler was to blame for "the zigzag course caused by his successive orders ... [and] OKH [cannot] tarnish its good name with these orders."[76]

The rigid defense tactic typical of World War I was used initially by the Russians in World War II; seeing its failure, they soon went to flexible mobile-operational warfare. Their execution of mobile warfare was seen by Halder as on the level of German Army standards. Quixotically, under Hitler's "no-retreat" philosophy the German Army gave up the mobile operational warfare so successful previously and wound up with an unimaginative, rigid defense which led to failure. Halder saw Stalingrad as emblematic of the disasters emanating from Hitler's mode of warfare, and repeated in miniature a thousand-fold as Germany's eastern catastrophe proceeded.[77]

Top commanders began to be relieved as 1941 ended. Commander in Chief von Brauchitsch left for health reasons in December and was replaced by the supreme commander himself. Now Halder reported directly to Hitler. Would this effect a compatible modus operandi? The next 9 months would tell.

By early September of 1942 Keitel bore news of Halder's impending dismissal. The supreme commander had increasingly reproached the military leadership for its incompetence and failure to grasp essentials. He refused to accept Halder's prognosis on the outcome of Stalin's defense of Stalingrad once Stalin had unleashed his new Russian Army of one and a half million men now being formed. What counted with the German Army in the task at hand was, "'not military skill but the ardor of the National Socialist creed'— something he [Hitler] could not expect from an officer of the old school." As Franz Halder says in his last *War Diary* entry (September 24, 1942), Hitler insisted not only in indoctrinating the General Staff with his fanatical ideology, but was "determined to enforce his will also into the army."[78]

10 The U-Boat Versus Surface Ship War

Initial Victories, Then Heavy Losses, Concern the Forces

Organization for an Effective Sea War

With reverses in Russia and North Africa by late 1942 and into 1943, one of the bright spots for Hitler and the Wehrmacht was the U-boat campaign. Not so successful, though had been the German Navy's use of large surface ships. So Hitler's military acumen, so often challenged, and rightfully so, was clearly on the mark in his assessment of the effectiveness of heavy surface ships as opposed to submarines and small surface ships in the battle to subdue Britain. As a result of his persistence on this issue, Karl Dönitz replaced Erich Raeder as navy chief in early 1943 with almost total emphasis on U-boats as opposed to large surface ships. The U-boat, which had posed a serious threat to Britain's survival since the start of war in 1940, then was defeated by anti-submarine technology developments in 1943 which made it non-productive, with two-thirds of the fleet being sunk by war's end.

Major Strategic Shift to U-boats

As time passed Hitler's tendency to second-guess his generals and admirals stimulated significant differences between Erich Raeder and himself over the issue of U-boats versus capital ships. Hitler and Raeder's successor, Karl Dönitz, then chief of U-boats, felt U-boats as opposed to surface ships would have a decisive effect on the war's outcome. As the map, "The German Ocean Access Problem" (Chapter 5) shows, German surface ships have a distinct operational disadvantage as compared to submarines given the country's geography.[1] When Hitler ordered the decommissioning of large surface ships, Raeder balked, maintaining surface ships deserved equal weight. Under the conditions Raeder resigned, being replaced by Karl Dönitz as Commander-in-Chief of the navy in early 1943.[2]

Though anti-submarine warfare ultimately took its toll on Germany's U-boat fleet with two-thirds—over 800 boats—destroyed, the experience of German capital ships in World War II was dismal, as illustrated in the table below. All of the major ships were sunk in action or scuttled.[3]

World War II German Capital Ships

Ship	Commissioned	Displacement (tons)	Armament	Fate[4]
Deutschland	1933	15.9	6 × 11"	Scuttled after bomb damage, May '45
Adm. Scheer	1934	15.9	6 × 11"	Capsized after bombing, April '45
Graf Spee	1936	16.2	6 × 11"	Scuttled, Dec. '39
Gneisenau	1938	38.9	9 × 11"	Scuttled, April '45
Scharnhorst	1939	38.9	9 × 11"	Sunk in action, Dec. '43
Bismarck	1940	50.9	8 × 15"	Sunk in action, May '41
Tirpitz	1941	52.6	8 × 15"	Sunk by air attack, Nov. '44

Hitler recognized the developing systemic problem and ordered the decommissioning of the capital ships in view of their lack of effectiveness. He apparently seized on this in early 1943 as a propitious opportunity to replace Raeder with the more dynamic Karl Dönitz, who had demonstrated his grasp of the issues key to Germany's survival. Dönitz, however, in a reflection of the Führer's confidence in him, convinced Hitler to retain the capital ships for political, economic and military reasons, though his and the navy's primary concentration from this point on was the U-boat.[5]

Raeder had proposed Admiral Carls, the most senior naval officer, as his replacement; however, he suggested to the Führer that if, indeed, he intended to give primary emphasis to U-boats, then Dönitz was the greatest authority and should become Navy Commander-in-Chief. Politics and personal bias, it appears, played a secondary role in the selection of Dönitz for this critical leadership and strategic role.[6]

When Dönitz proposed to Hitler that retention of the capital ships would be in Germany's interests both politically and militarily, his rationale was that decommissioning of the ships would not result in any appreciable increase in manpower or material, and breaking them up would make substantial claims on labor and technical resources. Dönitz went so far as to say he was unable to support orders for breaking them up and requested their cancellation. Hitler, though "disagreeably surprised," acceded to his request. His principle for successfully working for Hitler was always to do what it required to retain the latter's confidence. "I was always frank ... never concealed ... mistakes ... or any plans that had ended in failure. I did not hesitate, for example, to tell him in blunt terms my anxieties with regards to the U-boat war; and when, in May 1943, this collapsed, Hitler uttered no word of reproach."

Dönitz felt this approach paid dividends and on more than one occasion says he told Hitler, "That is something as Naval Commander-in-Chief I won't do," so his post-war memoirs claim.[7]

The relationship between Dönitz and Hitler developed slowly but at an accelerating rate as time passed. Between 1934, when Dönitz as captain of the *Emden* first met Hitler, until 1939 he encountered him three more times. Once war started their quarterly meetings consisted of military reports to Hitler on U-boat warfare. Before Dönitz's installation as Commander-in-Chief in early 1943 the meetings were always in group format; however, that changed once he became navy head. From that point on Dönitz spent much time at headquarters dealing personally and alone with Hitler on navy matters.[8]

According to Dönitz his ties to Hitler were three-fold: his oath, his personal agreement with the tenets of National Socialism, and lastly, a personal relationship with the Führer which now began to develop.[9] Though he maintained in his Nuremberg testimony that this personal relationship was apolitical and that he was never consulted on political matters, many of his speeches and public expressions show Hitler's political and ideological influence coming through. One such example is his address of December 17, 1943, to Navy commanders where he said, in part,

> I am a firm adherent of the idea of ideological education.... It is ... necessary for us to train the soldier uniformly ... that he may be adjusted ideologically to our Germany. Every dualism, every dissension ... or every divergence ... impl[ies] a weakness.... It is nonsense to say the soldier or the officer must have no politics. The soldier embodies the State.... He must therefore stand with his whole weight behind the State.... We can only [win this war] if we take part in it with holy zeal, with all our fanaticism.[10]

Dönitz's future elevation to head of state is clearly understandable and not surprising in light of his apparent political consciousness and dedication to the regime's tenets as reflected here.

Conduct of the War on Sealanes

Confronted with Britain's intransigence relative to surrender and its determination to fight following France's defeat, Dönitz had concluded the war would need to be conducted in such a way that eventually Britain would be prepared to listen to proposals for a negotiated peace. The best way would be by an invasion and occupation of England. However, SEALION, the OKW invasion plan, was held in disfavor by the Navy Command as being high risk due to Germany's sea and air power relative to Britain and was eventually discarded.

A second course was conquest of the Mediterranean basin and ejection of the British from the Mideast. Without German help, which was inadequate for allocation to the task, Italy could not accomplish this alone. Consequently, the remaining option — war on Britain's sea lanes of communication — promised the most direct and fertile approach.[11] For the Submarine Command this resolved into the equation of sinking more tonnage than could be replaced by the British and her allies as the war progressed.

Stemming from his World War I experience, one of Dönitz's initial concerns was

Mussolini, Dönitz and Hitler (L–R) on July 20, 1944, following the unsuccessful attempt on Hitler's life at his secure compound, Wolfsschanze (Wolf's Lair), at Rastenberg, East Prussia. The bomb carrier, Col. Claus von Stauffenberg, and an estimated 5,000 others suffered the ultimate penalty for this failure. Bibliothek für Zeitgeschichte, Stuttgart.

to develop a tactical solution to the single most destructive element to successful submarine operations in World War I, the convoy accompanied by armed escorts. Dönitz came away from World War I recognizing the futility of lone U-boat operations against armed convoys. Though the World War I German U-boat arm had achieved great successes, the escorted convoy system was robbing it of the chance to be a decisive factor. Zigzagging as a defensive counter, the huge lines of warships offered a fertile, though formidable, target array. The one or two ships sunk represented a poor percentage of the whole. The balance of the convoy—some 95%—would ultimately reach Britain or another destination.

Long waits for the successive—or no—convoys would then attenuate the U-boat's effectiveness; primitive wireless of the period and absence of radar further aggravated the problem, preventing inter-boat communication and coordination.

All this Dönitz had learned the hard way as a junior officer on the UB-68 in World War I. In one attack, the UB-68, alone, sank one ship, but was in turn sunk, though all hands were picked up by one of the escorts. Dönitz then languished in a British POW camp until repatriated in 1919 following war's end.

The obvious answer for Dönitz was a massed U-boat attack. However, it would be almost

20 years before he would have the resources and freedom to put such a concept into operational practice. That opportunity presented itself in Germany's rearmament in the mid–1930s. Exercises in the Baltic in 1937 and 1939 provided the chance to try out the "wolf-pack" approach, which was to prove effective in the first half of World War II.[12]

The major limitation of the "wolf-pack" approach once war came was always the insufficiency of operational boats available to the U-boat arm. Of the 46 boats on hand on September 1, 1939, when Poland was attacked, only 22 were operational against Atlantic sealanes, the rest either being unfit for the distant patrols or needed elsewhere for Channel and North Sea defense. Of the 22 boats operating in the Atlantic, a mere one-third would be in an attack mode at any given time, with the balance in transit. Dönitz, therefore, aggressively pursued prioritizing of U-boat construction, even at the sacrifice of other types of craft, so that by 1941 an average of 20 boats were entering service monthly.[13]

However, by 1943 the command "realized only too clearly what the unceasing expansion of the two greatest maritime powers in the world could mean in the future for the U-boat arm, which would be called upon to bear the burden of the fight [at sea] alone." Furthermore, improved surface location radar and anti-submarine air cover added increasingly to misgivings among the German Navy about the ultimate outcome.[14]

Germany, though posing a significant threat to Allied shipping early in the war, was ultimately doomed to lose the U-boat war. Of a grand total of 1,170 German U-boats, 863 became operational during the war; of these, two-thirds were destroyed. Against this, 148 Allied naval vessels and 2,759 merchantmen were sunk by U-boat action.[15]

One of the factors contributing to the ultimate failure of U-boat operations was the failure by Germany to foresee the critical need for a naval air arm and the need for efficient long-range reconnaissance aircraft. A second critical problem arose with the introduction in 1942 of short-wavelength (10cm) radar which enabled detection and location of U-boats as soon as they appeared over the horizon, both at night and in poor visibility by day.[16]

Reflections on the U-boat War

For Germany the surge in emphasis on the U-boat came too late. If Britain was to be strangled by severing of sealanes, it would have had to significantly precede the advance in anti-submarine warfare technology.

As it was, 1943 brought a dramatic rise in U-boat losses, primarily for the reasons noted earlier. As can be seen in the following table, 1943–44 was to spell the end of the German naval threat.[17]

Year	U-boat Losses
1939	9
1940	23
1941	35
1942	85
1943	238
1944	319
1945	157 (plus some 300 scuttled or surrendered at war's end)

Of the 40,000 men in the submarine force, 30,000 did not return; of the latter, over 80% were killed, the rest becoming POWs.[18] This is a poor commentary on the impact and results of the ideology promulgated by the regime and projected by the Naval Command, especially when compounded by ship and personnel losses incurred by the Allies.

11 The Africa-Italy Campaigns

Victory Becomes Tenuous

Hitler, in an effort to shore up failing Italian positions in North Africa, sent two of his top commanders, Erwin Rommel and Albrecht Kesselring, with German troops to the theater in early 1941. Victories were followed by retreat for Rommel as the superior, more heavily supplied Allied forces brought the North African Campaign to an end. When Italy changed sides in late 1943, bitter partisan warfare erupted against German troops in Italy. Kesselring, in trying to protect his troops against excesses by the partisans, then vastly overreacted against the Italians to control the situation. This conduct resulted in his post-war prosecution for war crimes by the Allies.

Rommel Recoups Italian Positions

Mussolini, anxious to second the actions of the Führer, made moves to extend his Italian presence in the southern area from the Balkans to North Africa. His action against Egypt in September of 1940, like the later 1941 incursion into Greece, inevitably required the Germans to recoup failing Italian positions. The Italians under Marshal Graziani had launched their attack against Egypt with eight divisions. Their objective was the capture of the Suez Canal so as to interdict and interrupt Britain's sea supply route. However, by December most of the Italian positions were overrun, and in January of 1941 Tobruk and most of Cyrenaica were in British control, with the Italians having lost some 100,000 men as prisoners.[1]

Erwin Rommel, whose stock with Hitler was high as a result of his successful campaign in France, was called upon to shore up the Italian forces then encountering a critical situation in Libya. Rommel, now a lieutenant general, was assigned to command of a German Afrika Corps in February of 1941.[2] In order to provide a commander in the theater capable of dealing with the Italian hierarchy, Albrecht Kesselring was appointed Commander-in-Chief South (Oberbefehlshaber Sud). Rommel, who had preceded Kesselring and was already subordinate to the Italian Command, now also reported to Kesselring.

Rommel meanwhile had embarked in North Africa with early successes against the British and Free French forces. After Rommel's entry the tide turned with successful joint German-Italian operations in the spring of 1941. Much of Cyrenaica was recaptured and, accordingly, Rommel's command was upgraded to a Panzer Group, giving him three German and six Italian divisions. (See map, "Rommel's North African Campaigns, 1941–43.")[3]

By August of 1941 Rommel marshaled his forces for the first attack on Tobruk, Britain's fortress and key port. However, he overextended his forces and the British Eighth Army pushed the German forces back to El Agheila.[4] During 1941 fuel and ammunition had not yet become the problem these assets would represent in the following year; however, the need to transport these vital elements overland from Tripoli and Benghazi posed a continuing problem.[5]

Rommel's 1942 campaign culminated in the retaking of Cyrenaica including Gazala

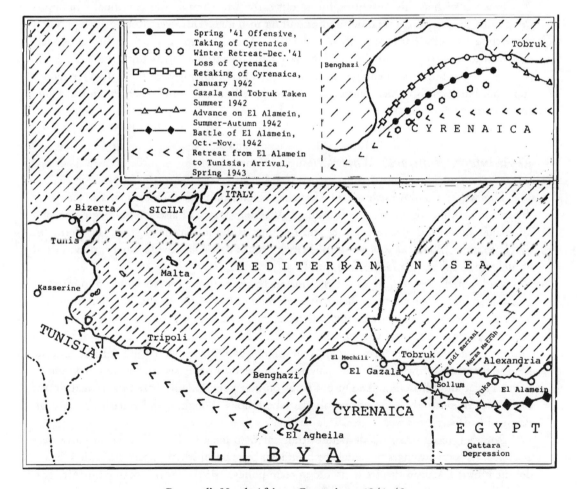

Rommel's North African Campaigns, 1941–43

and then Tobruk on June 21st. In the taking of Tobruk Rommel's forces captured the British commanding general, 33,000 men and abundant fuel and rations.[6]

Malta still loomed as a key objective, however; consequently it assumed a central position in the question of the next move after Tobruk. Field Marshal Kesselring, Commander-in-Chief southwest and Rommel's nominal superior, in agreement with the Italian Comando Supremo, argued for Malta as top priority. It had already given way in that position to Tobruk's capture. However, Kesselring, working with the Italian Comando Supremo, inevitably found himself at loggerheads with Rommel on the matter. Where strategic issues such as the capture of Malta before Tobruk had been seemingly settled, Kesselring found the order reversed "once Rommel got his propaganda machine working with Hitler, OKW and the Comando Supremo."[7] In the case of selecting between Malta and an incursion into Egypt, Rommel had conveyed his strong feelings directly to Hitler that Egypt should be invaded first and thereby pursuit of the British forces would not be interrupted. Influenced by success, Hitler went along with Rommel. This meant the Malta campaign would be abandoned because the Luftwaffe could not support operations both over Malta and into Egypt.[8]

In issues such as this Kesselring found out early that Rommel was continually in opposition with the Italian commander and unwilling to budge. However, Rommel's reputation at the time was sufficient to support his demands. His modus operandi, according to Kesselring, was to keep the Italians in the dark about his operational plans until the last minute because "he did not trust them." This compounded his problems with the Italian Comando Supremo. However, Rommel's successes in Africa paved the way for his independent and unilateral command approach.[9]

El Alamein, Rommel's Waterloo

This was to change, however. El Alamein, which Rommel's forces reached a week after the fall of Tobruk, now to be Rommel's Waterloo. It would also see the beginning of a sea change in relations between Hitler and Rommel as the tide turned against the Germans. By November of 1942 the well-supplied British Eighth Army had the Germans, now starved of fuel and supplies, in a losing position.[10]

Undoubtedly responding to the circumstances Hitler began on November 3 to interfere in command decisions affecting the tactical conduct of the battle. In this instance Rommel's objective was extricating German and Italian troops by a retreat to Fuka. However, the Führer ordered, "as to your troops, you can show them no other road than to victory or death." To Rommel, it appeared that "arms, petrol and aircraft could have helped us, but not orders." For the first time in the African Campaign he admitted to being stymied as to a next move. When Hitler and Mussolini, the Duce, finally, on November 5, authorized the retreat, it was too late for all except the armored and motorized divisions, though, with Kesselring's approval, Rommel had begun his withdrawal a day earlier.[11]

Rommel, recognizing his desperate straits, flew to meet with the Führer on November 28, 1942. He acknowledges he may have been less than tactful when he recommended "abandonment of the African theatre ... as a long term policy.... If the army remained in Africa, it would be destroyed." In response, "The Führer flew into a fury ... most of the staff officers present, the majority of whom had never heard a shot fired in anger, appeared to agree with every word the Führer said." It was a political necessity to hold a major bridgehead in Africa and, therefore, there would be no withdrawal. Hitler and his sycophantic OKW branded Rommel a defeatist for all his attempts at responsible assessment of the critical situation.[12]

Unhappy with Rommel's tactical retreats, though made under the adverse circumstances he faced, the Italians, Field Marshal Kesselring, Commander-in-Chief south, and Hitler's headquarters, OKW, pressed for and obtained Rommel's replacement in March of 1943.

Africa in Retrospect

Rommel attributed the ensuing defeat at El Alamein directly to the "idleness and muddle of the supply authorities on the mainland."[13] For Rommel, the pragmatist, the blame lay with those in charge on the mainland who were not directly threatened by the urgency of the situation which manifested itself in two ways. First, the Italian Navy, responsible for convoy protection, was staffed by officers, most of whom were not supporters of Mussolini and would rather have seen a German defeat than a victory. And, second, higher fascist authorities were too corrupt or too pompous to be effective. The few who tried to help could not overcome this disastrous bureaucracy.[14]

In the opinion of General Siegfried Westphal, Rommel's Chief of Staff at the time, blame for the reversal at El Alamein belongs as much to OKW and Hitler for allowing Rommel to embark on an attack in which they had no faith, with the result that they gave it little support.[15]

Italy's foreign minister, Count Galeazzo Ciano, concurred that transport of supplies to North Africa was the gravest problem confronting the African troops. Writing in his diary on December 1, 1941, commenting on the Italian Navy's efforts to deliver supplies, "Out of the whole convoy [of five ships] two ships arrived, one was forced to beach at Suda Bay, and two were sunk. The result is not brilliant." He adds that when accompanied by battleships, the losses were still staggering. "What is happening in the Navy is baffling. ... naval losses become more serious every day, and I wonder whether the war won't outlast our Navy."[16]

Rommel summed up the coming catastrophe well when he said that with America and its great industrial capacity in the war, if the Allies succeeded in countering the U-boat threat to their convoys, which they did, there was "little hope left for us."[17]

One of the root causes of failure of the North African Campaign, something Rommel could do nothing to counter, probably resided with the Italian people's lack of heart for this war. Undoubtedly the Duce put his finger on it when in March of 1942 he "had to admit the Italian people are not in the least for war ... [because] incentives are lacking [that] can be easily understood by the common people."[18]

This bore directly on Kesselring's role in Italy which was to facilitate a successful collaboration of two militaries. In that pursuit it required of him the development of a relationship with not only the Italian military commanders, but the Duce and the king. Though he was successful in developing excellent rapport with the hierarchy, he found the Italians inefficient and lacking the level of dedication to the war effort needed to support the troops. He felt if the Duce could not inspire a war-time spirit, he should never have entered the war.[19]

He saw no enthusiasm for the profession of soldiering on the part of the Italians.[20] Coming from a German field marshal who was on favorable terms with the king and Duce, this points to the basic problem with the Duce's overall war program and the cultural differences in the two societies.

Rommel, too, saw and experienced the residual of the malaise the Duce represented. He felt the Italians came with a lack of conviction, inadequate training, outmoded equipment, unqualified officers, lack of anti-aircraft weapons and low morale stemming from defeats before his arrival. Particularly harmful was the all-pervading differentiation between officer and man. While the men had to make do without field kitchens and often had to ask a German comrade for food, the officers refused to forgo their several-course meals, whereas Rommel and his staff shared common fare with the troops. Rommel was not surprised to see the consequent inferiority complex.[21]

By the end of 1942 Rommel felt he had been abandoned in Africa and appears to have turned away from Hitler in whom he had placed such implicit faith. The disaster at El Alamein affected Hitler as well in terms of confidence in Rommel's advice.

Whether winning or losing, Rommel was the most popular soldier in Germany; though he demanded too much and was overly severe, his soldiers sensed the depth of his feeling for them, saw his presence leading at the front and understood the great leadership skills he represented.[22] Hitler had allowed Rommel's prestige and notoriety to mount among the people for the obvious morale effects it brought. Even after he had in effect eliminated Rommel for political reasons near war's end, Hitler continued to profit from this popularity.

Rommel's popularity extended to the Allied lines to the extent it raised concern among Allied generals. Winston Churchill, caused inevitable complaints when, in the wake of Allied reverses in North Africa, he addressed the British Parliament in 1942, saying, "There was a great general fighting against us." Even when the tide turned in El Alamein in late 1942, and his losses mounted, Rommel remained the exemplary soldier to friend and foe alike.[23]

Perhaps a cooperative Rommel working with both Kesselring and the Italians would have produced in Kesselring, if not a victory, then a positive view of the Italians. Under the prevailing situation the antithesis developed, and Kesselring's evident disregard for the Italians would ultimately assert itself to his detriment. Tributary to the problems, he thought it was a mistake to leave Rommel in his command. Rommel in turn found Kesselring exhibited an uncomradely attitude, thinking only of himself and the consequences for the Luftwaffe of any decisions; he felt Kesselring was less than supportive when he diverted needed arms shipments and made destructive critical comments. Further, Rommel felt he was inclined to excessive optimism, expecting unrealistic results from the armies, especially where the Italians were concerned. On the positive side, he recognized Kesselring's ability to command high-level support and develop a liaison with the king and Duce.[24]

The three years in command of the Axis Italian-African theater influenced Kesselring's attitude toward the Italians negatively, from all appearances. Though he developed a rapport with the hierarchy, his perception and assessment of their army and its performance would contribute later to excesses in his treatment of the Italian people.[25]

The Tide Turns

Hitler's attention at this point was concentrated on the developing debacle in Russia, specifically focused on the mid-point of the Stalingrad battle. His generals—von Rundstedt is a case in point, Kesselring is another—were seeing the probability of Axis success diminishing as 1943 wore on. Hitler's asset allocation was directed to Europe where victory might be salvaged and preparations for an anticipated Allied invasion were paramount. With Mussolini's resignation in July of 1943 and Italy's armistice with the Allies in September of that year, the direction of the tide in the Italian theater was confirmed.

With the Duce's resignation, Kesselring met with the king to discuss Italy's intentions. There would be no change, the king said. Kesselring claims in his memoirs that he disbelieved this.[26] As noted by his then–Chief of Staff, General Westphal, the Commander-in-Chief, in fact, did everything in his power to preserve relations with the Italians, so much that he incurred suspicion on the part of Hitler and Göring of being "weak" and "Italophile." Confirming this opinion, Admiral Karl Dönitz remembered that Kesselring at the time actually did believe the new Badoglio government would remain with the Germans and thus he, Kesselring, opposed any intervention by Germany.[27] This is an interesting reflection on the bias in and/or revisionist tendency of most memoirs!

With the Duce's resignation, Karl Dönitz's representative attached to the Italian Naval Command, marine, Vice-Admiral Friedrich Ruge, reported that the new regime was favored by the populace and recommended Germany would only be discredited by efforts to reinstate the fascist regime. Hitler, by now more insular than ever, rejected Ruge's report, though the latter's comments were prescient as events would quickly show. Following the armistice the Italian fleet sailed to Malta to be interned and Italy entered into a state of war with the former ally on October 13, 1943.[28]

Bitter Reaction to an Unwanted War

If the Italian soldier appeared faint of heart up to 1943, Kesselring found the population by no means devoid of martial spirit as they waged bitter guerilla warfare against the German Wehrmacht following Italy's armistice and declaration of war on Germany.[29]

Partisan fighting against regular forces was nothing new to the Germans by this point. The German campaign in Russia, BARBAROSSA, had incited partisan fighting. In response OKW issued a directive of December 16, 1942, calling for the use of "all means without restriction, even against women and children, as long as it assures success."[30]

To counter the advent of partisan operations in Italy as sides were changed, Kesselring was given authority to direct all anti-partisan operations in his theater by OKW order of May 1, 1944, signed by Wilhelm Keitel. Kesselring then sent a message to the Italian populace via radio on June 28, 1944, warning "Badoglio followers and subversive elements ... not to continue the[ir] behavior." This broadcast was in response to the prior proclamation of Marshal Badoglio and British General Alexander to "kill the Germans in the back in order to escape reaction and to be able to kill more Germans."[31]

The Italian partisan war commenced full scale after the fall of Rome the first week of

June 1944. The Italian forces that had fought with the Germans, but only half-heartedly, now, with the full support of the Allies, proclaimed partisan war of the most brutal and murderous kind. This Kesselring felt was a complete violation of international law and contradicted every principle of clean soldierly fighting. Of the excesses that occurred during this period, he lays most of the blame on "[Italian] Partisan bands, neo–Fascist organizations and German deserter groups." Kesselring believed that only the smallest fraction should be blamed on the German Army.[32]

Mindful of the danger to his troops and their supply lines, particularly in central Italy, Kesselring accordingly issued a regulation of June 17, 1944, which called for the fight against the partisans to be:

> Carried on with all means at our disposal and with the utmost severity. I will protect any Commander who exceeds our usual restraint, in the choice and severity of the means he adopts in the fight. ... a mistake in the choice of the means to achieve an objective is always better than a failure to act.[33]

Then to add emphasis, a further order of July 1, 1944, titled Anti-Partisan Measures called for:

> all troops and police in my command to adopt the severest measures when attacked. Every act of violence committed by partisans must be punished immediately.... Where there are considerable numbers of partisan groups, a proportion of the male population in the area will be arrested and in the event of acts of violence being committed, these men will be shot.... Should troops ... be fired on from any village, the village will be burnt down. ... counter-measures must be hard but just.[34]

The call for action at any cost in the June and July orders, coupled with the absence of clarification of "hard but just," inevitably yielded a predictable end result, that of overreaction on the part of German troops and response by the Italians. The orders coupled with the political environment led to numerous hostage and/or reprisal incidents which would have near-term implications as well as post-war impact. By late August of 1944, Mussolini, then German-sponsored head of a fascist Italian government, had complained bitterly to the German ambassador about the methods used against partisans and punitive measures taken against local non-partisan populations. This spurred Kesselring to forward a cautionary edict to his commanders on August 21 relative to these incidents which, he wrote, "caused the greatest harm to dignity and discipline of the German Armed Forces.... [Some of these actions were] wrongly carried out and can only be considered as a 'Robber's Raid.'"[35]

By September the Duce had delivered "fresh instances" of the behavior of German forces which Kesselring found contrary to his August 21 order. Eleven specific instances were reported by the Duce. Borgo Ticino on August 13 is typical. Four German soldiers had been wounded by unknown assailants. As a reprisal the Duce reported masses of people were detained as they arrived from surrounding villages for a Boccia game. Thirteen men under 30 were picked out and shot. The village was then evacuated and partially destroyed by explosive charges and fire. Kesselring reported these incidents to 14th Army, saying the incidents "are revolting ... and are driving even the best elements of the population ... into the enemy camp." He further ordered the use of standing courts to "obviate the above mentioned misdemeanors."[36]

By February of 1945 Kesselring issued a moderating order on the subject of punitive measures. It undoubtedly would have prevented some of the counterproductive reactions and post-war recriminations on both sides had it been issued instead of the orders of June 17 and July 1. This new order delineated levels of illegal partisan activities, matched punitive measures appropriately and assigned clear lines of authority for imposition of these measures. This order sought to compensate for the excesses of summer 1944, but the damage that had been done would later prove a heavy burden for the Commander-in-Chief.[37]

Time now was Germany's enemy. Failure at Stalingrad behind them, Italy in opposition, North Africa gone and the prospect of a Normandy invasion facing them in mid–1944 caused many in the leadership, such as Karl Dönitz, to recognize that "with war on a number of land fronts ... once [the invasion] had succeeded ... [the] war could no longer be won by force of arms. To make peace was not possible since the enemy would have none of it until Germany had been destroyed."[38]

12 Aftermath in Italy

Defeat Impacts the Once-Aggressive Wehrmacht

In combating Italian partisan warfare, Field Marshal Kesselring was persuaded to issue such overreacting orders to his armies that uncontrolled and illegal reprisals against the Italian populace were conducted by German soldiers. As a result, at war's end Kesselring was tried by a British military court for these crimes, in a replication of the numerous similar trials of Wehrmacht leaders.

Excesses Endemic to the Period and Situation

The last year and a half of Kesselring's command in Italy, when he sought to combat illegal partisan warfare, proved to be the most fateful period of his career as a result of his overreaction to the partisans as the Germans retreated. For the excesses committed under his command as the German Army retreated through Italy, as discussed in Chapter 11, a day of reckoning came with unconditional surrender of German forces. Like the great percentage of his peers, such as von Manstein, von Rundstedt, von Brauchitsch and most other commanders , Kesselring entered the cycle of imprisonment, questioning, eventual indictment and trial; for Kesselring this meant testimony at Nuremberg, a holding period at Dachau, questioning in England and finally transfer to Venice-Mestre for trial by the British for war crimes where two counts were brought against him[1]:

1. Responsibility for the killing of 335 Italians in a reprisal for the ambush attack on Via Rasella in Rome on March 23, 1944, in which 32 German police were killed, and

2. Inciting by the orders of June 17 and July 1 the reprisal murder of innocent civilians

resulting from anti-partisan operations during the summer of 1944 (the prosecution brought as evidence "at least 1078 victims" under this charge)

Upon learning of the Via Rasella attack, Kesselring, General von Mackensen, Commander of 14th Army, and General Maelzer, the German Commandant of Rome, all independently recognized some reprisal was needed. While they made plans, the Führer's OKW order came through requiring a 10:1 ratio of Italians to Germans killed. The SD (a special branch of the SS) officer responsible for carrying out the reprisal, Obersturmbannführer (Lt. Colonel) Herbert Kappler, had, according to Kesselring's trial testimony, assured the Field Marshal that the ratio would be met by executing people already sentenced to death.[2]

Kappler, in testimony, denied having ever made this representation and even talking with Kesselring directly. However, when confronted with the Kesselring version and in the face of unanimity of Kesselring's staff officers' testimony, Kappler conceded it might have been possible he did speak to Kesselring, but still denied he had assured either Kesselring or 14th Army he had adequate victims who carried death sentences. He had spoken of those who were *todes wuerdig*, worthy of death, meaning they appeared guilty to the police but had never been tried by a court. In actual fact he had only four prisoners in custody who met the criteria so that many otherwise innocents were executed by the SD in what is known as the Ardeatine Caves Massacre. Recent research suggests Kappler may never, in fact, have spoken to Kesselring on the nights following the Via Rasella incident, thus corroborating Kappler's initial testimony. The evidence purports to show, circumstantially, that Kesselring was absent from his headquarters at Monte Soratte on March 23–24, but, instead, was at Liguria inspecting troops until March 26. In any event the issue is moot considering the ultimate trial verdict.[3]

Kesselring further claimed that a second order arrived from OKW the night of March 23, which turned the responsibility for the reprisal over to the SD, thus removing the Wehrmacht and him from responsibility. However, in a deposition he made while a POW in England in 1946, he described the entire affair but made no mention of this fact. The trial prosecutor, Colonel Halse, charged no such relief of responsibility ever occurred and that the earlier deposition, made before a defense had been contrived, reflected the real situation. In fact, the court suggested Kesselring's defense consisted of a "deliberate plan" on the part of his staff officers, and by implication, Kesselring, "to join together to give [false] evidence ... on behalf of their old master."[4]

The prosecution's case relied on the British Manual of Military Law; paragraphs 383 and 384 reflecting articles 46 and 50 of the Hague Convention which had been ratified by Germany. Under article 46 individual life and property must be respected, and under article 50, "No collective penalty ... shall be inflicted upon the population on account of acts of individuals for which it cannot be regarded as collectively responsible." Though the law may have been vague on the legality of killing innocents, the court found paragraph 459 to be specific in that "Acts done by way of reprisal must not, however, be excessive and must not exceed the degree of violation committed by the enemy." For the court this seemed the persuasive legal issue in charge one, the Via Rasella reprisal.[5]

To sum up, the court apparently heard the prosecution claim this was a terrorist act all out of proportion to the saboteurs' crime, against the defense claim the Germans had not exceeded the limits of coercion. The defense, however, claimed two mitigating points: the Field Marshal was of the understanding that those to be shot had already been sentenced to death, and, further, Kesselring was technically not responsible since Hitler and OKW had allegedly passed the responsibility to the SD for execution of the reprisal.

The basis for the second charge, excesses against partisans and innocent civilians, was found by the prosecution in Kesselring's partisan operations orders of June 17 and July 1, 1944. The first of the two orders instructs commanders to use the utmost severity beyond normal restraint and with impunity. The second order opens the door for "all troops" to adopt the severest measures immediately. Further, they are told to take hostages for eventual killing.[6]

Proof that things got out of hand, according to the prosecution, is found in Kesselring's orders of August and September responding to the Duce's complaints and admonishing German troops of the harm to the dignity of German Armed Forces caused by excesses against the population.[7]

This was a smoking gun for the prosecution, especially in light of the affidavit of German General Joachim Lemelsen, last chief of 14th Army under Kesselring. The affidavit, given in London in 1946 in his first year as a POW, freely stated that the order of June 17 about anti-partisan measures was "a great menace to discipline and order" among the troops. Though Lemelsen retracted this position in testimony during the trial, the fact that he had made it freely and read it to other German POW generals without complaint or disagreement at the time of writing was persuasive to the court.[8]

In addition to the eleven instances of excesses reported by the Duce, eighteen additional involving some one-thousand victims were investigated by the British and lodged as evidence; many were seconded by witnesses to the events. The defense characterized most as attributable to emotional Italians who were given to exaggeration, and they charged the events themselves were either legal or unfounded in fact.[9]

Kesselring's major defense for the legality of his June 17 and July 1 orders and for any alleged results was based on paragraph 358d of the U.S. Rules of Land Warfare (1940). This section allows hostages to be taken as insurance and subsequently put to death should illegal actions then occur. Kesselring claims in his memoirs that the court's ignorance of this document, which the defense had presented in evidence, heavily influenced the ultimate verdict. The prosecution's answer was that Kesselring, in order to smash the partisan movement, was inciting and ordering his troops to act in a way under the guise of reprisals which was in breech of the laws and usages of war. Incidentally, the 1956 revision of the U.S. Rules of Land Warfare specifically prohibits the taking of hostages (para. 497g) and restricts reprisals to military forces only, excluding civilians (para. 497).[10]

A Victim of the War

The Venice-Mestre trial judge advocate recognized the demonic environment emanating from Hitler's headquarters when he observed that had Hitler known that Kesselring was under the impression, if indeed he was as he claimed, that only those already sentenced to death, and not innocents, were to be subject to the Via Rasella reprisal, Hitler would have been irate, and might well have died of apoplexy, thereby ending the war![11] Though his onetime adversary, British General Sir Harold Alexander, Allied supreme commander, Mediterranean, had good words to say about him,[12] the British court was not so complimentary, finding him guilty on both counts.[13]

That demonic environment emanating from Hitler's leadership led many such as Kesselring to deviate from what would be considered a moral paradigm, one they had followed for much of their professional lives. Only when it became clear that victory was not possible and only defeat lay ahead, did Kesselring and others look to peace feelers in advance of capitulation in attempts to salvage their situation. Then only in the light of post-war convictions for excesses such as those of Kesselring and his armies in Italy did he, like so many others, seek to establish an excuse and seek rectitude in memoirs.[14] These same commanders would undoubtedly have performed within what we would consider acceptable bounds given a more reasonable leadership in Germany, but then there might not have been a war.

13 Invasion

The Tables of Victory Begin to Turn

The massive resources of the Allies had the Axis Powers in trouble everywhere except in the West by 1944, and there an invasion had been anticipated for two years. This set the stage for a dichotomy in thinking for the generals whose future and that of the country depended on victory. As the tide turned in the West in this last full year of the war, what could they do to salvage Germany? Their thoughts and actions turned to some kind of peace, irregardless of the dictum of "unconditional surrender" set by the Allied Leaders. A coup failed, as did attempts at negotiations which under intense battle conditions, the late stage of the war and its probable outcome were not acceptable to the Allies.

The Year of Retreat

Except for increased Allied air and commando activity coupled with spotty attacks by an embryonic resistance, comparative peace reigned in France in 1942. But on all other fronts potential defeat loomed: Rommel was in retreat in Africa, the Mediterranean posed a danger for the Axis, and the American-French-British forces in North Africa were on the ascendance; to make things worse, the first Russian winter of 1941–42 carried an ominous message for the future.

This is the deceptive quietude into which Hitler reactivated von Rundstedt in March of 1942 as Commander-in-Chief west, responsible for strategic and tactical authority in defense of the coast against invasion. While von Rundstedt speaks of cordial relations with Marshal Petain, Vichy French officers and authorities and the populace, the contradiction in and fragility and tentativeness of this relationship was the reality, and one that, in fact, did not escape him.[1]

By 1943, as the Axis position continued to deteriorate on the various fronts, von Rundstedt could anticipate the inevitable Allied invasion somewhere, sometime on his 2500-mile coastal front. Hitler was convinced every foot must be defended, a seeming corollary of his insistence that not a foot be yielded in retreat. By this point successful German Army mobility of the past had given way to rigid lines in a "fortress" mentality, according to von Rundstedt. He regarded Hitler's concrete and steel Atlantic Wall as a "propaganda bluff," similar in lethality to the West Wall of 1938, that earlier defensive wall built for similar reasons of bluffing the French as Czech negotiations over the Sudetenland were underway. Hitler had tied the commanders' hands further by insisting on issuing all orders. After 51 years of service this field marshal needed to ask before making the smallest decision. Troops were of second quality since the Eastern Front and Italy had siphoned off the bulk of first-line divisions. Von Rundstedt's command received older men and officers, often with artificial limbs. Some panzer divisions were with limited or no panzers! Luftwaffe assets counted in the few hundreds against an Allied force in the many thousands, a further detriment to mobility.[2]

By late 1943 the Commander-in-Chief and his staff reported to Hitler their belief that Brittany and Normandy would probably be the invasion points. Since artificial harbors — the Mulberries used by the Allies in the invasion — were unknown to the Germans, it was felt a harbor such as Cherbourg would be a necessity, but its lack of proximity to adequate coastal landing areas and its susceptibility to attack from two sides from the sea introduced significant uncertainty.[3]

Von Rundstedt's command in late 1943 encompassed Army Group B under Field Marshal Rommel and Army Group G under Col.-General Blaskowitz. Their combined total of 60 divisions was charged with holding the 2500-mile coastline. In the aftermath of the African defeat, Rommel had been assigned to command Army Group B with the task of organizing the defense against an invasion of France. Based on his initial inspections in the anticipated western battle area during the winter of 1943–44, Rommel formulated his defense plan. He believed that victory could no longer be gained by mobile armored warfare in view of the insufficiency of German industry and Allied air supremacy. His defense plan consisted of defeat of air and sea landings and a fight in the strongly fortified coastal strip. The plan called for extensive mine and offshore obstacle preparations and air landing obstacles. Rommel's inspection had revealed a dearth of landing defenses especially in the Normandy-Calvados coastal area, and, accordingly, a series of mines and underwater artificial reefs was constructed. These preparations may have been started too late to be fully effective, though in retrospect Allied resources could not have failed to overwhelm whatever defense the Germans brought to bear.[4]

Rommel insisted on his panzer divisions being held as close as possible to the shore, whereas von Rundstedt, Col.-General Guderian (then–Inspector General of Armored Troops), and General Geyr von Schweppenberg (Panzer Group West commander) all felt they should be held back as reserves for the entire front. Perhaps because Rommel had Hitler's ear, Hitler inclined to Rommel's view. Von Rundstedt's view was that the battle could not be won without credible reserves, especially if the Germans guessed wrong on the invasion point. A final compromise was driven with Hitler by von Rundstedt with four divisions being held in reserve near Paris, though Rommel's view carried for most of the troop placements.[5]

By April of 1944 German intelligence recognized massive preparations that dispelled any doubts that an invasion was imminent: the build-up of 75 divisions in Great Britain, embarkation of additional divisions from Southern Italy and the Mediterranean for the British Isles, and assembling of sizable and growing U.S. and British Naval assets in British harbors. Accordingly, the Supreme Command, OKW, as well as the Western Army Groups began a careful recording of Allied air and sea activity in an attempt to pinpoint the invasion date.[6]

Rommel prepared his troops for a momentary invasion. He had guessed the invasion point quite correctly as the area from Cherbourg on the Cotentin Peninsula to the coast of Calvados and on to the Somme, though the advent of the Mulberries introduced a key variable for him. OKW had predicted the landing would be on the coast of Belgium at the mouth of the Scheldt; to Rommel and Army Group B this seemed unlikely as the main Allied shipping was concentrated in the south-coast ports, in western England and in Wales. Rommel also postulated a secondary landing on the Mediterranean coast of France.[7]

When the Allies struck on June 6, Hitler's release of reserve panzer divisions was delayed — he was asleep at the critical 0100 hour. Von Rundstedt differed with a popular view that this meant the difference between success and failure for the invasion. The Allies carried the day based on materiel, air assets and seaborne batteries, and by evening on June 6 von Rundstedt and his staff recognized it was hopeless to defeat the landing.[8]

The first critical days passed without notable Allied reverses and with significant coordination of the various services and countries; a continuing flow of men and materiel was maintained so that from June 9th forward the initiative lay with the Allies.[9] The German Navy was not a factor as it totaled several destroyers, ten to fifteen torpedo boats, a few minesweepers, patrol boats, tankers, and repair ships. Of the forty U-boats available, only six ever put to sea in response to the invasion, and they achieved no success in view of Allied sea and air superiority.[10]

As to German operations, Hitler and OKW interfered daily with field commanders by sending an avalanche of "nervous orders." Hitler demanded unattainable goals without providing air or naval support for his troops. Still, the order from Hitler was, "Hold your ground. Do not yield a step."[11]

In spite of entreaties by Rommel and von Rundstedt both before the invasion and once the battle had commenced, Hitler issued a stern order reminiscent of Stalingrad which said, "Every enemy attempt to break through is to be prevented by tenaciously holding our ground. It is forbidden to shorten the front. It is not permitted to maneuver freely."[12]

Rommel requested strategic reserves to back up Army Group B of up to 15 armored and motorized divisions to be held east of Paris. Though promised by Hitler, no such reserves were furnished in time.[13]

By June both von Rundstedt and Rommel felt the situation could not be saved and arranged to meet with Hitler at Western Front Battle Headquarters, "WII," Margival, France, on June 17. They described the grave situation and asked him to negotiate with the Allies. Rommel warned that the German Front in Normandy would collapse followed by a breakthrough into Germany by the Allies, and, in a first overt sign that he would actively work for an armistice, he recommended the war be ended. Hitler would have none of this; instead he redirected the discussion to salvation of the situation through his new weapons combined with "fanatical resistance" of all Germans.[14] General Jodl, operations chief of OKW, who was present, recounted Rommel's statements to Hitler in his later testimony at Nuremberg, adding that Hitler simply ignored Rommel's attempts at a rational cessation. To Rommel's question, "My Führer, what do you really think about the further development of the war?" Hitler replied, "That is ... no part of your duty. You will have to leave that to me."[15] Hitler's promised reinforcements, especially air assets, never arrived.

As a final effort to prevail upon Hitler, von Rundstedt and Rommel met with Hitler in the presence of Keitel, Göring and Jodl at Berchtesgaden on June 29. In what General Bayerlein describes as an argument, Rommel asked Hitler how he imagined the war could be won — and both expected to be relieved of their posts as a consequence. The result was a lengthy discourse on "miracle weapons" and "final and total victory," a discourse which became lost in fantastic digressions, according to both generals. Again, Hitler monopolized the conversation, concentrating on salvation through wonder weapons such as the V1 and V2 missiles and new jet fighters.[16]

Not able to accept this sorry turn of events, von Rundstedt shortly advised Keitel that the war should be ended. Three days later Hitler retired von Rundstedt, blaming his deteriorating health and replacing him with Field Marshal von Kluge, but retaining Rommel.[17] This was not the first instance of von Rundstedt's plea to Hitler that the battles should be ended, nor would it be his last; however, he, unlike Rommel, von Kluge and many others, could not bring himself to deviate from his oath, his fear of being tagged a traitor or whatever else compelled him.

OKW — Hitler, Keitel and Jodl — had by now, according to Bayerlein, described Rommel to von Kluge, his new chief, as independent, defeatist and disobedient. They also convinced von Kluge, initially, at least, that the military situation was "not unfavorable." The result of all this was a contentious relationship between von Kluge and Rommel. This was reversed once von Kluge reached the field, had inspected the Normandy Front and had studied Rommel's recommendations to Hitler.[18]

On July 15 Rommel wrote to Hitler warning that "the unequal struggle is nearing its end" and asking the Führer to draw the political conclusions without delay. His fall from favor was precipitous from this point on.[19]

Hitler's "divide and rule" concept, used again in the invasion defense, was to work to the great detriment of the Germans in Normandy. Whereas Rommel attempted to implement a single unified command under himself of the three services plus the Todt construction organization, Hitler repeatedly refused. In contrast, Allied air, sea and ground cooperation was unified under General Eisenhower as supreme commander; coupled with overwhelming technological and force superiority, defeat of the Germans, who lacked in each area, was inevitable.[20]

The German "air fleet," for example, consisted of 90 bombers and 70 fighters operational out of a total of 500 German western aircraft assets. In the heat of the invasion none would be effective since Allied air power would render their bases inoperable before they could become airborne. In comparison, the Germans estimated Allied aircraft in England as about 17,000 at the inception of the invasion. As a further obstruction, Reichsmarschall Hermann Göring directed the Third Air Fleet from his far-removed base in East Prussia through his Commander-in-Chief Marshal Sperrle. The latter was ultimately blamed for the short comings and dismissed. Sperrle had attempted coordination with Rommel especially in view of the mutuality of tactical objectives and his political views, which were similar to Rommel's.[21] Recognition of his skeptical, though pragmatic and realistic assessment of the outcome, a mind-state the leadership could not countenance, undoubtedly led to his ousting from command. Moreover, it probably provided a clue as to his loyalties.

Col.-General Heinz Guderian's experience was similar. In December of 1944 while Chief of the General Staff, Guderian recognized the futility of the Western Campaign: the Ruhr had already been paralyzed by Allied bombing and the center of Reich armament was already in the East. Guderian therefore sought the transfer of troops from the Western Ardennes offensive to the Eastern Front. After trying Himmler without success, he again spoke to Jodl. "Far more dangerous," he found, "was Jodl's opposition to moving our defensive effort eastward." However, in the face of agreement of the Commander-in-Chief west, which Guderian obtained, Jodl angrily agreed to relinquish four divisions. Guderian states that needed tactical measures foundered on "the rocks of Hitler's and Jodl's

Field Marshal Walter Model, Commander-in-Chief of Army Group B, with Field Marshal Gerd von Rundstedt, Commander-in-Chief West, just before the start of the Battle of the Bulge, in December of 1944; von Rundstedt took a dim view of Germany's strategy in this last Ardennes campaign, feeling defense of the homeland was preeminent. Model, who had replaced Gunther von Kluge when the latter committed suicide in August, 1944 then committed suicide himself in the last month of the war. Ullstein bild/The Granger Collection, New York.

incomprehension."[22] Remote direction of the war inevitably tied the hands of responsible commanders.

Rommel's invasion defense performance elicits controversial comment from otherwise friendly peers. Col.-General Guderian, while holding Rommel in the highest regard, disagreed with his decision against concentrated armor attacks. He suggests that either Rommel had lost faith in the possibility of mounting a successful attack, or political considerations may have played a part in this decision, implying he might be laying the groundwork for some kind of armistice talks. General Freiherr Geyr von Schweppenburg, commander of the Caen Sector under Rommel's Army Group B, felt that the 2nd Panzer Group was initially held back in late June because of Rommel's knowledge and expectation of the 20th of July, 1944, attempt on Hitler's life, and he wished to have a "reliable" army division available for any emergency.[23]

With the obvious turning of the tide and the inevitable end by now clear, this surreptitious cleavage in the Wehrmacht leadership continued to develop as the invasion, the next to final campaign, proceeded. As a sign of the developing political pressure on the military it would not be long before Field Marshal von Kluge would dispatch himself on the way to a conference with the Führer in August of 1944. He had recognized he was under suspicion, and in fact it was Hitler's intent to replace him with Field Marshal Model and to inflict whatever other consequences can only be imagined. Two months later, Model, was replaced by von Rundstedt as Commander-in-Chief west, but still commanded Army Group B. Given the desperate straits of the battle in the Ruhr pocket, he had considered, in consultation with General von Mellenthin, the possibility of negotiations with the Allies. However, both decided against such a course reasoning that they were ignorant of higher level negotiations that might be going on, and, secondly, that they must keep fighting in order to protect the rear of the German forces in the East, who were trying to cover the escape of millions of civilians running from the Russians. However on the 21st of April Model committed suicide. In Model's case it appears the oath and his allegiance to Hitler and/or his ambition drove him, based on reports of associates. In the final analysis, he apparently felt little obligation to help rebuild the country.[24]

To Avert Total Debacle

On July 17, 1944, Field Marshal Rommel was seriously injured in an air attack on his command car and removed to a hospital, fatefully away during what was to be the key move of the resistance, a bomb attack on Hitler's life. Rommel's reaction to this attack on Hitler three days hence was one of surprise as he had presupposed the conspirators would pressure Hitler to sue for peace instead of attempting to kill him. He felt the attempt, if it had succeeded, would have only enhanced the aura surrounding Hitler and made a martyr of him in the eyes of the people. The best thing, thought Rommel, would have been to have confronted Hitler with a fait accompli.[25]

The bomb plot engineered by the Beck-Goerdeler group and implemented by Col.-General Klaus von Stauffenberg was executed, albeit unsuccessfully, on July 20, 1944. Hitler escaped with minor injuries and instituted a massive reprisal which cost the lives of most of the major conspirators as well as countless others, both military and civilian, who were suspected of complicity. The People's Court under its president Ronald Freisler became infamous for its handling and precipitous sentencing of suspects. The army established its so-called Court of Honor, which screened officer suspects and transferred those considered guilty from the army to People's Court jurisdiction. The Court of Honor was staffed by Field Marshals von Rundstedt and Keitel and three colonel-generals including Heinz Guderian, who proceeded to cashier and hand over to the court many former comrades such as Field Marshal Erwin von Witzleben.[26]

Rommel, out of the hospital and recovering at his home by early August of 1944, had premonitions of Hitler's wrath descending. It did in the form of a forced suicide on October 14, 1944, in the face of threats against Rommel's wife and son as well as his own relegation to the People's Court should he refuse the option offered. Rommel had become a national hero possessing great popularity with the German public. Hitler, therefore, used this to his advantage, providing a state funeral for Rommel; Germans were told at the time that he had died of an embolism.[27]

Though momentum was moving away from support for Hitler, positions of extremist supporters did not, and they are important, even if in retrospect they are only anecdotal. The day following the attempt on Hitler's life, his navy chief, Karl Dönitz, who typifies the loyal ideologues under Hitler, made a combative speech to the navy, saying,

> Men of the Navy! Holy wrath and unlimited anger fill our hearts because of the criminal attempt which should have cost the life of our Führer.... Providence ... did not abandon our German Fatherland in the fight for its destiny.... An insane small clique of generals ... contemplated this murder ... committing the basest treachery toward the Führer and the German people ... [should they have succeeded]. Destruction; of our people, enslavement of our men, hunger and nameless misery would have been the consequence.[28]

Two years later in post-war testimony at Nuremberg Dönitz still condemned the coup attempt, but in less strident terms, though sufficiently politicized that the President of the Court cautioned him about making a political speech.[29]

Fourteen years later writing his memoirs Dönitz's position on the matter was quite different:

> While ... I approve of the moral motives of the conspirators, particularly as they were aware of the mass murders that had been committed by the Hitler regime, I cannot help asking myself how I would have acted, had I known of the enormity of the crimes perpetrated by the National Socialist System.

Furthermore, he writes, the conspirators were wrong in their assessment of what they hoped to achieve; they could not have prevented defeat or the consequences. If Hitler had succumbed, the legend would have grown of a collapse caused solely by treachery of assassins, and that if Hitler had lived, the war would have been brought to a successful conclusion, the legend would contend.[30] Ten years (and twenty days, as his memoirs note) in Spandau Prison provided a sufficient contemplative period for Dönitz to moderate the severity of his ideas as to ideology and leadership. However, the questions that pose themselves are, 1. would they ever have so changed without Germany's defeat and his imprisonment, and, 2. without the pressure of legacy did they/would they ever really have changed? This was no Ludwig Beck!

All Appointments Are Temporary

Hitler was injured but not seriously by Col. Count Klaus von Stauffenberg's bomb. The persistent efforts of the resistance had failed once again, but the bomb ultimately effectively destroyed the conspirators and most suspected accomplices, both civilian and military.[31]

So once again — in September of 1944 — Hitler called upon von Rundstedt to lead an

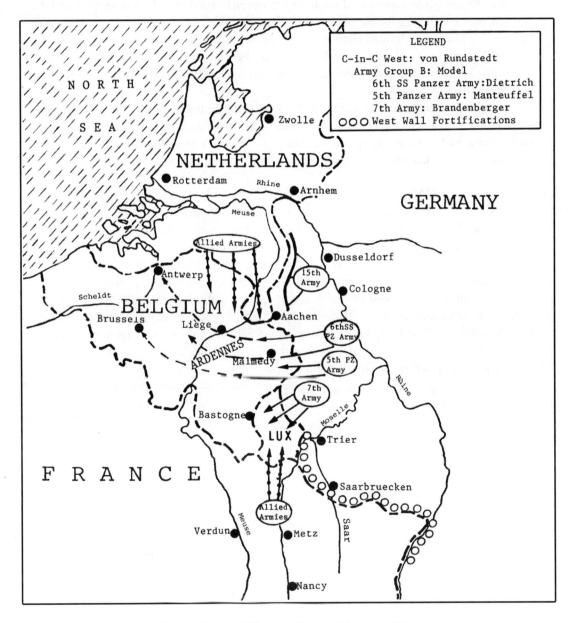

The Ardennes Offensive, Dec. 1944–Jan. 1945

army group, this time in what in retrospect wasted lives on both sides for no gain by the Germans: the Ardennes Offensive.[32]

Hitler's objective, one that metaphorically resembled the last bet of a losing gambler, was to separate the Allies, cut off the British from their source of supply and, in effect, produce a second Dunkirk. The plan, drawn up by OKW without consulting the field generals, called for driving the Allied Armies back from the Rhine near Aachen up through Belgium to Antwerp. (See map, "The Ardennes Offensive, Dec. 1944–Jan. 1945," page 119.)[33]

Von Rundstedt had concluded upon his recent reactivation that the war was lost and the prudent course militarily for the Germans was to wage a defensive war avoiding unnecessary fighting. He planned to draw all German forces behind a direct line from Zwolle (on the Zuider Zee) to Arnhem to the Meuse to the West Wall to the western slopes of the Vosges-Belfort. A compact, echeloned defensive counterforce would thereby be established against the coming Allied attack.[34]

In a last conference on December 2, 1944, at von Rundstedt's headquarters at Zeigenberg, Hitler would not be diverted. The offensive launched on December 16, in von Rundstedt's view, had "no adequate reinforcements, no supplies of ammunition, and ... [low] strength in tanks [that was] ... largely on paper." In addition fuel was in critically short supply.[35]

The Ardennes Offensive represented Stalingrad revisited to von Rundstedt. He had never seen any point to the offensive, which had extended the German flanks, making them susceptible to Allied counterattacks. Hitler's Ardennes Offensive produced two major negative results: first, it attrited German forces so they were irretrievably weakened for a Western defense; and second, it simply delayed the Western Allies, affording the Russians time to advance further into Germany, a development the Germans would long regret.[36]

Responding to the failed offensive and increasing collapse of the German lines, von Rundstedt's critical comments to Hitler brought his final replacement on March 10, 1945, by Field Marshal (Air) Kesselring. Hitler's armies would fight on, but a major emphasis now would be diverting troops from the Russian East to the Western Allies' areas of control, as it would take more than dedicated SS Divisions now to see victory.

14 Hitler as Commander-in-Chief

Revealing a Disjointed Organization Command

It's a wonder the war lasted as long as it did, given the disjointed organizational command structure existing between OKH and OKW, OKH and the field armies and Hitler with all of these entities.

Genesis of the Hitler Command Organization

The expanding Third Reich military meant promotions, improved status and career opportunities in the years leading up to the war. Hitler, however, had his own preconceived plans for the military structure so as to assure his control.

The major Blomberg-Fritsch upheaval of 1938, which introduced significant interference by Hitler into army affairs, set the stage for relations over the balance of the Third Reich's existence. This watershed event of the mid-years of Hitler's reign, a mere year and a half before the start of World War II, was the overt genesis and initiation of increasing cleavage between Hitler and his generals. The situation was further exacerbated by the dismissal of Ludwig Beck, Chief of the General Staff, who had presciently predicted Germany's military defeat.

Numerous incidents of interference and circumvention of responsible commanders and their consequent reactions are related by leading military figures such von Manstein, Guderian, Halder, Kesselring and many other top generals and field marshals. Often in these encounters where questions were raised, Hitler would lose his composure; in one such instance he was described as having "burst out in uncontrollable rage" while "trembling all down the left side of his body."[1]

Hitler was to find that members of the Wehrmacht officer corps were not all dedicated, loyal and consistent supporters of the Nazis nor of his invasive leadership. Of the eighteen wartime field marshals, eight were dismissed by Hitler, three — von Witzleben, von Kluge and Rommel — died as the result of complicity, or suspicion, in the failed coup of 1944; just two were in active service at war's end — Frederick Schörner and Wilhelm Keitel. Half of the six Luftwaffe field marshals remained at war's end. A similar ratio existed among the other senior officers, so that of the 36 colonel-generals appointed by Hitler, few survived the war in their positions. Distrust and disagreement on Hitler's part and/or their own disavowal of the Nazi regime were responsible for dissension in the corps.[2]

On September 25, 1942, Hitler replaced Col. General Halder with General Zeitzler as Chief of the General Staff. Guderian wondered if now Hitler would pay attention to the advice of his specialists. "The destiny of Germany was dependent on the answer to [this question]." Guderian's earlier observation at the time of the Blomberg-Fritsch crisis of 1938, that the head of the Reich distrusted the army leaders, turned out to be prophetic because the problem continued to grow over time. This widening gulf between Hitler and OKH was to have far-reaching repercussions. To the detriment of the war effort it manifested itself in circumvention of OKH and the responsible command chain and the disregard of recommendations and requests of responsible on-the-scene commanders.[3]

The Army High Command, having been gradually circumvented by Hitler's use of OKW and his key team of Jodl and Keitel, lost contact with Hitler's thinking and failed to recognize his intention of continued aggressive use of the military following the Polish success. Their Schlieffen-like plan for a Western attack (as described in Chapter 7), following the Polish Campaign had represented the Army Command's desire for a defensive fight. When it was ultimately supplanted by von Manstein's aggressive Ardennes attack plan, the army only suffered further loss of status with Hitler.[4]

A further and final consequence of this decline, in von Manstein's view, was the dismissal of Field Marshal Walther von Brauchitsch as army Commander-in-Chief and Hitler's assumption of the Commander-in-Chief role, and, therefore, direct army leadership in December of 1941. The army, and particularly the High Command, OKH, had now been eliminated as the authority for land war, its raison d'être, with Hitler working through OKW and his own team of Jodl and Keitel.

Himmler, Göring and Goebbels, according to von Manstein, were the main antagonists vis-à-vis the army, and directed against the army and its leadership a rabble-rousing campaign which bore fruit. Secondly, Hitler maintained that the generals were everlastingly hesitant to take action, and that his foreign policy successes had been against the opposition of the army generals. The reticence of the generals to effectively support von Fritsch as the latter sought exoneration from morals charges in 1938 may have also convinced Hitler he could call the shots with them from that point on; alternatively, von Manstein believed the inaction stemmed from the disbelief on the part of army professionals that the head of state could engage in such base intrigue as prevailed in the Fritsch case.[5]

As the war progressed von Manstein recognized the flaws in Hitler's leadership in the role he had assumed as supreme commander. He saw him as an amateur with an eye for opportune openings. He gives him credit for "a certain talent in the operational field ... with an ability to recognize possibilities of a technical nature.... [But] what he lacked ... was simply military ability based on experience ... for which his 'intuition' was no substitute," and real training in strategy and tactics.[6] "Yet his belief in his own superiority ... had disastrous consequences." He interfered with and hampered the smooth development of the Luftwaffe, rocket propulsion and atomic weapons programs, in addition. He overestimated the power of the will which led to his predilection for hanging on at all costs, and his "thirst for power and his ever-growing self-conceit" were most significant limitations as the war progressed.[7] He wanted to be another Napoleon, but had neither Napoleon's training nor genius.[8]

Hitler's eminence was based on the major advances he had brought to Germany, the political and economic gains as well as military reemergence. To maintain this momentum and to implement his initiatives — from large scale economic to major military moves — he had developed a loyal cadre around him. In the military, he had offered an expanding system with abundant promotional opportunities — he had over 20 field marshals at one time — and he had developed an organizational structure that facilitated his detailed orders to the field commands. The latter depended on an OKW cadre headed by his hand-picked team of Alfred Jodl and Wilhelm Keitel.

The "Intoxication of Ideology"

"Intoxication of Ideology," the phrase of Ludwig Beck, former Chief of the General Staff, used in reference to the Pied Piper–like acquiescence of the generals to Hitler's original plans for war, seems applicable to the Keitel-Jodl-Hitler relationship.[9]

Some observers, as Walther von Brauchitsch noted, attributed Hitler's sense of infallibility, which spawned much of this profile, to the encouragement of sycophants such as Keitel and Jodl. In the same sense von Brauchitsch is similarly guilty, though he did fall from grace early in the war.[10]

Men at OKW were observed to be "either in a state of permanent hypnosis, like Keitel, or of resigned acquiescence, like Jodl"; if these two officers had collaborated they could have prevented much of Hitler's evil from taking place.[11] Of course, there were more quite willing to step into their shoes for the obvious benefits of working closely with the supreme commander.

A close relationship developed between the three early in the war as Jodl took over the duty of daily noon and late-afternoon briefings to Hitler on the latest developments. Except when General Halder or the succeeding chiefs of the General Staff were present, Jodl conducted these war situation briefings himself. Despite OKW chief Field Marshal Keitel's efforts to see Jodl promoted to Chief of the General Staff, Hitler insisted on keeping Jodl in OKW; of course, he similarly hung on to Keitel despite recommendations by Guderian and others to replace him with a more competent and experienced field general.[12]

Albert Speer comments on Keitel's conduct as follows: "Constantly in Hitler's presence, he had completely succumbed to his influence. From an honorable, solidly respectable general he had developed ... into a servile flatterer ... not even trying to form his own opinion.... If he had offered resistance ... he would merely have been replaced by another Keitel." Keitel claims his repeated attempts to resign were rejected by Hitler, who obviously saw that he had in hand an obedient conduit for his plans.[13]

As Hitler's close team in OKW, Jodl and Keitel probably knew him as well as anyone; Keitel laid out Hitler's flaws as a commander,[14] which he observed, tolerated, abetted and lived with, as:

1. The need to find scapegoats in all instances
2. The circumvention of his experts, the generals, and the maintenance of the "stand fast, not one step back" order to the extent that whole armies perished (Stalingrad, Paulus' Sixth Army)
3. The unwarranted sacking of first-class commanders (von Rundstedt and von Leeb in the attack near Rostov-on-Don and Tikhvin in December of 1941)
4. His practice of causing opposing parties to compete with each other
5. The building of the Waffen-SS (Armed SS) at the expense of providing new young blood for the army (Hitler wanted a politically indoctrinated corps)
6. His use of Keitel as a military expert functioning as a secretary to carry out his demands and so implement his power and authority
7. His manifest self-deception regarding political and military issues

His comments overlay those of von Manstein; both saw Hitler as a user, interfering and degrading operations as he focused on short-term gains and with significant overreaching of his capabilities.

At the same time Keitel applauded Hitler in his post-war memoirs for having set an example of how centralized command could be successfully concentrated to the total exclusion of the Army General Staff and the Air Force, writing that,

> The Führer liked to immerse himself in every detail..., so wide was the sweep of his unparalleled inventiveness.... [T]here was no end to his questioning, intervening and sifting of facts, until ... his fantastic imagination ... [had been] satisfied.... [W]e often had conferences and briefings that lasted for hours on end with him.... His working ritual ... represented a marked divergence from our traditional ... [pattern of leaving the details] to lower echelons.[15]

Keitel apparently was so indoctrinated that even from his cell and in the war's aftermath, he could not see through the disaster that had been created by this man. At the same time as he reflected on the task he had inherited, he felt it was virtually insoluble, a fact no human could have foreseen. Hitler needed impotent tools, men who would render loyalty to him in the soldier's tradition; in this he succeeded with men such as Keitel, though the numbers diminished as time and the war wore on. In Keitel's perception, no other general could have overcome Hitler's maniacal plans, regardless of how much "tougher ... more critical and intelligent" he may have been.[16]

To the charge that he should have been stronger in order to correct this situation, Keitel responded, "Only people who — like me [Keitel] — have seen and heard the hundreds of cases where even senior commanders did not dare to stand up to the Führer at times like this and tell him what they thought and what they considered feasible, have any right to reject the accusation of 'feebleness' among the Führer's closest advisors."[17] "I was never permitted to make decisions; the Führer had reserved that right to himself even in seemingly trivial matters."[18]

Could another stronger personality have influenced a different outcome? If Keitel had succeeded in his several requests to resign, which were denied by the Führer, it's clear that his role would have been filled quickly, and not by a strong personality. Having developed the profile of what he needed to implement his directives, Hitler, in the flush of success, was not about to opt for a strong individual. A case in point is the attempt of both Guderian and von Manstein to convince Hitler to make such a change, as described below. As to Hitler's regard for Keitel in his position, Joseph Goebbels felt in early 1943, that "Bormann still has the Führer's confidence..., whereas Keitel is already on ice," and "the Führer has great regard for the personality of Keitel, but doesn't think much of his ability." In Göring's opinion, "Keitel ... was probably responsible that the ... campaign in the East did not function properly. He carried the Führer's commands to OKH with trembling knees."[19]

When a by-then-cynical Hermann Göring was asked at Nuremberg about the charge by a number of generals that Keitel had been a typical "yes-man," he responded, "I personally should be interested if I could see those who today consider themselves 'no-men.'"[20]

The truth is, however, there were, some even with relative impunity — Dönitz, von Manstein, Guderian, are representative; though all kept their necks, most lost their jobs. In the final analysis it is clear that "a Keitel" was necessary in the implementation of Hitler's Third Reich as he ran it, and that *this* Keitel was sufficiently pliable under Hitler's influence so as to succeed and remain as OKW chief.

Success with the Führer

Alfred Jodl made up the other part of the OKW team Hitler relied upon; according to General Walter Warlimont, Jodl's deputy Chief of Staff from 1939 to 1944, Jodl fulfilled the role of Hitler's toady, showing no loyalty to OKH officers, his peers, and reacting against them without evidence, but solely on Hitler's whim and request.[21]

To accommodate the demands of his situation, Jodl made his office in the Chancellery, and as a consequence he was always available to Hitler; accordingly, their relationship became more intimate, as did the latter's confidence in Jodl's abilities.

Alfred Jodl, at Nuremberg, described his role working for Hitler, telling prosecutor Roberts, "My only aim was to succeed with the Führer. ... at the end of five and one-half years I knew best how to achieve good results with ... [him] and avoid bad ones.... My aim was to achieve success, and I achieved it."[22] Here, Jodl was responding to questioning on a memorandum he had prepared for Hitler as the Germans groped for straws in early 1945 on the subject of advantages and disadvantages of repudiating various international agreements; when the analysis was referred to at Nuremberg as having been approached by a utilitarian rather than a moral basis, he explained that the memorandum basically recommended and concluded that rather than repudiate an agreement and thereby accept guilt, the preferred approach would be to ignore limitations which interfere with the war's conduct and then later explain away any consequences. As an example, should the British sink a hospital ship, any reprisal by the Germans should be explained away as a regretful mistake, and that satisfied the Führer.

General Franz Halder, who had adequate experience dealing with OKW and Jodl while at OKH from 1938 to 1942, expressed his opinion of Jodl in testimony at Nuremberg: Jodl believed in Hitler as a savior and, being very ambitious, "hoped to get a personal position for himself." Jodl told Halder as early as 1936–37 that he saw Hitler as a latter-day Napoleon.[23] Jodl's own view of his relationship with Hitler provides insight. As he told the Nuremberg court, he could write a book about the tensions and crises that arose in the years of his relations with Hitler.

Jodl described himself as belonging to that small group of officers who dared look the Führer in the face and confront him with reality, though this was not to be with impunity, as the following incident describes; the incident, which seems a combination of ego, embarrassment and anger balanced by the need on Hitler's part to retain Jodl in his established role, took place in August of 1942. Field Marshal Sigmund von List had reported a hopeless tactical situation faced by his Army Group A in the Caucasus. Hitler, who had never been impressed by List, was especially upset when Jodl flew to Army Headquarters to review the situation. Jodl's subsequent defense of Generals von List and Franz Halder as army Chief of Staff against unjustified criticism "caused a terrible outburst of rage" on the part of Hitler, according to Keitel. When the dust settled, Hitler had discontinued his practice of dinner meals with Jodl and Keitel — the latter for having arranged Jodl's visit — for the balance of the war. It was the end of January 1943 before Hitler would at least shake hands with either of these men who were his command links with the services![24]

Hermann Göring considered Jodl as having "a sergeant's mind in a marshal's body." Göring, for all his faults, was an intelligent and perceptive individual (with one of the four highest IQs of the major Nuremberg defendants).[25]

Hitler, comparing Jodl to Keitel, "felt the abilities of Jodl are much greater. He is in fact a very good and solid worker whose excellent General Staff training is revealed time and time again,"[26] observed Joseph Goebbels; the latter found Jodl a conduit for getting his propaganda requests executed by the German commander of Paris when other avenues failed. However, he felt that "Jodl does not seem to me to be too competent for evaluating a critical military situation.... He has been wrong in his prognoses."[27]

For all his faults, Goebbels was not off the mark regarding Jodl's ability to analyze field problems. General Hasso von Manteuffel, commander of panzer armies on the Eastern Front, felt that Jodl had lost contact with conditions at the front. This was particularly critical in fuel allocation where Jodl's calculations were insufficient to support planned drives. He observed Jodl's interpersonal relations as subservient to Hitler and arrogant to juniors, even including Manteuffel, who was commander of an army.[28]

Depending on whose ox is gored, viewpoints differ. Jodl apparently facilitated Field Marshal Kesselring's relationship with Hitler and OKW. As such Kesselring saw a different side of Jodl, describing him as "An astute and able strategist and tactician, ... placid, level-headed and an indefatigable worker, though one would have wished he had had more operational experience. He had an extremely difficult position, as Hitler was by no means easy to influence.... Those who presume to judge Jodl do not know what his diplomacy prevented and achieved.... Between Jodl and myself there were seldom any differences of opinion ... and I could always rely on his backing."[29] In other words he must have functioned as Kesselring's man at OKW.

The Supreme Commander Brings Ideas in a Vacuum

With the passing of time Hitler's circumvention took its toll on his commanders, and in this respect Halder found the same situation as von Manstein, Guderian, von Rundstedt and many other field commanders. Hitler had ordered, on July 19, 1942, over Halder's opposition, the diversion of armor to the Rostov area where no need existed, whereas the wing at Tsimlyanskaya was starving for armor support. "Now that the result is so palpable [critical outer wing at Tsimlyanskaya is starved for armor] he [Hitler] explodes in a fit of insane rage and hurls the gravest reproaches against the General Staff." The situation for Halder was growing intolerable with time; he characterized the "so-called leadership" on the part of Hitler as pathological, reacting to momentary impressions, and with a total lack of understanding of military command machinery.[30]

The Führer's proclivity to assume overriding command was to increase in intensity to the very end; even field marshals found it necessary to clear minor troop movements, and the effect on morale and success was extremely negative.

Halder as Chief of the General Staff and Walther von Brauchitsch as army Commander-in-Chief had an organic organizational problem in the Russian theater: the army group sectors — Army Group South under von Kleist and Army Group Center under von Bock — continually operated at cross-purposes with OKH. This irritated von Brauchitsch, who felt the field commands were ignoring OKH's orders. However, Halder understood the genesis of the problem and attempted to convey to von Brauchitsch in their meeting of June 27, 1941, that this was a natural consequence of OKH's remote location at Zossen. Distant army groups and armies construed their inputs as interference. We at OKH "cannot have a clearly detailed picture and so [we] should confine ourselves to assigning broad missions and not try to direct the movements of individual corps or even divisions."[31] To Halder, "the ultimate authority is the responsible authorities in the [army] groups. The armies execute."[32]

Where Hitler was concerned, though, a vastly different scenario prevailed. Defiance of his directives had dire consequences, especially where giving ground was concerned. Halder describes the lot of First Panzer Army, part of Army Group South under Field Marshal Gerd von Rundstedt, on December 1, 1941, during the first Russian winter. First Panzer Army, unable to prevent penetrations near Voroshilovgrad, had fallen back, and, "The Führer is in a state of extreme agitation over the situation. He forbids withdrawal.... These people [OKW and Hitler] have no conception of the condition of our troops, and keep grinding out ideas in a vacuum." Never mind that 9 km back an excellent defensive position existed for First Panzer forces at the River Mius (see the map "Eastern Europe, the Fatal Second Front," page 82).[33]

Halder recognized with regret that Commander in Chief von Brauchitsch had yielded to Hitler's demands and forwarded the order not to pull back. Von Rundstedt replied that he could not comply and that either the order must be changed or he, von Rundstedt, must be relieved of his post. For Halder, in a tight situation like this, the on-the-spot commander, especially where a top field marshal was concerned, should be allowed a free hand. Nevertheless, at 0200 on December 1 the Führer replaced von Rundstedt with von Reichenau, losing one of his ablest and most senior commanders, at least temporarily. Parenthetically, it is important to note that von Rundstedt would be hired and fired by the mercurial supreme commander twice more by the early part of 1945.[34]

Another dimension of interference with OKH's command prerogative was the relationship of the Army High Command with Hitler's OKW Supreme Command staff. Constant telephone dialogues, always about the same questions and rarely well thought-out, were distressing and time-consuming. The prime culprit was Field Marshal Keitel, Hitler's obeisant Chief of OKW, whose "undigested spoutings" Halder and staff found hardest to endure.[35]

Alfred Jodl, next in seniority behind Keitel at OKW, draws similar ire for, on July 30, 1942, feeding back as his own a directive based on one of OKH and Halder's own proposals. Submitted 6 days earlier, it called for a diversion of forces from Army Groups A and B south of the Don toward Stalingrad. Jodl, though, embellished Halder's order with what Halder calls "rankest nonsense," the diversion of First Panzer Army southwest instead of southeast, north of Armavir, where it was needed.[36]

In another instance of interference and misdirection, in the drive for Smolensk-Elnya-Roslavl in July of 1941, Hitler contradicted his own orders for this drive, and ordered a diversion of troops for the encirclement of Bialystok. Army Commander in Chief von Brauchitsch was afraid to push for the OKH approach which was to maintain the original push to Smolensk. The generals were split — Hoth and Guderian for the original plan, and von Kluge for agreeing with Hitler's changed plan.[37]

On a similar theme is Guderian's meeting of August 23, 1941, with Hitler and his staff, when Guderian proposed a continuation of the attack on Moscow, whereas Hitler had ordered redirection to attack Kiev. This was a carbon copy of Rommel's meeting with Hitler and staff in 1942 (discussed in Chapter 11, "The Africa-Italy Campaigns"), in which the assembled staff agreed with Hitler's every word and no intelligence was injected. It was a demonstration that Guderian and most other generals would become familiar with over the rest of the war especially as reverses increased.[38]

According to the Army High Command, Hitler's top command level — OKW as well as Hitler — simply distrusted everybody. Indeed, top-level officers had taken on the attitude of their leader, the supreme commander, whose mistrust of reports that did not suit his own wishes would increasingly militate against German successes.[39]

Attempts at Reorganization Draw a Blank

So concerned was Guderian with the continuing problem of interference by Hitler and its effect on command decisions, that in early 1943, after assuming the role of Inspector-General of Armored Troops, he approached Joseph Goebbels and raised the question of mismanagement by the Supreme Command, OKW, and asked Goebbels to intervene and urge Hitler to reorganize it; he suggested a new OKW Chief of Staff be appointed to replace the pliable and obeisant Keitel. With the necessary authority the new man would be able to lessen Hitler's direct influence on military operations. Goebbels recognized this as a "thorny" problem, but promised to do what he could since he admitted his own recognition of the deteriorating military situation. Guderian next tried Himmler, but the response was one of "impenetrable obliquity" so that he gave up pursuing the problem in depth. To the same proposal, Jodl's response to him was, "Do you know of a better supreme commander than Adolf Hitler?"[40]

Consequently, Guderian approached Hitler on his own in January of 1944, and stressed the need to get rid of the existing confusion in military command functions by appointing a general whom he trusted and who could solve this problem. However, "Hitler refused to part with Field Marshal Keitel. So distrustful was he that he immediately recognized my suggestion as an attempt to limit his powers. I achieved nothing. Besides, was there any general whom Hitler trusted? ... there was none."[41]

Rebuffed but not dissuaded, Guderian took a positive approach, recommending von Manstein for promotion to chief of OKW, replacing the weak Keitel. "Manstein is perhaps the best brain that the General Staff Corps has produced" was Adolf Hitler's response; however, he was not about to promote von Manstein in this instance. Von Manstein, able, energetic and impulsive, an organizer of genius, a difficult subordinate but a generous superior, as his peers describe him, would argue every point with the Führer, and he knew it.[42] In contrast, the OKW Chief-in-place, Keitel, had proven an obeisant and obedient link for Hitler with the field forces. Hitler had spent 10 years consolidating his control of the German military and there would be no return to the days when the army would dictate the demise of a Bismarck or a Brüning.[43] Promoting von Manstein would fracture Hitler's handpicked Supreme Command cadre. Instead, an antagonistic but upwardly loyal relationship would prevail between an iron-willed Hitler and a stubborn military talent, von Manstein, as long as he was employed.[44]

Probably equally threatening if not more so was an attempt by von Manstein in 1943 to get Hitler to transfer the military direction from himself to a fully responsible Chief of the General Staff; this fell on deaf ears. Hitler felt the prestige of the generals might impair his own in the eyes of the people.[45]

Following the July 20, 1944, coup attempt, Hitler replaced General Zeitzler with Guderian as Chief of the General Staff. Apparently Guderian, despite all his campaigning to change the command structure and to alter OKW tactical commands to the field, had determined just how far to go with the Supreme Commander; also, for reasons not embodied in Guderian's memoirs, Hitler may have had good reason to place confidence in him. In fact the conspirators who had attempted to recruit Guderian through General von Rabenau in confidential discussions in early 1943 (see Chapter 15) felt so; Fabian von Schlabrendorff, army officer and coup participant, in pointing to these discussions and Guderian's appointment as Chief of the General Staff following the July 20th coup attempt on Hitler's life, says it was clear "how he had paid his way to eminence."[46] Guderian charges these assertions are untrue, however.

However, in this new position Guderian now found his authority greatly limited by Hitler and the organizational structure; OKW basically controlled operations, with OKH, the army, in a secondary role. Guderian found his responsibilities as Chief of the General Staff limited to the Eastern Front. It appears that Hitler was once and for all attempting to extinguish what vestiges of power still remained in the Army General Staff.[47]

General Walter Warlimont, deputy chief to Jodl in OKW, comments on Guderian as Chief of the General Staff, saying, "In his impetuous and vivacious manner he would often use strong language at the briefing conferences ... [but] the change in Army Chief of Staff was unlikely to bring any change in the unhappy relationship between the two top level staffs of the Wehrmacht [OKW and OKH]. ... it did not enter the head of any senior army officers to make common cause with OKW or cooperate in opposition to the continuance of a war already lost."[48]

As the tide of battle inevitably reversed, Heinz Guderian was preoccupied with saving troops in the face of the advancing Russians. The 26 army divisions under Field Marshal Ferdinand Schörner were hopelessly cut off on the Courland Peninsula west of Riga, Latvia, and Guderian tried to convince Hitler that the position should be abandoned and the army transported across the Baltic Sea to safety. Hitler maintained his usual "no retreat" position so that the conversation became a confrontation, observed Albert Speer, Minister of Armament and Production, who was present. Guderian, faced Hitler across the marble table, both now standing. "It's simply our duty to save these people, and we still have time to remove them!" Guderian cried out in a challenging voice. An infuriated Hitler maintained his no retreat stance, and Guderian held firm, insisting on evacuation. Hitler prevailed, but had, for the moment, been confronted by a challenge amounting to insubordination.[49]

As a result of Guderian's persistent efforts to redirect and save the deteriorating military situation, Hitler finally relieved him on March 28, 1945, thus ending his active military duties. General Warlimont, in a position to observe from OKW, comments, "Guderian made desperate attempts to bring the horror to an end, but he was the only one [of Supreme Headquarters personnel and Hitler's entourage]. On 28 March he showed for the second time exemplary 'moral courage' in protecting his subordinates but on that very day he had to go."[50]

If Guderian was anything he was one who tackled apparently insoluble problems, and interference from Hitler was no exception. "There's no need for you to try to teach me," Hitler said to Guderian in one such encounter. Hitler then launched into a stereotypical almost tirade taking credit for leading the army successfully so far in the war, decrying the overall experience the General Staff who, even with their training, were no match for him. In this flight of Beck's "intoxication of ideology," Hitler had seemingly forgotten the fatal losses of Stalingrad, North Africa and the air war of 1940. Yet Hitler repeatedly confided, "I can't understand why everything has gone wrong the past two years."[51]

Hitler's A-Team in the Field

Finally, in a masterful demonstration of empathy for the thinking of his generals, Hitler's 12-year manipulation of Gerd von Rundstedt is revealing. Adolf Hitler, who perhaps knew von Rundstedt best, assumed a chameleon character in his relationship: when adversity struck he deactivated the field marshal, saying, "Well, he is an old man. He has lost his nerve. He just isn't up to the situation. He must go." When Hitler's mercurial nature brought forth some other general's firing and/or a need to fill an important command, he would rehire von Rundstedt, commenting on the great respect von Rundstedt enjoyed with the entire Wehrmacht leadership, saying, "He can push anything through, and I don't have anybody else that enjoys that sort of respect, who can push everybody else before him." When Hitler offered him the command in the West a second time, von Rundstedt's response was, "What ever you order, I shall do to my last breath."[52] Others such as Karl Dönitz appear to have been driven by both Hitler's leadership and the National Socialist ideology and probably a significant degree of nationalism in their dedication to the regime. This group comprised Hitler's most ardent supporters in the command structure. The extent of his dedication is exemplified in the details of his conference with Hitler on February 19–20, 1945; as to whether to renounce the Geneva Convention, Dönitz's response, in the presence of Jodl and Ribbentrop, was "On the contrary, the disadvantages outweigh the advantages. It would be better to carry out the measures considered necessary without warning, and at all costs to save face with the outer world."[53] It was inevitable that Hitler would select Dönitz as his successor to lead the Reich.

Franz Halder, as contrasted to Dönitz, was not driven to serve the Führer on the basis of ideology, but, instead by his dedication to the historic legacy of the Great General Staff, which preoccupied him if his writing is any indicator, as well as his drive for personal survival. That he succeeded in the latter is attested by his escaping indictment at war's end and subsequently working as a historian for the U.S. Army for 16 years until he retired.

Halder is sometimes credited with much of the prescient tactical planning of Germany's World War II campaigns: "the real brain behind [Germany's] victorious campaigns," writes General Walter Warlimont.[54] Though his significant miscalculations frequently emerge, as in SEALION and BARBAROSSA, as noted earlier, in fairness, Hitler's interminable meddling and pressure may, in part, be accountable.

15 A Futile Pursuit of Freedom

Support for the Führer Wanes at the Top

The facts show that brave men died on the gallows or in concentration camps because they dared against hopeless odds to effect the downfall of the organized terror Nazism had introduced to Germany. Without help from the outside world, the odds of success were nil.[1]

The Opposition Leadership Structure

In this environment Ludwig Beck assumed leadership of the major oppositional movements in Germany as the inevitable war he had predicted came to Europe. The consensus of the resistors had always been that if their attempts to overthrow the Nazis were to be successful, participation of the military in any coup attempt was mandatory. It followed that with the war on, only a respected general could effectively lead this movement, and Beck, with his appreciation of the broader national issues at stake and his eminent military background, was the ideal chief.[2]

"Beck was the only general with an unimpaired reputation, the only general who voluntarily resigned. No one among the military men could surpass him in personal or soldierly capacity," was the post-war comment of Hans Gisevius, one of the few anti–Nazi collaborators to survive the war.[3]

Beck's civilian counterpart was Carl Goerdeler, former mayor of Leipzig, who, if faulted, continually represented the sanguine viewpoint as each coup attempt was conceived and pursued. Beck, on the other hand, was persistently cautious and conservative so as not to bring disrepute on the opposition movement if no putsch was forthcoming or if they showed little possibility of success.[4]

Beck, therefore, sought and pursued plans and/or negotiations in only five situations that he felt promised a reasonable chance of success:[5]

- November 1939 after the Polish Campaign in an effort to head off an attack on France
- Spring 1940 in a second effort to coalesce military support to abort the attack on the west
- Early 1943 after the Stalingrad and Tunis disasters
- Late 1943 as reverses met Axis efforts on every front
- July 1944 post-invasion when the end was inevitable

Beck and Goerdeler and their associate conspirators contacted one field marshal and general after another but drew little support in their efforts to construct coups. Von Manstein, von Rundstedt, Rommel, Halder, von Brauchitsch and many other top officers were among those pursued by Beck and his associates, but as Beck said at the time of Stalingrad, "We were deserted."[6]

Attempts at Support Bear Little

When war with Poland was a scant few months off, Beck wrote to both von Brauchitsch and his own successor, Franz Halder. Not surprisingly only Halder responded by meeting with Beck. On all matters of principle Beck was right, Halder agreed: war would mean the end of Germany. The Gestapo dictatorship was unendurable, and unless Hitler were deposed, Germany and Europe would see no peace. As each respective coup plan came to the fore, Halder agreed to everything, but beyond rhetoric, there was never any action — consensus was he had no will.[7]

Memoirs often "spin veils" intended to deflect the reader's perception of the true train of events, said Albert Speer; he could have been alluding to Franz Halder's testimony at the Nuremberg Trials as well as Halder's post-war retrospective, *Hitler as Warlord*. What Halder considered a rational explanation in both instances as to why no action could be taken to arrest Hitler's onslaught is contradicted by observations of oppositionists who had attempted to work with Halder, such as Ulrich von Hassell and Hans Gisevius. For example, Halder had met with von Hassell on April 6, 1940, to discuss plans for a coup designed to prevent the attack in the west. According to von Hassell "Halder, who had begun to weep during the discussion of his responsibility ... had got cold feet."[8]

Hans Gisevius sums up the attitude of the opposition towards Halder's efforts, saying, "there was occasion after occasion when ... Halder was willing to venture a first step without daring to take a second.... [He is a] 'little man' ... [whom] Hitler has picked out [as] an obedient functionary."[9]

Of stiffer timber was Erich von Manstein. One of the characteristics distinguishing him is that he did adhere to a strict code in relations with Hitler and the state. By this code von Manstein directly expressed his disagreements with Hitler, suffering dismissal in 1944 with no further recall as the final result. Despite disagreement and dismissal he refused, though efforts were made to recruit him, to participate in any of the coup plans or attempts. In fact, though he had reflected some measure of interest and agreement when confronted with a conspiracy proposal in 1943 by General Henning von Tresckow, he ultimately declined. If reports of his subsequent actions are true, the characterization is not flattering to von Manstein. According to some observers, he reported this incident to Hitler's adjutant, Major-General Schmundt, saying that von Tresckow's attitude toward National Socialism was negative, an indictment which apparently limited Tresckow's future military career.[10]

As the reverses of 1942 accrued, Ludwig Beck attempted to persuade von Manstein by letter that further military operations had become senseless for Germany and that the first consideration should be Germany's survival; only an intact army could protect the country's borders and simultaneously maintain internal order. The mistake of allowing the revolutionary upheaval of 1918 to repeat, Beck wrote, must be avoided by the firm hand of an intact army. Von Manstein's response to Beck, as he told the Nuremberg court in 1946 was "a war was only lost if you yourself consider it lost."[11]

Others such as Col. Count Klaus von Stauffenberg, the bomb carrier in the July 20, 1944, unsuccessful coup attempt, endeavored to enlist von Manstein but with no success: von Manstein would not participate, but did allow that he would refrain from reporting Stauffenberg's plan to the Gestapo.[12]

Von Manstein's position, as he stated after the war, was that a commander during wartime, though he disagreed with the leadership, even when he realized the war would be lost could not pull the rug out from under his loyal German troops, nor contravene his oath by participating in a coup. Too, he felt a coup such as the attempt on Hitler's life of July 20th could have, if it had been successful, caused chaos in Germany.[13]

Beck and his co-conspirators recognized only too well that success depended on active participation of the OKH leaders, von Brauchitsch and Halder, but the latter's own personal agendas prevented this ever being realized.[14] For those in leadership positions who were not so encumbered, they still were in a tenuous position relative to taking action. Field Marshal Erwin von Witzleben, who was dedicated and would ultimately suffer for that posture, was rarely in command of troops when needed; Generals Georg Thomas and Hans Oster and Admiral Wilhelm Canaris in OKW were important collaborators, but had no resources for more than intelligence and coordination. As intermediaries Thomas and Oster constantly risked their own safety. Field Marshals such as the constantly wavering von Kluge could not be won over until too late.

The Resistance: Considered and Declined Again

By early 1943, with the failure of two Russian winters and the collapse of the North African Campaign a matter of history, the long-smoldering embers of the resistance movement flared. Looking for broadened support, General Friedrich von Rabenau, Chief of Army Archives, brought Dr. Carl Goerdeler to meet with Heinz Guderian to discuss the very same problem Guderian had been attacking, that of curtailing Hitler's initiatives as Chancellor and Supreme Commander but in a more extreme way. Goerdeler described Beck's current efforts to bring about a coup d'état, whereby Hitler would be interned on the Obersalzberg. Guderian, finding the plan without foreign support, with no provision for replacing the other National Socialist leaders and no plan for a provisional government, felt it was unworkable.

In his opinion, "The weaknesses and mistakes of the National Socialists and the personal errors that Hitler made were then plain to see — even to me; ... But, Goerdeler's plan would be harmful ... and incapable of being put into practice." Guderian, therefore, asked Goerdeler to give up his plan.[15]

Harboring early misgivings about Guderian's real politics, the conspirators realized he would not join them unless success was first assured, and that in case of failure there was a good chance Guderian would betray the conspirators. Von Rabenau, therefore, warned Guderian not to betray the conspirators, that he was already deeply involved as a result of their discussions and that in the Reich it was not only he who lights the fire, but he who reports its outbreak that was also punished![16]

On Oath and Duty to Country

Shortly before the coup attempt of July 1944, Guderian was "utterly horrified" to learn that Field Marshal von Kluge and others planned to arrange an armistice with the Western Powers without Hitler's knowledge. However, six months later, in January of 1945, the situation had so deteriorated that Guderian solicited a meeting with Foreign Minister Joachim von Ribbentrop and proposed they see Hitler together and recommend an armistice. Ribbentrop could not believe the Russians would be at the gates of Berlin in the not too distant future; he refused to accompany Guderian to see Hitler on the subject and insisted no one know of their conversation. Nevertheless, Ribbentrop did relay Guderians's comments to Hitler, who subsequently advised Guderian that any further statements of this nature would be regarded as high treason.[17]

However, on March 21, 1945, Guderian approached Heinrich Himmler, the Reichsfuehrer, while the latter was talking informally with Hitler and asked to talk to Himmler alone. Hitler walked away and Guderian proceeded to ask Himmler to use his foreign contacts to seek an armistice. But nothing could be done with him, for "He was afraid of Hitler."[18]

Even as the war situation became desperate, Guderian maintained complete support for Hitler, if his performance in Headquarters Situation Meetings as late as January of 1945 is representative. He apparently decided against a direct confrontation to broach the subject of the lost war. While others such as Albert Speer pursued this subject with Hitler, a fact which Hitler relayed to Guderian, the latter continued to defer any discussion of the looming catastrophe or its mitigation with the Führer. In this meeting of late January, attended by some two dozen high-ranking Wehrmacht officers, Hitler and Guderian engaged in a lengthy dialogue concerning the retreat in the East. During this encounter Guderian was constantly admonished by Hitler that German troops would succeed even as Guderian continued to give conditional or less than positive estimates of their situation, to which the latter would then agree. Tactics, welfare of his troops, and army organization issues, but not a lost war, were as far as Guderian would go with Hitler, shrewdly assessing the point of no return.[19]

The opposition situation is well stated by Guderian and portrayed by the profile of his experiences; he recognized the need to maintain a safe position, avoiding confrontation with Hitler and demonstrating active support of the regime while covertly deploring its existence as soon as the tide turned toward defeat, though never making a serious counter move. As a result this survivor who played it safe ended the war without ever being indicted or charged, whereas active resistors such as Beck, von Kluge, von Witzleben, Rommel, and Canaris, to name a few, recognized and worked for a solution timely enough to prevent the destruction Hitler offered and paid the price.

An Alternative Plan Emerges

By 1944 Rommel had concluded the war was lost and was concerned that a small group could control and dictate the nations' welfare on a whim despite the obviously looming catastrophe.[20] Rommel finally recognized the growing amorality of the regime and the corruption of the judicial system, both of which seemed to him a precursor of inevitable destruction of the German state. He finally saw Hitler as a monster manifesting senseless greed in the most brutal forms: dreams of power through conquest, the lust for killing and destruction, and the rule by terror, fear and vengeance, writes his Chief of Staff in the invasion campaign, General Hans Speidel.[21] He condemned Hitler's excesses in human and military matters and in affairs of state, his disdain for European unity and lack of feeling for humanity.[22]

The time for action had arrived for Rommel who met in February of 1944 with key resistance leader Dr. Carl Goerdeler. In this meeting the possibility of a legal change of government and means of ending the war were discussed. Key military leaders, including Beck, Quartermaster General of the Army; General Eduard Wagner; General Alexander von Falkenhausen, the military governor of Belgium and northern France; General Karl Heinrich von Stuelpnagel, the military governor of France; and numerous others were in concurrence that a way must be found to end the war before the inevitable catastrophe.[23]

Rommel and Stuelpnagel found von Rundstedt a listener to their views but only that. It is clear von Rundstedt had recognized the hopelessness of the struggle as early as the fall of Stalingrad, and had made his views known to the Führer following the invasion. He was dismissed for this last expression, but refused to join any action against the regime. In fact he was shortly rehired by Hitler for the Ardennes Campaign.

General Wagner met with Rommel in May of 1944 to coordinate conspiracy preparations in the West for a coup and/or peace which would include OKH. Rommel, however, objected to plans to assassinate Hitler which would thereby martyr him, according to General Speidel. He said Rommel's plan was to use reliable troops to seize and arrest Hitler for subsequent trial before a German court.[24] A different Rommel position is described by Hans Gisevius in testimony at Nuremberg when he said Rommel proposed not only the assassination of Hitler but also of Göring and Himmler.[25]

Lt. General Fritz Bayerlein, Chief of Staff to Rommel in 1941–42 in the Afrika Corps, said Rommel's conversations with his wife and son before and after the Normandy invasion confirm his rejection of a coup d'ètat. Rather than killing Hitler, he favored negotiations with the Allies, circumventing Hitler, so as to present him with a fait accompli. Rommel and his then–Chief of Staff, Hans Speidel, made contact with the Allies before the invasion and discussed the possibility of such negotiations. However, Rommel's injury as the result of the air attack on June 17 removed his further leadership and/or involvement.[26]

Despite the "unconditional surrender" dictate established by the Allies at Casablanca in

1943, the army conspirators developed a plan they hoped to put into effect before the invasion so as to conclude an armistice. However naïve and unempathetic from the German standpoint, and though such would be received without merit by the Allies, they intended to submit the proposal to Generals Eisenhower and Montgomery, but without Hitler's participation, according to Hans Speidel. The Germans felt it critical to initiate negotiations for the armistice before the invasion, key points of which were[27]:

- German evacuation of occupied Western territories and withdrawal behind the West-Wall (also known as the Siegfried Line)
- Surrender of administration of occupied territories to the Allies
- Suspension of Allied bombing of Germany
- Armistice, not unconditional surrender, followed by peace negotiations
- Arrest of Hitler and trial before a German court
- Temporary assumption of power in Germany by the resistance forces of General Beck and Mayor Goerdeler and trade union leader Leuschner
- Continuation of fighting along a reduced line in the East

Rationale for Action against the Oath

Rommel had his loyal supporters as would be expected, especially from a Chief of Staff. In this case, Hans Speidel, his last chief, describes what he perceived as Rommel's approach to the opposition question: "Rommel," he writes, "struggled to determine at what point obedience must end for a general who feels responsible for the fate of the nation, and at what point human conscience would demand insurrection. He did know the difference between obedience to God and ... to man.... It was clear to him that only the highest military leader was qualified, entitled, and obliged to undertake this ... responsibility and decision, not the individual soldier or officer."[28]

Though Rommel was welcomed by many in the resistance, he was criticized by some for coming to their support late in the game when his own military catastrophe loomed, and then maintaining a background role, so they perceived, so as to allow the movement to profit by his popularity later on. Of these late adherents to the opposition, Hans Gisevius, long-time co-conspirator, testified at Nuremberg that "it is ... difficult to know whether these gentlemen, when they joined our group, came as the fallen might, as people who wished to save their pensions, or as people who, from the beginning, stood for decency and honor."[29]

The invasion proceeded before substantive progress could be made, if indeed meetings of substance occurred and if the Allies would have entertained this last proposal, so that the issue became moot. Beck was a determined man with a respected past who relished little the repeated rebuffs he had experienced since 1938. Yet he had continued to lead a campaign even as he had before his resignation, though reaching the end of his rope repeatedly. As the plans for each successive attempt were frustrated, he had finally consented to assassination as the only answer, having previously rejected this extreme measure for religious and political reasons.[30]

On July 20, 1944, the final coup attempt was executed. A bomb which was to kill the

Führer was by chance mispositioned so that Hitler was only moderately injured. His revenge was quick and by evening the primary participants were dead. Beck, as coup leader, was given the option of dispatching himself. Colonel Count Klaus von Stauffenberg, the bomb carrier, Colonel of the General Staff Merz von Quirnheim, General of the Infantry Olbricht and Lieutenant Werner von Haeften were summarily shot on orders of Col. General Freidrich Fromm, commander of the Reserve Army. Many more, including General Fromm, would suffer the same fate as the Führer took his revenge, concluding any further resistance efforts before war's end.[31]

16 Aggression's Price

Twelve Years of Rampage Have a Cost

The German people and their military and civilian leaders, ill used by a despot, were destined to suffer as payment for the short-term gains they had made. This brought a new approach to a system of laws for adjudicating international criminality which gave closure to two wars.

The Führer's Will, Dönitz's Inheritance

Following Hitler's suicide in a Berlin bunker on April 29, 1945, Karl Dönitz received a communication from Martin Bormann advising that he, Dönitz, was Hitler's designated successor. At the time Dönitz felt that Hitler, wishing the war brought to an end had nominated him feeling a senior officer of the Armed Forces would be best able to do this. "That this assumption was incorrect I did not find out until the winter of 1945–46 in Nuremberg [postwar war-crimes trials], when for the first time I heard the provisions of Hitler's will, in which he demanded that the struggle should be continued."[1]

Once in the leadership role, "My policy was simple — to try to save as many lives as I could."[2] Implementing this objective entailed maintaining active forces in all services with the single objective of moving as many troops and civilians as possible into the British and American areas of jurisdiction and away from the control of the Russians. Unconditional surrender documents ending all action were signed by General Jodl, as Dönitz's representative, in Rheims on May 7, 1945.

By now the reader may not be surprised that many of his peers and associates described Dönitz as an ardent Nazi, enjoying Hitler's complete confidence[3]; though his memoirs are mostly apolitical, comments of his peers as well as his speeches to both the navy and the country provide added and pertinent insight.

Signing surrender documents at Reims, France, May 7, 1945: for Germany, from the left, Maj. General Wilhelm Oxenius, Col. General Alfred Jodl, Admiral Hans Georg von Friedeburg; for the Allies, Major General Walter Bedell Smith (middle) and General Frederick Morgan. Ullstein bild/The Granger Collection, New York.

As one of the Reich's five major culpable military leaders — Göring, Keitel, Jodl, Raeder and himself— Dönitz drew ten years' imprisonment at the Nuremberg Trials, with his term ending on September 30, 1956. Dönitz, according to Albert Speer, his fellow prisoner in Spandau Prison for these ten years, attributed his appointment as Hitler's heir to the Chancellorship as being based on Speer's recommendation. Ready to depart Spandau, Dönitz said to Speer, "Because of you I've lost these eleven years.... But for you Hitler would never have had the idea of making me Chief of State. All my men have commands again. But look at me! Like a common criminal. My career is wrecked."

Speer responded that the war had killed millions and more millions were murdered in camps by Nazi criminals, and "All of us here were part of the regime. But your ten years here perturb you more than fifty million dead. And your last words in Spandau are: your career!"[4] Further Speer felt this was a man for whom the tragedy of the recent past is reduced to the question of what mistakes led to the loss of the war[5]; and that his book of memoirs, published in 1958, "wraps in silence or spins a veil around" his real role in the Nazi government, one in which he had been held in higher esteem than almost any other officer in the services, and was considered by Hitler as a true National Socialist.[6]

A Myopic Worldview

Dönitz's memoirs present a self-characterization he would have us accept, and which he probably believed to a great extent himself. His profile is further fleshed out by comments of his peers and his Nuremberg testimony. What is revealed appears to be not simply a military professional but an individual who, once caught up in the Nazi *Weltanschauung* (worldview), hoped for fulfillment of Hitler's dreams of world hegemony.

Hjalmar Schacht, once economics minister and Reichsbank president, and himself not the personification of innocence in Hitler's rise to power, said informally while imprisoned at Nuremberg that for some — meaning here Dönitz — the narrow feeling of duty in such militarists prevented their taking proper action to avert the destruction brought by the war.[7]

In fact Dönitz demonstrates this in his post-war memoirs when he fails to perceive the issues driving United States policy prior to the entry of the U.S. into the war. He believed the wishes of the American people diverged from those of President Roosevelt; Churchill's influence and relationship with Roosevelt were responsible for this, he felt, and led to the Lend-Lease Act, American ships protecting convoys and joint British-American naval conferences while Britain was engaged with Germany.

Dönitz observes that America had, though being in a state of neutrality under international law, aided Britain from 1939 on with arms as well as financial credits; this led to U.S. entry into the war because "so important a debtor could not, obviously, have been abandoned to his fate."[8] His failure to mention Pearl Harbor is probably a clue to insular thinking; Hitler himself exemplified this characteristic, an attitude possibly attributable to National Socialist Germany's own isolation from the world outside Europe as well as the regime's proclivity to construct its own reality. After all, this approach had worked for the past 8 years.

However, President Roosevelt pointed up the life or death issues at stake for the U.S. in his December 29, 1940, fireside chat, saying, "If Great Britain goes down the Axis Powers will control the Continents of Europe, Asia, Africa and Australia and they will be in a position to bring enormous military and naval resources against this hemisphere. It is no exaggeration to say that all of us in all the Americas would be living at the point of a gun ... economic as well as military."[9]

Dönitz refers to this as a "quite fantastic picture" which had the desired effect. However, one only need refer to the chronology of the Third Reich from the early 1930s through the Rhineland, Anschluss, Sudetenland, Poland and the fall of France, the Pact of Steel and the Tri-Partite Pact to recognize the modus operandi and obvious threat to the then-noncombatants. It is surprising that Dönitz would have written this rationalization after the war and in the face of the proven logic of Roosevelt's arguments. Either his objective was to absolve his administration of any more fault than had accrued by war's end and/or he was trying to justify Germany's and his own actions.

A Better Hand Than He Deserved

The Nuremberg Trials which followed the surrender were without precedent. Consequently, under the leadership of Chief U.S. Prosecutor Robert Jackson, new legal ground was forged. Though Dönitz was critical, if he had been realistic, he should have looked upon the tribunal as having dealt him a better than average hand, given his role in the total war. He criticized the tribunal's creation of new legal principles endowed with retroactive validity as being a breach of recognized legal principle, *nulle poena sine lege* (no penalty without prior law). Yet compare this reaction to his earlier aggressive response to Germany's 1939 abrogation of the 1935 Anglo-German Naval Treaty: rather than objecting, he used the event to request and gain top priority for U-boat construction over that for capital ships.

In an informal conversation in his Nuremberg cell Dönitz condemned the anti–Christian character spawned by the Nazis and at the same time emphasized the guilt of war on the politicians: "There are two classes of people [here] in that dock: soldiers and politicians. The soldiers only did their duty ... but the politicians [profited handsomely and] ... brought the Nazis to power and started the war! They are the ones who brought about these disgusting crimes."[10]

In his testimony Dönitz claimed to be unaware of the extermination program, the slave labor program, concentration camp conditions and the extent of the camps. However, a memorandum signed by Dönitz in late 1944, which was distributed to Hitler, Keitel, Jodl, Speer and the Supreme Command of the Air Force, discusses shipping losses and states as a remedy, in part, "Furthermore, I propose reinforcing the shipyard working parties by prisoners from the concentration camps ... 12,000 concentration camp prisoners will be employed in the shipyards as additional labor (Security Service [SD] agrees to this)."[11]

Responding to British prosecutor Sir David Maxwell-Fyfe on May 10, 1946, Dönitz agreed he as well as the whole German people knew of the existence of the camps, but knew nothing of camp conditions. He personally knew of only two camps: Dachau and Oranienberg. He had understood that employing prisoners to work in shipyards meant better food conditions for them, but was unaware of adverse camp conditions. When asked whether 12,000 working alongside non-prison workers would not have told of the deplorable camp conditions, he claimed ignorance except to say he guessed they had orders not to talk.[12]

Of the five major military defendants, Dönitz was dealt with most lightly; the others receiving hanging, except for Raeder's life sentence. At first he viewed the indictment as just an American joke,[13] but eventually began to take it seriously, his defense obtaining important documents from American Admiral Nimitz that probably saved his life.[14] Surely, in retrospect Dönitz must have recognized his major aggressive military and close political role to Hitler could have drawn the ultimate sentence. On the other hand, his regret was probably not that he erred, but that he got caught, and the German campaign toward hegemony was aborted.

Caught in Hitler's Trap

Wilhelm Keitel probably recognized his first-tier Nuremberg presence combined with his role in the Supreme Military Command made him a terminal case. Though he obfuscated in much of his testimony at Nuremberg in responding to questioning, in the end he made a forthright statement attempting to explain his behavior and actions as OKW chief: the Führer had a "forceful and convincing way, stating the military and political necessities and making felt his concern for the welfare of his soldiers ... [and] our people.... [B]cause of that ... [and] the ever increasing emergency, ... in which we found ourselves, I convinced myself and often allowed myself to become convinced ... of the rightness of the measures. So I would transmit ... and promulgate [the orders] without ... [being] deterred by any possible effects" Despite a growing conflict of conscience and accusations of weakness, "it never entered my mind to revolt against the head of state. ... loyalty is sacred to me. I may be accused of having made mistakes, and also of having shown weakness towards the Führer, Adolf Hitler, but never can it be said that I was cowardly, dishonorable, or faithless."[15]

Keitel's memoirs, written during his months at Nuremberg prior to execution, are candid, seeming not to transfer responsibility and to state finally his acceptance of his guilt, to the extent he could comprehend it. Though he stated that he would have been proud to have participated in a victory, if he were in the same position again, "I would choose death rather than let myself be drawn into the meshes of such ruinous methods.... I believed [but] I erred, and I was not in a position to prevent what ought to have been prevented. That is my guilt."[16] It seems apparent that on the one hand he wanted Nazi victory, while at the same time he professes that he would not become involved if he had it to do over. That is questionable since a pliable individual like Keitel can almost always be swayed by an Adolf Hitler–like personality, especially when the offer is promotion and power and applause. Next time if it is not Keitel, it will be some other similar personality. Keitel seems to be saying what he felt the prosecution wanted to hear, not necessarily the full range of his feelings.

In his defense Keitel claimed obedience under the military code left him no alternative course, especially in Hitler's Third Reich where the Führer Principle (*Führerprinzip*) demanded unquestioned obedience to the next higher echelon of leadership. Keitel was demonstrably a weak man, never qualified for the responsible authoritarian role required by his position at OKW. This was widely recognized by his fellow generals, men such as von Manstein and Guderian, who felt strongly enough to engage in efforts with Hitler to make a change. But he was precisely what Hitler needed. This was the Peter Principle applied.

Plea of a Two-Dimensional Soldier

The catseat occupied by Alfred Jodl at OKW produced an obvious predicament — no way existed to leave with impunity, especially for one so outspoken in his respect for the oath he had taken on August 2, 1934. Accordingly, he joined his OKW partner in the Nuremberg dock.

Before discussing Jodl's final plea at Nuremberg in which he reveals his narrow understanding of a normal healthy philosophy, consider his writing in 1938 that "War ... serves the preservation of the state and folk.... These high goals give it its total character and ethical justification."[17] Given this early outlook and worldview, Jodl's final plea is understandable when he said, "the ... German Wehrmacht were confronted with an insoluble task; namely to conduct a war they had not wanted under a Commander-in-Chief ... whom they ... only trusted within limits; to conduct a war ... with methods which frequently were in contradiction with their operational principles and their ... opinions which had been disregarded.... They did not serve the powers of Hell and they did not serve a criminal but rather, their own

Four former Nazi general officers wait to testify at Nuremberg War Crimes Trials: L to R, Field Marshal Sperrle (Air), Col. General Heinz Guderian, Col. General (Air) Hans Stumpf, and Field Marshal (Air) Erhard Milch. Ullstein bild/The Granger Collection, New York.

people and their own country.... No man can do more than to reach the highest goals possible for him. That ... has been my guiding principle ... and for that reason ... no matter what verdict you may pass upon me, I shall leave this courtroom with my head held high as when I entered it many months ago."[18]

Jodl's plea is important in its honesty. It reveals the discord in his thinking and actions in situ, that is during the war years under Hitler's influence, as compared to much of his testimony at Nuremberg. After years under that influence Jodl apparently had lost what most would construe as a proper moral compass. While he told the court he decried the increasingly onerous decrees he handled and had finally lost respect for Hitler's humanity, his final plea belies that position. If he had only been able to view with sobriety the de facto results of the Wehrmacht's service, his plea might have been contrite instead of defiant. Conventional wisdom points to some combination of the lure for power, the attraction of some form of ideology and the underlying imperative of loyalty to oath and country. Some combination of these motivations underlay Jodl's actions. The contradiction is that had Ludwig Beck succeeded in derailing Hitler's plans, he could have doubtless relied on the likes of Alfred Jodl for honorable service in the interests of *Volk* (people) and country. However, Jodl, "the good soldier" most countries rely on for service if not leadership, had subscribed to these opiates so long that even in retrospect he could not hear the message the tribunal was sending.

Justice with Varying Leniency

A microcosm of the treatment of the vanquished countries of World War II was the leniency shown to some of the Third Reich's top military leadership. The Moscow Declaration of November 1, 1943, was intended to bring the prime participants of the war to justice as an example and deterrent against future aggressions.[19] And the Nuremberg Trials served this purpose for Germany very well. However, in many cases leniency was shown, if not initially, then ultimately to the key men responsible for conducting the war. Consider the cases of Heinz Guderian and Franz Halder, who were never charged, or others, such as von Manstein, Kesselring and Raeder, who were charged, convicted and sentenced to prison; and Gerd von Rundstedt, charged but never tried due to ill health; and von Brauchitsch and Strauss, who succumbed before their trials. All except Strauss appeared as witnesses at Nuremberg and in most cases gave white-washed versions of their part in the war.[20]

Rundstedt at War — A Question of Morality Emerges

Gerd von Rundstedt appeared at the Nuremberg Trials in August of 1946, not as a defendant but as a witness. In this role he euphemized his and Germany's role in the war, saying it was defense against Poland, there was no order to shoot prisoners, the onerous Commando Order was never employed in the West, and scores of other rejoinders concocted to represent him and his role as chivalrous, workmanlike and compassionate of the adversary, both civilian and soldier alike.[21]

On the evidence, von Rundstedt's creativity at war tells a far different story. "*Arbeitstab Rundstedt*" (Rundstedt staff) was created in April of 1939 and by early May had developed an elaborate scheme of aggression directed at Poland. In the third week of the war, September 24th, von Rundstedt wrote to OKH recommending unrestricted bombing of Warsaw. "A restriction in the use of air force (including incendiary bombs) endangers its success. Incendiary bombs ... cannot be confined to military objectives since their aim is ... the weakening of their [the Poles'] will to resist."[22]

The list of discrepancies in his testimony involving transgressions is long: ill treatment of civilians, prohibited treatment of POWs, support of forced labor by deportations, destruction and looting of evacuated areas when retreating in France in 1944. The message is clear: this senior soldier of the German Army was giving full and creative support to aggression; orders were not just to be carried out apolitically.

Commanding Army Group South in the 1941 attack of ally Russia, von Rundstedt was charged with enforcing the Commissar Order, described in Chapter 9.[23] "The order was simply never carried out," he testified. The facts are different in that from the evidence scores of Soviet POWs were killed as a result by late 1941 by 6th Army, part of von Rundstedt's Army Group South.[24]

As to a second onerous order issued by OKW in October of 1942, there was the Commando Order (described in Chapter 9). "We commanders ... agreed to make it ineffective," testified von Rundstedt. If so it may have been because von Rundstedt had already issued and signed his own Principle Order No. 13 in July of 1942, known as "Enemy Parachute and Airborne Landing Attempts," which said much the same: parachutists taken prisoner, whether in uniform or not were to be turned over to the Gestapo. Regardless of his post-war protestations to the contrary, Nuremberg investigations found that von Rundstedt did promulgate the order to his armies. Killings pursuant to the order following the invasion in 1944 were attributed in major part to von Rundstedt by the tribunal's findings.[25]

The tribunal heard evidence that of 3,600,000 Soviet prisoners taken between June and August of 1942, only several hundred thousand — 5% — were alive and still able to work by the end of that period.[26] In part responsible for this sordid tale was the "Reichenau Order" issued by von Rundstedt's 6th Army commander, Field Marshal Reichenau, in October of 1941. This order called for "annihilation" and "pitiless eradication" during BARBAROSSA, the Russian Campaign. "I [do not] recollect that I had seen that order before I came to England [after the war as a POW] and my Chief of Staff spoke about it," was von Rundstedt's position. In fact, he had transmitted the Reichenau Order to his armies with a cover letter he personally signed and which stated, "I thoroughly concur with its contents."[27]

How did von Rundstedt square his disclaimers and euphemistic testimony at Nuremberg with the above evidence?[28] Did he have a responsibility as the army's senior soldier and trusted leader to risk his personal fear of being branded "for all time the greatest traitor to my fatherland," as he said in testimony, by following a more rational dictate and thereby diverting Hitler in some manner?[29] As the end approached, von Rundstedt struggled with the "bitter conflicts of conscience" this dichotomy had spawned, observed his last Chief of Staff, General Siegfried Westphal.[30] Perhaps Hitler's words were prescient — after 50 years of service the field marshal's ability to innovate had irreparably dissipated. General Hans Speidel, Rommel's respected Chief of Staff in the West in 1944, writes of von Rundstedt, "eminent strategist, a master of the tools of war, but in the last years of the war he had lost, with advancing age, his creative drive and his clear sense of responsibility to the nation."[31]

Von Rundstedt was one who recognized on repeated occasions the inevitability of failing military ventures; as key resistance figure Hans Bernd Gisevius stated at Nuremberg, in his opinion, "loyalty to the German people required continuous opposition to the Nazi regime."[32] Apparently von Rundstedt did not accept that premise and the importance of his own legacy in history overwhelmed his ability or incentive to join the Witzlebens and other key military to head off the inevitable.

An Aggressive Stance Begets Prosecution

Three of Hitler's most successful, ardent and/or aggressive military figures — Field Marshals von Manstein and Kesselring and Grand Admiral Raeder — underwent prosecution of criminal charges, the latter at Nuremberg, the first two in British courts. All three were to suffer prison.

Von Manstein came under British jurisdiction following Germany's capitulation, spending his first years of incarceration awaiting judgment at Brigend Camp, Wales, England. He felt impelled to insist he had never been approached by anyone to bring him into the anti–Hitler conspiracy. Another issue he pressed in informal conversations was that the war would have been won by Germany if only Hitler had left the military leadership to the generals.[33] Of course, this is highly problematical given the ratio of forces and resources against the Germans.

The mindset, philosophy and xenophobia inspired by the National Socialists seems to have drawn on an age-old German nationalism and militarism, as epitomized by von Manstein's view, expressed post-war, that "We ... regarded the glory of war as something great." Even despite the loss of a son and the knowledge that under orders of the generals "youths went to their death by the million," von Manstein was still able to state this position to the Nuremberg court in 1946.[34] The insight this provides enables an understanding of the dichotomy in his thinking and conduct that emerges in a review of the facts, one probably typical of a great many of his peers.

Von Manstein is outspoken on the chivalry of the German soldier. "There was no question of our 'pillaging' ... [an] area. That was something the German Army — unlike certain others — did not tolerate." Particularly in the Ukraine the soldiers were on excellent terms with the population, and with regard to monuments and churches, these were spared in his area, he says.[35] He explained at Nuremberg that by 1943 the transport of grain and cattle from the Ukraine was carried out because of the dire straits of Germany and could not be considered as looting, but was, instead, simply "State requisitioning of State property."[36]

In contrast, his memoirs are silent on the BARBAROSSA Order of May 13,1941, which called for the ruthless treatment of people in the conquered areas and leniency toward soldiers accused of excesses against the population. Responsibility for putting these orders in play was negotiated by the army and the SS whereby the Einsatzgruppen (Deployment Group) assassination squads operated in the army's wake. Otto Ohlendorff, SS chief in charge of Group D, one of four Einsatzgruppen operating in the Russian theater, testified at the Nuremberg Trial, describing meetings with von Manstein, then commanding officer of the Eleventh Army to which Group D was attached. Since the work of the SS was to take place in the operational areas of the armies or army groups, support by the army was required for without such support the activities of the Einsatzgruppen would not have been possible, Ohlendorff said. SS operations with the advance of the Eleventh Army were the subject of "oral consultations with von Manstein, the Chief of Staff and me," testified Ohlendorff. However, he said he recognized the army leaders were "inwardly opposed to the liquidations.[37] In a total, 90,000 people were liquidated by his Einsatzgruppen D between June 1941 and June of 1942 said Ohlendorff.[38]

Von Manstein, in questioning at Nuremberg, admitted he may have once met Ohlendorff at headquarters, but denied all knowledge of extermination activities and thought that the group's activities involved "political screening of the population."[39]

On October 10, 1941, General Walther von Reichenau issued the so-called "Reichenau Order" to his Sixth Army troops; its particularly cruel manner of treating the people in occupied countries was endorsed by Hitler with his recommendation that other commanders issue similar orders. Accordingly, von Manstein issued his own such order on November 20, 1941, to Eleventh Army. It said, in part,

> The German soldier ... comes as the bearer of a racial concept and as the avenger of all the cruelties which have been perpetrated ... on the German people.... The food situation at home makes it essential ... that ... the largest possible stocks be placed at the disposal of the homeland ... in enemy cities a large part of the population will have to go hungry. ... nothing ... may, out of a misguided sense of humanity, be given to Prisoners or the population.[40]

Von Manstein's Eleventh Army files at war's end were replete with documentation of reprisals; scorched earth orders; the ordering of POW's to dangerous work gangs, although prohibited; and collaboration of Eleventh Army with Minister of Eastern Territories Rosenberg in the confiscation of all cultural institutions and their archives and possessions.[41]

Von Manstein was tried in Hamburg, Germany, by a British military court in a trial starting in August of 1949. Like his earlier performance as a witness at Nuremberg, von Manstein again lost credibility through contradictions between his testimony and documentation presented by the prosecution.[42] The British military court convicted him and sentenced him to eighteen years, though he was released in four years; he died in 1973.

Albrecht Kesselring, like von Manstein, came under British jurisdiction at war's end. As Commander-in-Chief South, responsible for Italy and North Africa, he was charged and convicted for the excesses of German forces as they retreated through Italy in 1943–45, as discussed in Chapter 12. His memoirs present an interesting contrast to the court findings, however. He prefaced them by stating his intent to present the material in the most objective fashion, acknowledging that subjectivity naturally creeps in. However, his memoirs frequently demonstrate his inclination to describe events more as he would have wished them than as they were in reality. His defense, as given in his memoirs, is, in the light of the evidence either unrealistic or disingenuous. When he describes the Italian theater, he makes a claim contrary to the evidence, saying, "German soldiers were guided by humane, cultural and economic considerations to an extent which conflicts on this scale have very seldom admitted."[43] Kesselring developed what appeared to be an effective liaison with the Italian hierarchy—the King, the Duce and the Italian military Comando Supremo—and, in another facet of unrealistic thinking, believed the Italians would remain German allies after Mussolini's departure. In fact he never seemed to recognize the extent of antipathy always present in Italians for the Germans.[44] Had he empathized on this point, how much farther would the situation have deteriorated as the German armies retreated?

Kesselring, given to philosophizing, maintains that in his view the organic core of the Nazi and fascist states contained the inevitable seeds of collapse, given they were unanswerable to any "outer or inner laws."[45] Prescient words, but would he and his fellow generals have articulated this belief given a German victory? Not likely, based on a review of his actions. Although the British commuted his death sentence to 21 years, he was released in five years, perhaps lending credence to claims he makes in his memoirs of dissatisfaction with the verdict on the part of former adversaries.[46] He then became president of the right-wing organization, the Stalhelm, that had lobbied for his release. Considered to be Nazi-oriented, at least in its antecedents, his association tends to confirm the perception in his memoirs of his subscribing to Hitler's National Socialist agenda.[47] Of course this could be gratitude for support as well as political naïveté. The evidence points to a confirmed supporter of the regime who endorsed and espoused the ideology involved.

Death for a Holy Cause

Another of the leading military proponents under Hitler and seemingly as ardent an ideologue, one who was fundamentally involved in the initial growth of rearmament in the early days of Hitler's reign, was Erich Raeder. As the first grand admiral under Hitler, Raeder was one of the 24 leaders indicted at Nuremberg. Of the trial charge of preparing for aggressive war, Raeder claims he did what any naval officer would do in the face of orders, and that, "Wars are not brought on by ... precautionary preparations of the military, but by the intentions, actions and omissions, and errors of politicians and statesmen."[48] That sounds very much like the observation of fellow admiral Karl Dönitz.

Raeder's post-war position relative to Nazi ideology, as expressed at Nuremberg, was that though he may not have entirely agreed with the National Socialist government — the Nuremberg Laws are an example he gives of disagreement — it was not possible for him to express or react to his personal views and his speeches to the navy and/or the nation had to be guided and moderated accordingly. In fact, however, his articulation of this ideological responsibility as given by his March 12, 1939, "Hero Commemoration Day" speech to the nation, is heavily political; he stresses the unity of the party with the Armed Forces in attitude, spirit and ideology; the young soldier should be indoctrinated to carry forth the "great tradition of death for a holy cause, knowing that the blood will lead the way towards the freedom of their dreams."[49] Apparently violence extolled on a relatively non-cerebral plane was not unusual, given the leader's example.

In contrast, Raeder was said by Pastor Gericke, the American Lutheran cleric at the Nuremberg prison, to be the most devout of the defendants. Accordingly, the party's attitude toward religion was important to him. While he thought the Hitler regime would bring a religious renewal, he found instead that some in the leadership, such as Joseph Goebbels, were behind the formation of a new movement which he felt was more closely akin "to the super-race myth of the Nordic Gods than any aspect of ... Christ."[50] He also found that despite early assurances, Hitler's attitude towards the church gradually changed; symptomatic of this was persecution of Martin Neimoller, World War I U-boat captain, a cleric by World War II, who spent the bulk of this war in Dachau for his persistent protestations against the regime.[51] Raeder claims to have felt the Nazi attacks on the Christian churches and the party's treatment of minorities would eventually lead to a parting of the ways with Hitler.[52] None of this ever happened as their parting was on a strictly business basis over naval strategy.

Raeder decries the acts of the Nazis against humanity, saying these crimes were without justification and a cause for shame on the part of every decent German.[53] Though he says "there existed a limit beyond which I would not have consented to follow Hitler," this limit apparently was never reached.

Keeper of the Grail

Fate and politics smiled on both Franz Halder and Heinz Guderian. Both were deeply involved in the major campaigns for Germany. Their careers are relevant more than fifty years later as the world attempts to resolve current political and military issues. Both demonstrated loyalty to their oath and country with equal dedication; Halder seemed carried away in the aura of the German General Staff and his responsibility to its legacy. Guderian, the constant field general, never wavered in his support of Hitler, though his ideological bent is questionable. Survival in the field seemed his major motivation.

Halder allowed his dedication to the General Staff as the "keeper of the grail" to induce him to support a despot while he ignored where his actions were leading the country. In our democratic, Western worldview, his dedication toward duty, honor and country would have placed emphasis properly on the welfare of flag and country, though perhaps he was not strong enough to buck the momentous tide. Comments of conspiratorial contacts, as described in Chapter 15, would lead to that conclusion. However, in his position as Chief of the General Staff, "when he took the floor [in briefings] he was the personification of the German General Staff both in knowledge and judgment, in style and approach," according to General Walter Warlimont, who had observed him for years from OKW.[54] On the other hand, Hermann Göring criticized Halder's military ability and averred that he had repeatedly pointed out to the Führer that Halder should be replaced with a chief who knew something about war.[55] Such comments by the Reichsmarschall, an acknowledged failure as the leader of the Luftwaffe, and made from a prison cell, might merit less than full weight. However, in some respects his evaluation of Halder has credibility when one considers his planning for both SEALION and BARBAROSSA. As to Göring, he seemed preoccupied with criticizing those around him, especially those he considered lower in the pecking order.

Halder was arrested following the July 1944 attempt on Hitler's life; surviving, he was spared the fate of fellow prisoners such as von Witzleben and Canaris and the immediate coup participants. Never charged by the Allies, he spent the last 16 years of his career working for the U.S. Army Historical Division.

Equally fortunate, Heinz Guderian, though arrested and incarcerated by American forces in May of 1945 in the Tyrol, was never charged and ultimately freed. The Poles had sought him for his role in putting down Polish partisan operations as German forces retreated through Warsaw in 1944. However, American-British policy by 1947 tended to retain custody of such potential defendants in view of increasing political polarization involving the Eastern Bloc countries.[56] All charges against Guderian were dropped in mid–1947; released in 1948, he retired to semi-activity, devoting himself to his memoirs.[57]

From Beck to Keitel, Extremes

There seems to have existed a morality distribution among Germany's generals, with Ludwig Beck willing to stand up to the Führer at one extreme; in contrast were the Keitels at the opposite end of the spectrum. The positions of many shifted against the regime as the war wore on and prospects of catastrophe became obvious, but not enough to turn the Hitlerian movement around.

Beck represented an anathema to the great majority of the Wehrmacht officer corps, at least while Germany ascended. Some assessment of typical thinking might be found in the memoirs of Wilhelm Keitel, who wrote from his cell in Nuremberg while awaiting execution, "I cannot say what kind of motive led Beck to move into the camp of the 'resistance movement,' the first step along the road towards his later high treason. ... was it his injured vanity? Or his own designs on the office of Commander-in-Chief of the Army?"[58] Beck clearly explained his rationale when he said in his proposal to von Brauchitsch of July 1938, that *when an officer's knowledge, conscience and responsibility forbid execution of a command, he had a higher responsibility to refuse to perform.*

However, Keitel clearly failed to understand the scope or intent and depth of this statement. Also, perhaps a degree of anger and jealousy combined with latent respect for Beck's actions were present in Keitel's thinking. Beck's statement did not represent a moralizing position nor one made for personal gain, and in fact it cost the writer his life. Many in the military leadership who had previously hesitated to collaborate in the resistance took definitive measures to finally head off the inevitable debacle. Their individual and personal objectives were widely disparate. However, the Keitels represented the significant majority; at least in the military, who were either not sufficiently prescient to understand the warnings, or felt so trapped by the system that their action was precluded, or had bought into Hitler's National Socialist dogma, which produced its own peculiar cerebral myopia.

Conclusion

The Military's Napoleonic Dreams
Lead to Catastrophe

If fear of the past as prologue had not failed to pose its eternally ubiquitous threat, there would be no issues here, no questions and no defenses to consider. Contemporary events confirm this concern, however.

The Political Leadership Vacuum Filled

Hitler and his Nazis had promised Germans relief from the Versailles burdens, and indeed they had fulfilled that promise. To gain and keep power, the Nazis needed the army as much as the army needed them, at least until Hitler could gain control of the armed forces. For the Reichswehr to bring to fruition all the technological military preparations that had proceeded in the inter-war period, this aggressive repossession of sovereignty was necessary, and they applauded it. Though the regime's excesses elicited early concern among the politicians who brought Hitler to power as well as among the generals, they thought they could control him. They underestimated Hitler's political senses, and sooner than later he was the supreme commander of a recalcitrant army, enthusiastic navy and air force and endeared leader, if not dictator, over a newly fully employed civilian population.

Though war looked likely to some in the army if Germany was to regain territories lost as the result of the World War I settlement, Hitler's political victories of the late 1930s dispelled this as a realistic possibility for most. That Hitler had his own personal agenda for European hegemony could have been seen by reading *Mein Kampf*, but in the euphoria of good times and regained sovereignty, this was a footnote to the history of the period.

Some cautioned that the world's resources far outweighed those of Germany, but the regime's implied promises of a growing Wehrmacht with rising opportunities for promotions, victories and the glory and personal material increases incident to victorious war-making made such warnings fall on deaf ears of the generals, if not the population.

Military Politics in the Struggle for War or Peace

Ludwig Beck's attempt to recruit the generals against Hitler's plans represents one of the major historical pivot points of the twentieth century. When the Commander-in-Chief of the army, von Brauchitsch, put those plans to the Führer, all of the latter's fiery determination, built on wrathful vengeance over twenty years from frustration, failure and societal rejection, overwhelmed the counsel for reason.

General Beck was accused in the late stages of the war of being "weak and reserved" and in need of "backbone stiffening." That this was so in 1938 is doubtful as it took significant fortitude to express his position against Hitler's plans at that time; what it required was an aggressive crusader more politically attuned and equal to Hitler in this arena to overcome the army's vacillation. The army, not withstanding the regime's SS forces, could still have determined the outcome for peace instead of European aggression, especially at this early point. It was always the necessary ingredient where a coup or control of the government's direction was concerned. That is, with no army, there could be no war. On this thin subjective thread of rejection the deaths of 50 million people and the disruption of the world was resolved.

"Great Victories" Lie Ahead

The generals must have seen this, because though they embarked on the Prague invasion with some trepidation, in the victorious aftermath of their subsequent *Blitzkreig* against Poland, they reveled in the performance of their armies who had now been "blooded." This was the fatal step the Wehrmacht generals took as they were carried away by "Napoleonic dreams" being spawned by their successes in Poland, Norway, France and the Balkans, out of which grew the cult of "the greatest general of all times."[1]

In this mode of thinking, base drives became manifest among the Wehrmacht leadership. These men were, for the most part, high-achieving individuals who had selected militarism as their preferred life's work. As individuals they responded in different ways to the psychological and material stimuli Hitler delivered. One extremity is represented by von Manstein, Kesselring, Dönitz and Jodl, for example. Von Manstein was vocal about his philosophy, even at Nuremberg, when he told the court, "we regarded the glory of war as something great." Jodl referred similarly in documents during the Polish Campaign when he wrote of "This wonderful campaign in Poland ... [as] a grand opening" in his letter to the police president of Bruenn, Moravia, and reminded him not to relieve the pressure on the Czechs. In fact he viewed war as ethically justified and serving the state's ends.

This thinking found its genesis not only in the Nazi culture of the period, but was a legacy of the mid-nineteenth-century view expressed by Field Marshal Graf Helmuth von

Moltke (the Elder) who felt, "Eternal peace is a dream. ... without war the world would sink into materialism." Their own contemporary, Hans von Seeckt, carried it further, saying, "War is the highest summit of human achievement." Under Hitler this was all amplified.[2]

Compare the attitude just described with the response of Beck, whose orientation was not against war, but towards a rational assessment of the balance of power and against opportunistic and materialistic political-military adventures. This camp was joined in the prewar period by troop commander Field Marshal Erwin von Witzleben, Generals Georg Thomas and Hans Oster, Abwehr Intelligence Chief Admiral Wilhelm Canaris and others in continuing active efforts against war plans and then to subvert the war once it had started. In many of these cases, Canaris, Oster and Thomas for example, the impetus to assist a conspiracy had found its genesis in Beck's arguments. In view of their ultimate sacrifices and the obvious risks, their dedication certainly encompassed the elements of Beck's balance of power philosophy and the orientation away from marginal war.

A middle group appeared to readily accept plans for war and its execution, but only so long as it promised success. Generals are hired to fight wars and serve, and in Douglas MacArthur's words they are to be dedicated to *duty, honor and country*. Who then can condemn those that embark along this road, as did Rommel, von Kluge, Guderian, Raeder and the vast majority of others? Diversion from this road comes for some when the war looks lost, when, as Rommel felt, the fate of the nation demanded insurrection on the part of the military leadership. However, that fork in the road never came for others such as Raeder and Guderian, though they both saw the loss coming.

Some, von Rundstedt is representative, also recognized the ultimate futility repeatedly as key reverses such as Stalingrad, the 1944 invasion and the Ardennes Offensive developed. How had their oath to *duty and honor* forsaken *country* by so wide a margin?

My Army Must Not Stand Idle!

No timely plans had been prepared for an invasion following the fall of France, and it ultimately became obvious to Hitler that failure in this tactical endeavor could mean destruction of his underlying *strategic* program and aspirations.

Most key Wehrmacht leaders were highly critical, though, when Hitler moved instead to open a second front against Russia. Vastly underrating the task, they nevertheless followed Hitler's leadership. Apparently the lure of "Napoleonic dreams," even in the face of their knowledge of that earlier venture's demise, overruled the military leadership's judgment. The promise of "great victories" was all they saw now, said an Austrian expatriate, an observer who fought with the British against them in North Africa and Italy.[3]

The Oath, Orders and Obedience — The Soldier's Responsibility

In Germany obedience to authority represents a historical paradigm and mandate. The oath to Hitler, taken at garrisons throughout Germany on August 2, 1934, upon Paul von Hindenburg's death, represented a personal moral and ethical responsibility for each soldier.

Alternatively, military orders represented a legal mandate where failure to comply carried dire consequences. The German soldier of the Third Reich shouldered both of these obligations; the immediate issue would be military orders, while the fulfillment of the oath would impact late in the war. Additionally, for senior officers both mandates would converge to provide an additional dilemma.

In this authoritarian environment the question of disposition of questionable orders was inevitable, especially once the defensive phase of the war had commenced for the Germans, and Hitler's frailty as a commander had been confirmed through major losses. From a principled viewpoint Beck had counseled von Brauchitsch on this point to prepare him for his presentation of the third memorandum to the generals; he wrote, "soldierly obedience has a limit where their knowledge, their conscience and their responsibility forbid carrying out of an order." Absent a receptive hearing for their advice and views, it was incumbent upon them to resign, he concluded. Given the political strengths of the respective leadership — the army versus the party — the counsel proved academic.

Wars are replete with orders ranging from reasonable to questionable or unacceptable from a humanitarian or tactical viewpoint and/or illegal under international law. Von Manstein felt no commander can defend with impunity his acceptance of an order against his better judgment if its execution results in a loss; success or not weighs heavily on the final verdict of the commander's action. It is clear in his order of December 1942 to General Paulus, Sixth Army commander at Stalingrad, however, that he was stretching the orders from Hitler, and his obligation under the oath, when he did issue an order to Sixth Army to break out southwest of the pocket; the Supreme Command had continued to refuse such relief, given Hitler's belief that any relinquishing of territory was tantamount to defeat. As Hitler's order said, more or less, on this occasion, "No Army Group Commander, and certainly no Army Commander, has the right to give up a locality or even a single coordinated trench system without my prior sanction."[4] Or, "where the German soldier stands there he remains and no power on earth will drive him back," a statement along the same line from his political speeches. A further insight into Hitler's state of mind is given in this wireless reply to Sixth Army, "Surrender is forbidden. Sixth Army will hold their positions to the last man...."[5]

In this action here von Manstein embarked, however briefly, on a course contrary to his oath to Hitler — briefly, because his overall obedience to the oath was otherwise unblemished, as far as the records show. When anti–Hitler conspirators, such as Ludwig Beck, approached him, he declined with the rejoinder that he could not fail to support his troops by such deviation.

General Paulus encountered this dual responsibility — the oath and superior orders — in executing his Stalingrad responsibilities. Friedrich Paulus was a soldier who felt his first duty was obedience.[6] In his last letter to his wife from the cauldron at Stalingrad, he wrote, "I stand and fight — those are my orders."[7] Paulus toyed with the entreaties of von Manstein at Don Army Headquarters to consider a breakout, but by the time he could have, and had an order in hand from von Manstein, fuel was insufficient for movement of armor. In totals, 90,000 troops of the German and Romanian armies under Sixth Army command were sacrificed in surrender. Paulus was thereby relieved of his obligations under the oath, something he obviously was conscious of during the decision period.

Stalingrad produces a precise focus on the terrible consequences of the oath, obedience to orders and allegiance to Germany during this period where the leadership — Hitler — refused to employ reason and informed tactical direction and thereby overruled the generals. In early January of 1943, as the end approached, Generals von Hartmann, Pfeffer, von Seydlitz, Heitz, Strecker and Schlömer debated and considered whether suicide might be a solution for their men and themselves in the face of impending collapse. Hartmann felt "An officer must die in battle," and another refused to shoot himself for the sake of a "Bohemian lance-corporal." In the final analysis none had faith in Hitler any longer, reports an imbedded war correspondent. Only Paulus himself had the right to order an end to the fighting, they felt.[8] Some did surrender, though, when there was no ammunition left or a T34 threatened to crush them in the snow.[9]

Some commanders resolved the problem by extricating themselves from command rather than disobey. Von Rundstedt tendered his resignation in late 1941 when his request for a defensive retreat from Rostov was denied. This was unusual for him, however, as even in the face of the Ardennes Offensive, which he knew could never succeed, he carried out a campaign antithetical to his own recommendations. But as Hitler and even the generals said, he was old and tired of bucking the tide, and also fearful of a traitor's legacy. The impetus that drove von Rundstedt even in the face of having years before predicted defeat was sufficiently strong so as to overcome those conclusions and convictions. Ideology, dedication to the regime, the oath to Hitler of 1934, blind loyalty to the country regardless of any transgressions, or the broad cloak of nationalism or any combination of these factors were the driving forces for many in the military; many of these factors influenced civilians as well and were amplified by aggressive indoctrination in youth programs. As to von Rundstedt, the legacy of the Wehrmacht and all that implies and the reticence to be involved in what could be termed a traitorous act appear to have been the deciding issues for him.

Resignation or pursuit of a losing situation were no solution to the problem, however, and others sought more definitive resolutions as the political balance and pressures of war changed. Kesselring's rationale for bridging this dilemma late in the war, according to his post-war memoirs, was that as a senior commander, working in concert with other senior individuals, he had certain prerogatives of latitude. The senior officer's role as "responsible advisor to the Head of State" would justify unilateral actions under extreme circumstances, he claimed. The "extreme" case for him was contact with the Allies to abort further hopeless losses in 1944–45. This, of course, raises the question of why, if he actually felt this way at the time, he would not have exercised this prerogative earlier to avert the 1944 excesses of his retreating troops in Italy, when, in fact, the court found he had exacerbated the situation.

Erwin Rommel saw his responsibility to the nation as dictating the need for insurrectional action, though, again, it was late in the war when he acted on this position and really after the point of no return had been reached. Like Kesselring, he felt that as a high military leader he was "qualified, entitled, and obliged" to take this responsibility. To reinforce this commitment Rommel, according to peers, knew the difference between obedience to God and man (orders), and acted accordingly once his political awareness had matured, or one might say, as the cataclysm closed in. Here, again, is a military leader who was apolitical for most of his professional career, only to have politics become preeminent when the implications of the regime's extremes became clear. He was hired to mount winning military campaigns, not play politics; he did this well, but when the war turned against him, he then decided to act, which seems the story of many of the Wehrmacht leadership.

Recognizing the excesses of the National Socialists, and, finally the catastrophe they had wrought, Guderian asks rhetorically, "What should have been done?" It was the duty of those opposed to say so to the German people without ambiguity, if not inside Germany, then from abroad, he maintains in his post-war memoirs. Nevertheless, for obvious reasons, very few dared to express these contrary opinions in Hitler's presence, and "of those few even fewer are still alive," an approach that he obviously recognized early and that guided him in his response to this dilemma.[10]

The question of motivations driving the German military leadership to act against the government during the war range from one extreme of justified insurrection based on either saving the country from destruction or the imperative of honor and decency to the other extreme of simply saving themselves, their families and their possessions. Their professional jobs and commitments were to support the regime militarily, and anything less broached the question of treason, which became reality if they joined the active resistance. Such action required a firm and final commitment, regardless of which of the above rationale applied.

Though von Manstein's position on this question and the numerous rationales he gives represent loyalty and are defensible, the circumstances that had descended on the Germans by late 1942 to early 1943 could be construed to dictate at least some consideration on the part of a senior commander of an attempt to avert the looming catastrophe. The increasing debacle in Russia provided sufficient clues, and an increasing number of von Manstein's peers found justification for either peace overtures or direct coup collaboration. This must represent a classic case where the question of what leadership a commander owed his troops with respect to the country's and their own longer term welfare presents itself. Of note on this point are the reflections of Erwin Rommel and Albrecht Kesselring, who felt that they had a responsibility for leadership on a higher level when necessary; Kesselring, though he felt obedience to the legally constituted government was required to prevent *coups d'état,* did at the same time claim to have attempted to collaborate to contact the Allies near war's end to effect an armistice.[11] Others, such as Karl Dönitz, had little patience with any path other than following the constituted leadership, even in the face of 75% loss of submarine crews, that is some 24,000 men over a 5-year span. An extreme case represented by that leadership's actions on this point was the sacrifice of 250,000 men at Stalingrad against the best military judgment. That leadership in turn influenced von Rundstedt and many others to continue supporting it despite repeated acknowledgment by these generals of campaigns that should not have been undertaken or that were destined to fail. BARBAROSSA and the Ardennes are examples. Hitler, himself, set the tone for influencing the generals and the populace in his early 1945 message through the media which proclaimed the slogan, "Victory or Destruction," one that had been his constant theme as defeat threatened during the last years of the war.[12]

The plans of action to counter the regime, for whatever reason, seem to have usually involved the seizing of power by the resistance leadership with the subsequent placing of a civilian in control. In the early stages, 1938 and pre–Poland, the plans had called for General von Witzleben or the Commander-in-Chief of the army to be placed in power, followed by Goerdeler or another civilian appointed to that position. Later, Rommel's notes indicate, Beck and Goerdeler would assume leadership and that military dictatorship was eschewed. Of course, none of this came to pass, but detailed plans had been laid for governing in the key cases of which we have details.

There existed a spectrum of opinion, attitude and dedication when it came to allegiance to the Führer stemming from the oath and its implications among the Wehrmacht leadership, and presumably the troops. One group never wavered in support of the Führer, and presumably the oath may not have been the prime imperative. A mix of ideology, nationalism, professionalism and ambition may well have been basic with this group.

As discussed previously, then–Chief of the Army Staff, Ludwig Beck, felt it was the "darkest day" of his life. Nevertheless he persevered in the service of the Führer until relieved in 1938. Whatever thoughts he had for action against the legally ensconced leadership, and he had many serious misgivings, would await his dismissal.

What may have made the oath so emphatic and singular, but acceptable, in many taker's minds is the impact of precursor events. Hitler had engendered significant loyalty in the Reichswehr, the pre-war army, by elimination of the SA challenge to the army's eminence in the Night of the Long Knives. The leadership of the brownshirts, the SA, in the person of Captain Ernst Roehm and his adherents, would no longer challenge the army's position of power. This was a carte blanche rationale for agreement with whatever Hitler presented at this point.

Too, this was a leader who was already promising growth of the military during this period of fiscal austerity. Then again, the general case of nationalism and allegiance to central leadership was an age-old foundation of German society.

There was justification for such abject obedience in the religious sense as well, as propounded by Dietrich Bonhoeffer in his *Letters and Papers from Prison*. To this theologist, Christian conscience demands such "subjection to the will and demands of authority."[13] In the philosophical concepts of cultural authority, religious consciousness and nationalism, the oath, despite personal questions that arose that August day, was taken out of hand, even despite the surprise it engendered to the more thoughtful takers. Again, we look in retrospect at the Third Reich as a criminal conspiracy, and that certainly entertains the issue that leadership would be taking the Wehrmacht on malevolent adventures most could not predict and which many would not have approved.

The two Supreme Command officers most relied upon by Hitler in conduct of the war and the issuance of directives to the field forces, Alfred Jodl and Wilhelm Keitel, never wavered in their support of the Führer. For Keitel, more than the taking of the oath seems at stake; one is impressed that he succumbed to Hitler's "unbridled dictatorship" on a continuing basis, as he wrote. Keitel proceeded in what he himself described as an "obedient and faithful" fashion in a "soldier's tradition."[14]

For Alfred Jodl, the oath meant ascribing to the will of the people who had placed Hitler in office, according to his testimony at Nuremberg.[15] Jodl showed a narrow field-of-view in terms of the broad consequences of his service to the oath and its effect on the Fatherland in future years.

Admiral Dönitz, one of the top German leaders of the period, considering his performance and persistence, came away dissuaded that the "Führerprinzip, the principle of dictatorship, as political principle is false." Under this concept one is to obey the dictates of the next higher echelon in command and on to the top. It is appropriate, he says, to the military, but can lead to abuse of power when applied to the political spectrum. Of course, these are pronouncements made in captivity in his memoirs and at the Nuremberg Trials. He had been one of the most enthusiastic supporters of the regime, it must be remembered. Is the essence of the Führerprinzip, that is, the Führer Principle, not a necessary element in the structure of successful military forces worldwide? As he stresses, above, it is indeed a necessary element of such activities. The problem arises when it is applied to civilian purposes, and, most relevant here, when it is promulgated by political leadership pursuing aggressive strategies. In the Third Reich two factors were responsible for Germany's debacle. First, Hitler announced his aggressive plans early on in *Mein Kampf*, then followed them by political moves that, to the observant, were a precursor to large-scale aggression. Once Poland was vanquished in 1939, his ultimate goal was clear for all to see.

Second, notwithstanding the warning Beck had given that Germany could not win against the forces of the world, Hitler made the fatal mistake of preempting his generals on tactical issues. They recognized his Napoleon-like error in the invasion of Russia, as Guderian and others so cogently observed in 1942.

The case of Heinz Guderian is reflective of the single-minded adherents like Dönitz, Keitel, Jodl, and von Manstein; he supported the leadership as long as he was needed, from army group commander to chief of the Army Staff, to the onerous Court of Honor, where he presided over trials of and condemned fellow officers. Though approached by the anti–Hitler conspirators, he declined any cooperation, even as the prospects of Germany's demise in the war grew.

A surprise departure from obedience to the Führer was Rudolf Hess. His flight to England in 1941 just as hostilities were heating up yielded only life in prison, first in England, then for the rest of his life in Spandau. His wife, Ilse, writes that he only sought peace in this endeavor. However, some departure from prudent thought seems present in this adventure.[16]

Another departure from obedience as a prime paradigm turned out to be Hermann Göring. In the late stages of the war, April 1945, he sent a communiqué to Hitler in his bunker suggesting he, Göring, take over given that Hitler might be immobilized, and this per Hitler's own 1941 decree to this effect. The result was a political catastrophe for Göring, leading to his arrest and the redesignation of Dönitz as Hitler's successor. Apparently survival and position had preempted the years-long loyalty and obedience Hitler had expected of his number two.[17]

Of course there existed a group of men like General Beck who saw the oath and its implications for what it portended. Still on active duty, such men as Admiral Canaris, head of the Abwehr intelligence service, Field Marshal Erwin von Witzleben, Generals Oster, Olbricht, Fromm and many more were co-conspirators and eventually met their fates at Hitler's hands for the 1944 attack on his life. Most, though not all, were on active duty: Beck deferred action until his retirement in 1938, then led the plotters. One, General Franz Halder, often professed sympathy with the group's agenda, but in the end always withheld any support. Halder, in his role as Chief of the Army Staff, had been Hitler's primary planner for BARBAROSSA, the Russian Campaign, and had become inactive when replaced in 1942.

The Following Orders Predicament

Following "Superior Orders" became a standard defense after the war for Wehrmacht members charged with war crimes. Following such orders is a two sided coin since the order recipient must consider his duty to his commander, but must also weigh the legality or not of the order. In World War II *The British Year Book of International Law 1944* required the soldier to obey legal orders at the expense of court-martial if he did not. As to orders the soldier considered illegal on their face, he could use Superior Orders as a defense if his safety was in jeopardy for not obeying, but he could not use such a defense if there was no danger to him for declining the order. The soldier in the field is more often than not between the Scylla of an illegal order and the Charybdis of disobedience since in the heat of battle he may face his own execution for refusing what he considers an illegal order. While the doctrine of Superior Orders as an absolute defense was generally accepted by the U.S. in the *1940 Rules of Land Warfare* and Great Britain in *The British Year Book of International Law 1944*, it was subject to the test of legality as above with the gray area of the soldier's degree of jeopardy.[18] The 1956 revision in the U.S., *The Law of Land Warfare*, recognized the mitigating circumstances of the gray area as a defense, yet reaffirmed the requirement that all soldiers are bound to obey only lawful orders.[19]

The pre–World War II German Code of Military Law held that the soldier's immunity from protection by virtue of superior orders ceased if he knew of the unlawful nature of the order. Finally, apparently disavowing a definitive stand, the Peace Conference in Paris in 1919 left it up to the courts to decide in each case.[20]

The Superior Orders in question were initiated by commanders such as Keitel, Jodl, von Manstein, Kesselring, and countless others who carried out the orders of the Supreme Commander, and thus suffered the judgment of Allied courts. In their own defense, since they as commanders were held responsible for the many onerous orders sent down, many of these same commanders, like others defending themselves, claim to have deliberately disregarded and not to have implemented onerous OKW orders such as the Commissar and Commando Orders. Where true, whether their motivations were humanitarian and chivalrous or were based on their recognition of the future legal consequences is problematical, as is the validity of many of their claims based on the evidence presented. In any case, the relevant body of law governing adjudication of such issues has evolved through successive wars over the centuries, whereas the events they apply to vary only in the technology used.

Dreams and Illusions, but Not the Genius of Napoleon

Many in the military lost respect for Hitler's leadership for varying reasons including military inadequacy, his inhumanity, and his single-minded march into the abyss. Jodl, who early on found Hitler to be "a genius," eventually recognized his inhumanity, or so he said after the fact, and felt it was deleterious to the country's future. Halder, von Brauchitsch, Jodl, Keitel, and even von Manstein are only a few of the many who found Hitler inordinately persuasive. There are many anecdotal tales of key officers meeting with Hitler to convey a pressing need for change, only to come away without change and convinced action was not needed — convinced at least in the short run. Some, such as von Manstein, removed themselves from the issue; others, like Jodl, continued dedicated support, probably so constricted or inflexible in their thinking that any other course meant a conflict with duty, loyalty, and assuredly, forfeiture in any participation in the "great victories" that might accrue in the event of success. Others — Wilhelm Keitel is typical — were so under the Führer's dominance that only at Nuremberg did they finally acknowledge their failure to recognize the immorality of their conduct, and that under obvious duress. While a loyal and dedicated core never wavered in their support — including Karl Dönitz, Albrecht Kesselring and Erich Raeder, while the Führer would have him — a significant leadership group coalesced in 1943–44 (admittedly late in the game) to take mitigating action against the fatal consequences of Hitler's leadership.

Wehrmacht Leadership in Perspective

Realistic self-assessment of abilities and their accomplishments, recognition of the regard and perception of others for them and posterity's position on all this seems to have been a deficiency with many of the Wehrmacht leaders.

Erich Raeder and Erich von Manstein, for example, viewed themselves in this light and described their performances as apolitical and strictly military in pursuit of an honorable and chivalrous tradition. Both excelled to a point militarily; however, their respective efforts to move into the political arena are apparent. Raeder took the initiative in surreptitious naval construction years before Hitler's seizure of power. He then continued under Hitler, and, additionally, injected the state's ideology into the navy, as well as attempting to influence the direction of the war. He would have gone after the Mediterranean and control of the Mideast instead of Russia, and he pushed for this with the Führer.

Von Manstein had gone beyond his military oath sufficiently to embarrass himself as a witness at Nuremberg; his memorandums and actions in support of the racist SS Einsatzgruppen agenda during BARBAROSSA were presented by the prosecution, to his dismay and with impact on his reputation. Apparently he failed to recognize the political dimension this support was to bring and its later repercussions.

Wilhelm Keitel and Alfred Jodl, the dual facilitators for Hitler's war directives, viewed themselves similarly, asserting their actions had been fully justified by their military oath, their roles and their responsibilities. From this point, though, they differed: Jodl maintained to the end the justness of his actions, seeming to see a higher calling than would justify criticism. Keitel claimed retrospectively to have seen the error of his "obeisant" performance, though he objected strenuously to that characterization, which had been made widely. He would have savored victory, but, if given a second chance, would choose death rather than repeat his role. Where did he really stand and for whose ears was he talking? He sounds very much like Albert Speer who in his memoirs says he recognized the malevolence of Hitler's program, but after release from Spandau Prison was able to fantasize about how he would have grown and prospered in Hitler's world government had it succeeded.[21]

The consensus of Hermann Göring, the Führer and others seems to have been that

Keitel and Jodl fit well as the Führer's obeisant and/or obedient toadies, carrying out his orders; their lack of military expertise, though not their primary raison d'être, when coupled with that of Hitler, served to cripple tactical operations.

Others, such as Heinz Guderian and Franz Halder, made great issue in memoirs and/or at Nuremberg witness testimony of their liaison and sympathy for the anti–Hitler resistance. However, neither assumed more than a rhetorical role, and they backed off when the call to action came. Conspirators found Guderian sufficiently unreliable to justify warning him against betrayal; Halder simply lacked fortitude.

Though he described himself as the Keeper of the Grail, charged with perpetuating the spirit of the General Staff greats of the past — von Moltke, Gallwitz, von Hindenburg, and Ludendorff— and serving one's superiors obediently, this is not easily accepted in light of the above. His pursuit of the General Staff credo, "Perform well, without being conspicuous," and his dedication to not retreating from fulfilling the long cultivated "spirit of the German General Staff" greatly influenced Halder's dedicated approach to his military oath. Retrospectively, however, Halder came to realize this service of his was to a master who destroyed more than he created.[22]

However, Halder was no Ludwig Beck and accordingly accommodated the Führer until such time as Hitler chose to replace him. His modus operandi seems consistent with the conformist persona implied in his writings and actions. Throughout he straddled the fence, with one leg on the side of continuity of the institutions of government and the oath, while the other labored on the side of correcting the obvious destructive military path Hitler pursued, though in this last instance only to a point. No new ground was actually to be plowed, as the anti–Nazi plotters would find.

A regime such as the Third Reich was fertile ground for men with autocratic political and personal inclinations. That is the sense implied by the memoirs, post-war testimony and peer comments regarding Karl Dönitz and Albrecht Kesselring. Kesselring became president of the right-wing Stahlhelm after release from prison in 1952; this association plus his writings and conduct before capitulation makes a statement about his personal politics, one that implies his dedicated acceptance of the ideology of the regime. He would have thrived given a German victory.

Dönitz, however, in his final plea at Nuremberg, whether honestly or disingenuously, volunteered that the Führer Principle (*Führerprinzip*) worked well for the military, but had proven a failure when applied to civilians. That is, absolute obedience to one above can and needs to be employed, however judiciously, where military discipline is involved, but, in Western eyes, such a philosophy would be rejected if employed with the civilian populace. In reality Dönitz may have been writing for Western consumption in this memoir citation, whereas he may have favored such an approach if it meant winning a war or attaining a goal he felt important. For an appreciation of Dönitz's politics and the extent of his support of the regime, consider an excerpt from his February 15, 1944, speech to the commanders in chief when he said, in part, "From the very start the whole of the officer corps must be so indoctrinated that it feels itself co-responsible for the National Socialist State in its entirety. The officer is the exponent of the state; the idle chatter that the officer is non-political is sheer nonsense."[23] And later, on Heroes' Day, March 12, 1944, he said to the German people, "What would become of our country today if the Führer had not united us under National Socialism! ...

we would long since have succumbed to the burdens of this war and ... the merciless destruction of our adversaries."[24]

Albert Speer, one of Hitler's inner circle, who had spent half of his twenty-year sentence at Spandau Prison with fellow prisoner Dönitz, felt the ex-admiral was completely preoccupied with his own misery, even upon release, and was not the least concerned with the havoc their regime had caused.

Chronicle of the Race to the Abyss

No key Wehrmacht officer could claim isolation from the war's major plans and milestones. They were set forth in Hitler's seventy-four war directives, commencing with Number 1, Fall Weiss, the Polish Attack Plan, dated August 31, 1939, and finally ending with Number 74, "Declaration to the German People on Roosevelt's Death," dated April 15, 1945.[25] Nor can a perceptive reader of the war directives be immune from the psychological state of the supreme commander relative to the war's progress.

When there was that last opportunity to arrest the aggressive direction of the government that would lead to war and the defeat Beck had predicted, only a minority of the officer corps was so inclined to action. Once this moment — 1938, before the Czech adventure — had passed, the reality was that the momentum of the forces in power, with its apparatus of terror, could not be stopped. The military represented the critical force needed for such a countermove, but once war had started, it was always perpetually involved with its own and the country's survival.

Nevertheless, a small and less than critical mass existed in the military leadership from 1938 on when Hitler's war plans became obvious. Though the opposition grew as inevitable defeat loomed, efforts in 1944 to effect cessation of hostilities or to eliminate Hitler were in vain. It is safe to conclude that most of the officer corps had some clue that a coup was planned, especially as the German position deteriorated. After all, Beck and his military and civilian co-conspirators attempted to recruit among the military for the coup. Most of the leadership would have no part of it; a commander cannot pull the rug out from under his loyal troops was von Manstein's position. Some maintained a foot in both camps (von Kluge), and betrayal came from some quarters for obvious reasons. Once the attempt was made and failed, some of the uninvolved key leaders willingly, via the Court of Honor, collaborated with the Supreme Commander and condemned their brother officers.

If Ludwig Beck had been stronger politically and as or more persuasive than Adolf Hitler, the catastrophe for Germany would have been avoided. As it turned out the great rewards Hitler promised coupled with the momentum he had established by the late 1930s turned the tide for the army leadership, and the revolt of the generals Beck had attempted to foment never occurred. With this foundation, Hitler was able to command and direct these talented men in the Wehrmacht though he was, as it inevitably turned out, clearly unqualified to do so. This magnified the foibles and weaknesses as well as the strengths of these leaders who were asked to perform a task which, based on the world balance of power, could never have succeeded in the long run. They, and the country, paid for this misguided venture, though it took our thinking to a new level relative to aggressive war.

One of the most important systemic lessons represented by the tenure of the Third Reich is that short of external assistance and/or defeat, once the totalitarian regime has established itself there is slim chance to arrest such a movement. Rommel, for example, was powerless and without resources to protect himself in 1944 against Hitler's vengeance despite alliance with a resistance network of key military and civilians. In every instance where a coup might have been mounted — during the failing months of BARBAROSSA, or prior to the Sudetenland issue, or as the invasion succeeded — either troops and a cooperative command were not available or were involved in a campaign or a peace treaty such as Munich precluded action.

Lessons from the German Experience

The conditions that nurtured the continuance of the German militarist spirit and its manifestation in the twentieth century hopefully will not recur in that country nor among its close neighbors, Austria and Hungary. However, the environment for politico-military adventures is recognizable in other parts of Europe, Asia and the Mideast as well. This group of military leaders that emerged in the Germany of World War II is not unlike, in fact is undoubtedly similar to, military leadership emerging in each potential and actual problem area — Asia, Africa, the Mideast and elsewhere. In essence it's bound to replicate itself wherever humans strive for power despite any world efforts by organizations such as the United Nations (UN), North Atlantic Treaty Organization (NATO), or others to impede it.

The Wehrmacht leadership represented a distribution ranging from what can be typified as liberal, pragmatic and politically critical to the extreme of reactionary and subscribing to all tenets of the authoritarian regime. All of the German leaders can be said to have responded to the calling of *duty, honor and country,* but with significantly different emphasis on each of these elements. Those differences represent an important litmus test as to their place in this distribution, and in the final analysis, their loyalty and support of *country*. Beck and von Witzleben and their co-conspirators represented the politically critical; Halder and Guderian found it impossible to do more than speak of an opposition position, and Guderian is charged by his critics of crossing the line of betrayal. Rommel finally emphasized *country*, as did many of his peers, when defeat loomed and/or he saw the inhumanity of the Nazi movement, though one is persuaded that the latter issue was not the controlling factor for him. Von Manstein is typical of those who abided by the government line to the end, though openly questioning the soundness of its military strategy. Post-war more than a few felt, with regrets, that had the military been given a free hand the war could have been won. Finally, Kesselring and Dönitz on the spectrum's right seem to have exemplified and supported the regime's objectives and would have welcomed victory and all it implied.

In Germany, undoubtedly the result of the country's particular history, the military was key to taking the timely action that would have been necessary to preclude and abort the Nazi movement. They elected not to do so and, as a consequence, external military forces were required to accomplish this. In today's world and its political climate organizations such as the UN, NATO and possibly the new European Force are/or will be striving to function as the first line of this external force and so head off major conflagrations. While we can be fairly sure that these military-political forces currently involved in counter-democratic actions have many of the same base motivations and characteristics found in the Third Reich, we are in the early and rudimentary phase of dealing with them effectively.

The German experience shows that the majority of the military will go along if they perceive future glory and power and are caught up in so-called Napoleonic dreams, until persuaded otherwise by events. Alternatively, a terror apparatus serves the authoritarian powers well in gaining the support of those less aggressively inclined. This analysis of the German experience, of course, does not provide a panacea for dealing with a regime intent on aggression and hegemony; however, its most important contribution is in providing a framework for understanding the range of motivations of many military leaders, whether in an authoritarian or democratic regime, and in predicting their potential moves.

Appendix A
*International Military Tribunal Indictments**

Count 1   The Common Plan or Conspiracy

a. Nazi Party as the Central Core of the Conspiracy
b. Common Objectives and Methods of Conspiracy
c. Doctrinal Techniques of the Conspiracy
d. Acquiring Totalitarian Control of Germany: Political
e. Utilization of Nazi Control for Foreign Aggression

Count 2   Crimes Against Peace

Count 3   War Crimes

a. Murder and Ill-treatment of Civilian Populations in Occupied Territories and on the High Seas
b. Deportation for Slave Labor and for Other Purposes of Civilian Populations in Occupied Territories
c. Murder and Ill-treatment of POWs
d. Killing of Hostages
e. Plunder of Public and Private Property
f. Exaction of Collective Penalties
g. Wanton Destruction of Cities, Towns and Villages Not Justified by Military Necessity
h. Conscription of Civilian Labor
i. Forcing Civilians of Occupied Territories to Swear Allegiance to a Hostile Power
j. Germanization of Occupied Territories

Count 4   Crimes against Humanity

a. Murder, Extermination, Enslavement, Deportation and Other Inhuman Acts Committed Against Civilian Populations
b. Persecution on Political, Racial and Religious Grounds in Execution of Count 1, Conspiracy

*IMT, *Trial of the War Criminals,* 1:29–68.

Appendix B

Chronology of the Third Reich

1922	Aug.	Collapse of the German monetary system
1923	Nov. 8	Hitler leads Munich Beer-Hall Putsch against President von Kahr's government
1924		Post–World War I inflation threatens life in Germany; Hitler is incarcerated in Landsberg Fortress for 1 year
1925	April 26	Hindenburg is elected president of Weimar Republic; first edition of *Mein Kampf* is published
1926	Sept. 8	Germany joins the League of Nations
1930	Sept. 14	Hitler's party gains in Reichstag elections, becoming the second strongest
1931		Economic crisis in Germany: foreign credit is overextended, exports diminish in a contracting world market, tax revenues diminish
1932		Unemployment reaches six million in Germany
	May 30, 31	Bruening resigns as chancellor, is replaced by von Papen
	July 31	National Socialists gain 230 seats (36%) in Reichstag elections
	Dec. 2	von Schleicher replaces von Papen as chancellor
1933	Jan. 30	President von Hindenburg asks Hitler, leader of the strongest opposition party, to form a government, replacing von Schleicher, who resigns
	Feb. 27	Reichstag fire
	Feb. 28	Emergency decrees give Göring broad police powers
	Mar. 23	Enabling Act passed — Hitler gains access to totalitarian power; originally intended for 4 years, never rescinded; all publications, except Nazi controlled, are suppressed
	April/May	The Gestapo is established under Göring
	May	Labor unions are dissolved; "Burning of the Books" organized by Goebbels
	June/July	Political parties are dissolved, Nazis become the only legal party
	Oct. 14	Germany leaves the League of Nations
1934	June 30	"Night of the Long Knives": killing of SA leader Ernst Roehm and other

		potential threats to Hitler: Ernst, Strasser, von Schleicher, at behest of Hitler, Himmler, Göring
	Aug. 1	von Hindenburg dies
	Aug. 2	Amalgamation of president and chancellor posts: Hitler assumes both
	Aug. 2	Armed forces take an oath of loyalty to Hitler
1935	Mar. 16	Versailles Treaty armament restrictions are renounced and conscription is introduced by Hitler
	Sept.	Nuremberg Laws are passed denying Jews rights as citizens
	June 18	Anglo-German Naval Conference and Agreement supersedes Versailles naval restrictions; Abwehr is established to serve as a secret police and secret service under the army; Admiral Canaris heads it, General Oster sets it up
1936	Mar. 7	German remilitarization of Rhineland
	April	Himmler is appointed chief of all Third Reich police forces
	Oct.	Hitler presents 4-year economic plan to party congress emphasizing armament expenditures
1937	Sept. 7	Hitler says Versailles Treaty dead
	Nov. 5	Hossbach Meeting—Hitler reveals aggressive war intentions to von Neurath, von Fritsch, Göring, Raeder and von Blomberg, insisting on secrecy; Italy withdraws from the League of Nations
1938	Jan./Feb.	von Blomberg, von Fritsch crises; they are replaced by Hitler with himself as minister of war and Commander-in-Chief of all armed forces (OKW) and Brauchitsch as Commander-in-Chief of the army, replacing Fritsch
	Feb. 4	von Ribbentrop is appointed foreign minister
	Mar. 12	Austrian Anschluss
	Aug.	Col.-General Ludwig Beck, Chief of the General Staff, resigns over Hitler's aggressive actions, is replaced by Franz Halder
	Sept. 29	Munich Agreement to avert war with Czechs; Chamberlain, Daladier, Mussolini, Hitler meet; Sudetenland is ceded to Germany; a planned army coup against Hitler is defused
	Nov. 9	Kristallnacht—Jews are assessed financial penalties, excluded from economic life
1939	March 15	Czechoslovakia is occupied by German troops
	April 26	Germany repudiates the Anglo-German Naval Pact
	Aug. 23	Russo-German nonaggression pact
	Sept. 1	Germany invades Poland
	Sept. 3	England and France declare war on Germany
1940	June 10	Italy declares war on France and Britain
	June 22	France accepts armistice, is occupied by Germany
	April 9	German invasion of Denmark and Norway
	May 10	German invasion of Netherlands, Belgium and Luxembourg; SEALION—proposed plan for invasion of England—begins
1941		Rommel achieves victories in North Africa
	April 6	Germans begin Balkan Campaign against Greece and Yugoslavia
	June 22	Germany attacks Russia
	Sept. 25	Hitler replaces Halder with Zeitzler as Chief of the General Staff
	Dec. 11	Germany and Italy declare war on the United States
	Dec. 19	Hitler relieves Field Marshal von Brauchitsch as Commander-in-Chief of the army, assumes role himself
1942	Nov.	Rommel is defeated at El Alamein by British forces
	Nov. 7–8	Anglo-American forces land in North Africa

1943	Jan. 14–24	Casablanca Conference decides on the unconditional surrender of Germany as the terms for peace
	Feb. 2	German Sixth Army is defeated at Stalingrad
	May	Surrender of Afrika Corps and Italian troops
	July 10	Allies land in Sicily
	July 25	Mussolini resigns
	Sept. 3	Italy surrenders, signs armistice with Allies
	Oct. 31	Italy under Badoglio declares war on Germany
	Nov. 28	Teheran Conference of Roosevelt, Stalin, Churchill
1944	Jan.	The Abwehr comes under Himmler, SS; Canaris is relieved
	June 6	Normandy Invasion
	July 20	A coup attempt on Hitler's life fails
		People's Court — trials and executions of estimated 5000 implicated in the coup attempt
	Dec.	Battle of the Bulge and the last major German campaign, in through the Ardennes
1945	Feb. 12	Yalta Conference of Roosevelt, Churchill, Stalin
	Mar. 7	Allied forces invade Germany
	April 28	Mussolini is shot
	April 30	Hitler commits suicide
	May 7	Germany signs surrender agreement at Reims
	Oct.	Nuremberg Trials of leading members of Third Reich government commence
	Aug.	Japan formally surrenders
1946	Oct. 16	Executions of 10 Nuremberg defendants; there are subsequent trials at Nuremberg of other important Nazi leaders
1947	July 18	Seven Nuremberg defendants are incarcerated at Spandau
1987		The last of Nuremberg's Spandau prisoners (Hess) commits suicide and the prison is dismantled

Appendix C

Treaties and Agreements

Treaty of Versailles — May 1919

Called for ceding of German Territory, reparations, Alsace-Lorraine, loss of Polish Corridor and isolation of East Prussia, establishment of Danzig as a Free State, cession of Sudeten area to Czechs, 15 year administration and occupation of left bank of Rhine (Rhineland) and Saar by League of Nations, demilitarization of Rhineland, confiscation of colonies, military limits.

Treaty of St. Germain — September 1919

Limitation of Austrian boundaries to 32,000 square landlocked miles, breaking up Austro-Hungarian Empire.

Treaty of Trianon — June 1920

Reduction of Hungarian territory to Austria, Romania, Czechoslovakia, Yugoslavia, military limits.

Little Entente — 1924

Czechoslovakia, Romania, Yugoslavia; objective: common defense against a resurgent Hungary.

Dawes Plan — 1924

Worked out a long-term schedule of reparations payments for Germany.

Treaty of Locarno — 1925

Conclusion of five pacts; most significant was Rhine Pact between Germany, France, Great Britain, Italy, and Belgium guaranteeing existing boundaries.

Kellogg-Briand Peace Pact (Pact of Paris) — 1928

Renunciation of war as an instrument of national policy, solutions of future disputes to be resolved by pacific means; signed by approximately 62 nations, including Germany, the United States, Belgium, France, Great Britain, Italy, Japan, Poland. Basis for Nuremberg crimes against peace charge.

Young Plan — 1929

Scaled down German reparations payments.

German-Polish Non-Aggression and Friendship Pact — Jan. 26, 1934

Excluded force from settlements and agreed to

resolve mutual problems as explicitly defined in the Pact of Paris; ten-year term.

Franco-Soviet Treaty of Mutual Assistance — May 1935

London Naval Agreement— June 18, 1935

Provided for 100:35 ratio between Britain and Germany of total naval strength and within ship classes, except for submarines, where parity was agreed upon.

Austro-German Pact— July 11, 1936

Germany recognized Austrian Sovereignty.

Anti-Comintern Pact— Nov. 25, 1936

Germany and Japan agreed to jointly combat communist influence; joined by Italy November 6, 1937.

Munich Conference — September 29, 1938

France, England, Germany and Italy agreed to ceding of Czechoslovakia's Sudetenland to Germany; German troops entered Sudetenland October 1, 1938.

British-French Guarantee of Military Support to Poland — March 31, 1939

German Protectorate of Bohemia-Moravia — March 16, 1939

Hacha-Hitler signed decree as such; Tiso places Slovakia under German protection, March 17, 1939.

British-Polish-French Mutual Assistance Agreement— March 30, 1939

German-Italian Alliance — May 23, 1939

"Pact of Steel" bound Italy and Germany to engage jointly if war came.

German Non-Aggression Pacts with Norway — Sept. 1939, Denmark — May 31, 1939

German-Russian Mutual Assistance Pact— August 23, 1939

To assure Russian neutrality; adjunct secret pact divided Poland and assigned spheres of influence in the Baltic States.

British, French, Polish Formal Mutual Assistance Treaties — August 25, 1939 and May 19, 1939

Tri-Partite Pact— Sept. 27, 1940

Germany, Italy and Japan upgrade Anti-Comintern Pact to political, military, economic alliance. Established axis powers of World War II.

Appendix D

Comparative Army Ranks

German	*U.S.*
Generalfeldmarschall	General of the Army (5 stars)*
Generaloberst	General (4 stars)
General (der Infanterie, etc.)	Lieutenant General (3 stars)
Generaleutnant	Major General (2 stars)
Generalmajor	Brigadier General (1 star)
Oberst	Colonel
Oberstleutnant	Lieutenant Colonel
Major	Major
Hauptmann	Captain
Oberleutnant	1st Lieutenant
Leutnant	2nd Lieutenant

In his twelve years in power, Hitler appointed nineteen army field marshals. The U.S. Army, in its entire history from George Washington forward to this date, has named only five men to the rank of five-star general of the army, and these were first appointed in 1944: H.E. Arnold, Dwight Eisenhower, Douglas MacArthur, and George C. Marshall. These were followed by Omar Bradley in 1950. Five others were appointed to the rank but at the four-star level: George Washington (post), John J. Pershing (post), U.S. Grant, William T. Sherman, and Philip H. Sheridan.

Appendix E

Definitions

Anschluss— Annexation/union of Germany with Austria in 1938

Barbarossa— The German Campaign against Russia, 1941 on

Comando Supremo— Italian Supreme Command

Fall Gelb— Operation YELLOW, plan for action against the West

Fall Gruen— Operation GREEN, plan for action against Czechoslovakia

Fall Weiss— Operation WHITE, plan for action against Poland, Führer War Directive No. 1

Hossbach Conference— Hitler's November 5, 1937, statement of European aggression plans

Manstein Plan—1940 plan for German Western attack

NSDAP— Nazi Party, Nationalsozialistische Deutsche Arbeiterpartei

OKH— Oberkommando des Heeres, the Army High Command

OKL— Oberkommando der Luftwaffe, Air Force High Command

OKM— Oberkommando der Marine, Navy High Command

OKW— Oberkommando der Wehrmacht, the Supreme Command, Hitler's military staff

Panzer— Armored military units

Reichswehr— Designation for the army during the inter-war period up to 1935

SA— Sturmabteilung, Hitler's storm troops, "brownshirts," private paramilitary force developed in early 1920s, faded after Roehm purge of 1934

Sealion— Planned invasion of Britain

SS— Schutzstaffel, combination of all German police organizations under Heinrich Himmler; expanded once Hitler had seized power

Truppenamt— The Troop Office, the subterfuge for the Army General Staff, outlawed by Versailles

Waffen SS— Militarily armed SS units deployed with army

Wehrmacht— Armed Forces of Germany, so designated from 1935 on

Appendix F

Significant Figures

Badoglio, Pietro. Head of state succeeding Mussolini upon Italian armistice, 1943

Bayerlein, Lt. General Fritz. Chief of Staff to Rommel, 1941–42, Africa

Beck, Col. General Ludwig. Chief of the German General Staff, 1933–38

Benes, Eduard. Czech President, 1935–38

Blaskowitz, Col. General Johannes von. Commander-in-Chief Army Group G under von Rundstedt, France, 1944

Blomberg, Field Marshal Werner von. German Defense Minister to 1938

Blumentritt, General Guenther. Operations chief under von Rundstedt in Poland and France, 1939–40; Chief of Staff to von Kluge's Fourth Army, Russia, 1941; Chief of Staff to von Rundstedt, 1942–44

Bock, Field Marshal Feodor von. Commander in Chief Army Group North, 1939; Commander-in-Chief Army Group B, France, 1940; Commander-in-Chief Army Group Center, Russia, 1941; Commander-in-Chief Army Group South, Russia, 1942

Brauchitsch, Field Marshal Walther von. Commander-in-Chief German Army, 1938–42

Canaris, Admiral Wilhelm. OKW chief of intelligence, Abwehr; anti–Nazi conspirator; executed 1945

Carls, Admiral Rolf. German commander Naval Group North, 1943, Raeder's first selection for his replacement, over Dönitz

Chamberlain, Neville. British Prime Minister, 1937–40

Ciano, Galeazzo. Italian Foreign Minister, 1936–43; Mussolini's son in law; executed by Italian Fascists, 1943

Daladier, Eduard. French Prime Minister, 1938–40

Darlan, Admiral Jean François. Chief of all Vichy French Forces, assassinated 1942

Dönitz, Grand Admiral Karl. Chief of the German Navy, 1943–45; successor to Hitler as Chancellor upon the latter's death

Falkenhausen, General Alexander von. Military Governor of France

François-Poncet, Andre. French Ambassador to Berlin, 1931–38; to Rome, 1938–40

Fritsch, Col. General Werner Freiherr von. Commander-in-Chief German Army until relieved in 1938

Fromm, Col. General Friedrich. Commander of the German Reserve Army, 1944; partial conspirator, executed 1944

Galland, Adolf. German fighter pilot, Luftwaffe commander of fighter forces in the West until war's end

Gisevius, Hans. German vice-counsel in Zurich, Abwehr anti–Nazi conspirator, survived

Goebbels, Joseph. German propaganda minister

Goerdeler, Karl. Mayor of Leipzig until resignation in 1937 in protest against Nazis; anti–Nazi conspirator, hanged in 1945

Göring, Reichsmarschall Hermann. Chief of the Luftwaffe, second in Third Reich hierarchy until late in the war

Groener, Lt. General Wilhelm. Reichswehr officer, Minister of Defense, 1928–32

Guderian, Col. General Heinz. Cmdr. XIX Tank Corps, Poland, 1939; Cmdr. Panzer Corps, France, 1940; Cmdr. 2nd Panzer Army, Russia, 1941–42; Inspector General of Armored Troops, 1943; Chief of the General Staff, 1944–45

Halder, General Franz. Chief of the German General Staff, 1938–42

Hammerstein, General Kurt von. Commander-in-chief German Army until resignation/firing 1934

Hassell, Ulrich von. German ambassador to Italy, 1932–38; anti–Nazi activist, hanged 1944

Heinkel, Ernst. Pioneer German aircraft manufacturer

Heinlein, Konrad. Leader of German minority in Sudetenland, led Nazi precipitation of Munich crisis

Henderson, Neville. British ambassador to Berlin, 1937–39

Heydrich, Reinhard. Key deputy to Himmler and SS leader; Reich protector of Moravia-Bohemia, 1941–42 when he was assassinated

Himmler, Heinrich. Reichsfuehrer, SS commandant

Hindenburg, President Paul von. Reichs president 1925–34; Commander-in-Chief German Army World War I

Hossbach, General Friedrich. Recorder of minutes of Hitler's Nov. 5, 1937, meeting where plans for aggression were laid out

Jeshonnek, General Hans. Chief of Staff, Luftwaffe, 1939; in disfavor due to Allied bombings, suicide 1943

Jodl, Col. General Alfred. Chief of Operations, OKW

Keitel, Field Marshal Wilhelm. Chief of Staff, OKW, 1938 to war's end

Kesselring, Field Marshal Albrecht. Commander-in-chief South, Italy-Africa, 1941–44; Commander-in-Chief West, 1944–45

Kleist, Field Marshal Ewald von. Commander of Panzer Group Kleist in France, 1940; commander of Army Group A in Russian Campaign, 1941–43

Kluge, Field Marshal Hans Günther von. Commander-in-Chief Army Group Center, Russia, 1941; Commander-in-Chief West 1944, relieving von Rundstedt

Laval, Pierre. Vichy government head after 1940; executed in 1945

Leeb, Field Marshal Wilhelm Ritter von. Commander Army Group C, 1940, in the West; Army Group North, 1941–42, Russian invasion

Liddell-Hart, B.H. British historian, author, critic, armor expert and innovator

List, Field Marshal Sigmund von. Commander-in-Chief Army Group A, 1942

Loerzer, General Bruno. Luftwaffe corps commander, World War I associate of Göring

Ludendorff, General Erich. Chief of the German General Staff, 1914–18

Mackensen, General von. Commander German 14th Army, Italian theater, 1943–44

Maelzer, General. German commandant of Rome, 1943–44

Mahan, Capt. Alfred Thayer. U.S. Naval Officer and author in 1890 of *The Influence of Sea Power on History 1660–1783*

Manstein, Field Marshall Erich von. Chief of Staff, Army Group A, 1940; Commander-in-Chief 11th Army, Russia, 1941; Commander-In-Chief Don Army Group, Russia, 1942–43

Milch, Field Marshal Erhard. De facto chief

executive officer of Luftwaffe; pre-war managing director of Lufthansa

Model, Field Marshal Walther. Commander 3rd Panzer Division in 1941 in Russia, Commander-in-Chief West, 1944; commander Army Group B late 1944–45 in Ardennes

Molotov, V.M. Russian foreign minister, 1939 on

Moltke (the Elder), Field Marshal Helmuth von. First Chief of the Great German General Staff, 1870–88

Moltke (the Younger), General Helmuth von. Chief of the General Staff, 1906–16; modified 1905 Schlieffen Plan for World War I

Mussolini, Benito. Il Duce, Premier of Italy until 1943

Neurath, Constantin von. German foreign minister, 1932–38; defendant at Nuremberg, sentenced to 15 years in Spandau

Oster, General Hans. Chief of Staff to Admiral Canaris, OKW; anti–Nazi collaborator, executed 1945

Papen, Franz von. Chancellor, 1932; ambassador to Austria, 1933–38; to Turkey, 1938–44

Paulus, Field Marshal Friedrich. Commander-in-chief German Sixth Army, 1942–43

Raeder, Grand Admiral Erich. Chief of the German Navy 1928–43

Rathenau, Field Marshal Walther von. Commander army formations in Poland, France, the Anschluss; Sixth Army commander 1941, Russia; commander Army Group South, Russia, 1942

Roehm, Captain Ernst. Retired Reichswehr officer, commandant of Hitler's SA brownshirts until murdered in 1934

Reinhardt, Col. General Georg-Hans. Pre-war German Chief of Army Training Section; later Panzer Group commander, Eastern Front

Ribbentrop, Joachim von. German foreign minister, 1938–45

Rommel, Field Marshal Erwin. Commander-in-Chief Afrika Corps, 1941–43; Commander-in-Chief Army Group B, France, 1943–44 under von Rundstedt

Ruge, Vice-Admiral Friedrich. Commander German Naval Forces West, 1944

Rundstedt, Field Marshal Gerd von. Commander-in-Chief Army Group South, Poland, 1939; Commander-in-Chief Army Group A, France, 1940; Commander-in-Chief West, 1942; Commander-in-Chief Ardennes, 1944

Schacht, Hjalmar. German economic minister 1934–37; president of Reichsbank 1923–30, 1933–39

Schlabrendorff, Fabian von. Co-conspirator with von Treskow in 1943 bomb attempt on Hitler's aircraft; survived war

Schleicher, General Kurt von. Reichswehr officer to 1934; chancellor 1932; Minister of Defense 1932–34

Schlieffen, Field Marshal Alfred Graf von. Chief of the German General Staff, 1891–1906; author of plan to attack the West

Schmid, Lt. General Josef. Luftwaffe intelligence chief

Schörner, Field Marshal Ferdinand. Commander-in-Chief Army Groups Center, A, North on Eastern Front, 1944–45

Schuschnigg, Kurt von. Austrian Chancellor, 1934–38; replaced by Arthur Seyss-Inquart during Anschluss

Schweppenberg, General Geyr von. Commander, Panzer Group West, under von Rundstedt, 1944

Seeckt, Col. General Hans von. Chief of post–World War I Reichswehr to 1925

Speidel, Lt. General Hans. Chief of Staff to Rommel, 1944; post-war German Army officer

Sperrle, Col. General Hugo. Commander-in-Chief Third Air Fleet, 1944

Stauffenberg, Col. Count Klaus von. Bomb carrier in 1944 coup attempt on Hitler's life, executed 1944

Stumpff, General Hans-Juergen. Chief of Staff, Luftwaffe, 1937–39; Commander-in-Chief Air Fleets in Battle of Britain, Norway

Thomas, General Georg. Chief of War Economy and Armaments Office, OKW, 1938–44; anti–Nazi conspirator with Admiral Canaris

Todt, Fritz. Head of organization that built West Wall, major road and other construction projects; succeeded on his death by Albert Speer

Treskow, General Henning von. Chief of Staff, Army Group Center, Russia; anti–Nazi, attempted bombing of Hitler's aircraft in 1943; suicide in 1944 after failed coup on Hitler

Udet, General Ernst. Luftwaffe commander, World War I associate of Göring

Wagner, General Eduard. Army Quartermaster General; anti–Nazi, suicide after failed coup attempt of 1944

Warlimont, General Walter. Deputy Chief of Operations under Alfred Jodl, OKW, 1939–1944

Westphal, General Siegfried. Chief of Staff to Rommel, 1941–43; Chief of Staff to Kesselring, 1943–44; Chief of Staff to von Rundstedt, 1944–45

Wever, Lt. General Walther. First chief of the Air Command Office, de facto General Staff, in 1933; killed in 1936 air crash

Wilhelm II, Kaiser. German monarch, deposed in 1918 at conclusion of World War I

Wilson, President Woodrow. U.S. president, 1913–21

Zeitzler, General Kurt. Chief of the General Staff, 1942–44; replaced by Guderian

Chapter Notes

Introduction

1. Fritz Fischer, *Germany's Aims in the First World War* (New York: W.W. Norton, 1967), 104–6.

2. Woodruff D. Smith, *The Ideological Origins of Nazi Imperialism* (New York: Oxford University Press, 1986), 168–70; Friedrich Naumann, *Central Europe*, trans. Christabel M. Meredith (London: P.S. King and Son, 1916), viii.

3. Fritz Redlich, *Hitler, Diagnosis of a Destructive Prophet* (New York: Oxford University Press, 1998), 54; Wolfgang Förster, *Generaloberst Ludwig Beck, Sein Kampf gegen den Krieg* (Munich: Isar Verlag, 1953), 100–105, 109–13, 116–21, 122–13; trans. of cited passages, Gary Steiner.

Chapter 1

1. J.M. Keynes, *The Economic Consequences of the Peace* (New York: Harcourt, Brace and Howe, 1920), 65–66; International Military Tribunal (IMT), *Nazi Conspiracy and Aggression* (Washington, DC: U.S. Govt. Printing Office, 1946, 10 vols.), 7:590–91; H. Foley, *Woodrow Wilson's Case for the League of Nations* (Princeton, NJ: Princeton University Press, 1923).

2. Keynes, *Economic Consequences*, 61. Following his role as observer at the peace conference in 1919, Keynes discusses the impact on Germany and Europe of the impossible terms laid down by the Versailles Treaty.

3. Günther Blumentritt, *Von Rundstedt, the Soldier and the Man*, trans. Cuthbert Reavely (London: Odhams Press, 1952), 22–27. This is a biographical essay on von Rundstedt, whom the author, Blumentritt, served as Chief of Staff from 1942 to 1944; John W. Wheeler-Bennett, *The Nemesis of Power* (London: Macmillan, 1953), 90.

4. Wheeler-Bennett, *Nemesis*, 182, 266–68, 323–24.

5. See note 3.

6. Robert Seager II, *Alfred Thayer Mahan, the Man and His Letters* (Annapolis, MD: Naval Institute Press, 1977), 500.

7. Keynes, *Economic Consequences*, 35–70 passim.

8. International Military Tribunal (IMT), *The Trial of the Major War Criminals* (Nuremberg: Allied Control Authority for Germany, 1947, 23 vols. Transcripts, 17 vols. Documents), 3:185–86; Friedrich Ruge, *Der See-krieg*, trans. M.G. Saunders (Annapolis, MD: U.S. Naval Institute Press, 1957), 20.

9. Keynes, *Economic Consequences*, 57–62.

10. Erich Räder, *My Life*, trans. Henry W. Drexel (Annapolis, MD: U.S. Naval Institute, 1960), 137.

11. Ibid., 138–39.

12. See note 11.

13. IMT, *Trial of The War Criminals*, 14:152–53; International Military Tribunal (IMT), *Nazi Conspiracy and Aggression* (Washington, DC: U.S. Govt. Printing Office, 1946, 10 vols.), Sup A:977–78, D854.

14. Robert K. Massie, *Dreadnought, Britain, Germany, and the Coming of the Great War* (New York: Random House, 1991), 172–73.

15. Ibid., xxiv.

16. Ibid., 909–11; Seager, *Mahan, the Man*, 501.

17. Räder, *My Life*, 34–35.

18. IMT, *Trial of The War Criminals*, 13:597; IMT, *Nazi Conspiracy*, 6:970–71, C156.

19. IMT, *Nazi Conspiracy*, Sup A:977–78, D854.

20. Erich von Manstein, *Lost Victories*, trans. Anthony Powell (Novato, CA: Presidio Press, 1982), 109, 124.

21. Heinz Guderian, *Panzer Leader*, trans. Constantine Fitzgibbon (New York: E.P. Dutton, 1952), 20, 26; B.H. Liddell-Hart, *The Rommel Papers*, trans. Paul Findlay (New York: Harcourt, Brace, 1953), 299.

22. F.W. von Mellenthin, *German Generals of World War II* (Norman: University of Oklahoma Press, 1977), 56–57; Hans Speidel, *Invasion 1944*, trans. Theo R. Crevenna (Chicago: Regnery, 1950), 112; F.W. von Mellenthin, *Panzer Battles*, trans. H. Betzler (Norman: University of Oklahoma Press, 1956), 43.

23. Erwin Rommel, *Attacks* (Vienna, VA: Athena Press, 1979), 250.

24. Franz Halder, *The Halder War Diary 1939–1942*, ed.

Charles Burdick and Hans-Adolf Jacobsen (Novato, CA: Presidio Press, 1988), 454.

25. Konrad Heiden, *Der Führer*, trans. Ralph Manheim (Boston: Houghton Mifflin, 1944), 398.

26. Ibid., 406.

27. IMT, *Trial of the War Criminals*, 15:285.

28. Adolf Galland, *The First and The Last*, trans. Mervyn Savill (London: Methuen, 1955), 1.

29. Ernst Heinkel, *Stormy Life*, trans. R.C. Murray and J.A. Bagley (New York: E.P. Dutton, 1956), 10.

30. Ibid., 13, 17.

31. Ibid., 18.

32. Richard Suchenwirth, *Command and Leadership in the German Air Force,* ed. Harry R. Fletcher (New York: Arno Press/USAF Historical Division, Air University, 1969), ix.

33. Heinkel, *Stormy Life*, 65, 70–71.

34. Ibid., 73–74.

35. Ibid., 74; IMT, *Trial of the War Criminals*, 22:424.

36. Galland, *First and Last*, 6–7; Suchenwirth, *Command and Leadership,* 18–19.

37. Heinkel, *Stormy Life*, 123.

Chapter 2

1. IMT, *Trial of the War Criminals*, 1:217.

2. IMT, *Nazi Conspiracy*, Sup B:1547.

3. Räder, *My Life*, 184.

4. Ibid., 165–71.

5. Ibid., 193; IMT, *Trial of the War Criminals*, 14:162.

6. IMT, *Nazi Conspiracy*, 6:414–18, 3704PS, 3706PS.

7. IMT, *Trial of the War Criminals*, 22:279.

8. Ibid., 21:40; Ulrich von Hassell, *The Von Hassell Diaries 1938–1944* (New York: Doubleday, 1947), 197. Von Hassell, former ambassador to Rome and anti-Nazi activist, observed and provides critical comment on von Rundstedt's de facto attitude as coup plans developed.

9. Blumentritt, *Von Rundstedt*, 31. Rundstedt's remarks underscore the substantial support for the monarchy among the senior military and landed class that continued through the Weimar period.

10. Ibid., 34.

11. Speidel, *Invasion*, 14.

12. Wilhelm Keitel, *The Memoirs of Field Marshal Keitel*, trans. David Irving (New York: Stein and Day, 1966), 48. Hitler's expansion of the Reichswehr during the mid-1930s provided opportunities in the military which over-balanced, for most members, any hostility toward National Socialist policies; this was at least part of von Rundstedt's agenda.

13. IMT, *Trial of the War Criminals*, 21:23.

14. Blumentritt, *Von Rundstedt*, 39.

15. IMT, *Trial of the War Criminals*, 15:284–87; Heiden, *Der Führer*, 406.

16. See note 15.

17. Ibid.

18. Blumentritt, *Von Rundstedt*, 35.

19. Robert J. O'Neill, *The German Army and the Nazi Party 1933–1939* (New York: Heinemann, 1966), 50.

20. Wheeler-Bennett, *Nemesis*, 395; Hans B. Gisevius, *To the Bitter End*, trans. Richard and Clara Winston (Boston: Houghton Mifflin, 1947), 278–79.

21. Franz von Papen, *Memoirs*, trans. Brian Connell (London: Andre Deutsch, 1952), 335–36.

22. Wheeler-Bennett, *Nemesis*, 339; Richard Brett-Smith, *Hitler's Generals* (San Rafael, CA: Presidio Press, 1977), 4.

23. IMT, *Trial of the War Criminals*, 12:242.

24. Heinrich Oppenheimer, *The Constitution of the German Republic* (London: Stevens and Sons, 1923), Appendix.

25. See note 21.

26. See note 4.

27. IMT, *Trial of the War Criminals*, 15:294.

28. Ibid., 14:161–62; IMT, *Nazi Conspiracy*, 6:827–28, C23.

29. Speidel, *Invasion*, 157–58.

30. See note 29.

31. IMT, *Trial of the War Criminals*, 14:162–63; IMT, *Nazi Conspiracy*, 6:970–71, C156.

32. IMT, *Trial of the War Criminals*, 14:159; IMT, *Nazi Conspiracy*, Sup A:979–80, F855.

33. IMT, *Trial of the War Criminals*, 14:152–573; IMT *Nazi Conspiracy*, Sup A:977–78, D854.

34. Guderian, *Panzer Leader*, 30, 32–33; B.H. Liddell-Hart, *The German Generals Talk* (New York: Morrow Quill Paperbacks, 1979), 25, 32.

35. See note 34.

36. Klaus-Jürgen Müller, *The Army, Politics and Society in Germany, 1933–45* (New York: St Martin's Press, 1987), 85.

37. Albrecht Kesselring, *The Memoirs of Field-Marshal Kesselring*, trans. Wm. Kimber (Novato, CA: Presidio Press, 1989), 25, 26, 31.

38. Suchenwirth, *Command and Leadership,* ix–x, 18–22, 115–16, 132–34.

Chapter 3

1. IMT, *Nazi Conspiracy*, 6:946–47, C135.

2. Guderian, *Panzer Leader*, 29, 30.

3. Ibid., 31, 35.

4. Raeder, *My Life*, 187.

5. IMT, *Trial of the War Criminals*, 14:154.

6. Raeder, *My Life*, 188–89.

7. Karl Dönitz, *Memoirs: Ten Years and Twenty Days*, trans. R.H. Stevens (Annapolis, MD: Naval Institute Press, 1990), 9, 10.

8. Ibid., 10, 29.

9. IMT, *Trial of the War Criminals*, 14:170; IMT, *Nazi Conspiracy*, Sup A:954, D806.

10. Räder, *My Life*, 230–38.

11. IMT, *Trial of the War Criminals*, 14:160; IMT, *Nazi Conspiracy*, 6:827–28, C23.

12. Dönitz, *Memoirs*, 10, 12.

13. Keitel, *Memoirs*, 27.

14. Walter Warlimont, *Inside Hitler's Headquarters 1939–45*, trans. R.H. Barry (Novato, CA: Presidio Press, 1964), 12.

15. Fabian von Schlabrendorff, *The Secret War against Hitler*, trans. Hilda Simon (New York: Pitman, 1965), 72–73, 149–51, 158–59.

16. See note 15.

17. IMT, *Trial of the War Criminals*, 22:294–95; Telford Taylor, *Sword and Swastika* (Chicago: Quadrangle Books, 1969), 95.

18. See note 17.

19. Muller, *The Army*, 56.

20. IMT, *Trial of the War Criminals*, 15:351.

21. IMT, *Nazi Conspiracy*, 6:951–52, C139.

22. Ibid., 5:1100–1103, 3308PS, 6:974–76, C159; IMT, *Trial of the War Criminals*, 20:602–3.

23. IMT, *Trial of the War Criminals*, 15:352.

24. Andre François-Poncet, *The Fateful Years*, trans. Jacques LeClercq (New York: Harcourt, Brace, 1949), 194–96. François-Poncet, an economist by training and experience, was ambassador to Berlin from 1931 to 1938; he viewed "Hitler and his gang" and National Socialism as an "odious ... spectacle of tyranny trampling human values, exalting brutality and glorifying savagery" (ibid., x). Fluent in German, he had frequent opportunity to talk directly with Hitler.

25. Kesselring, *Memoirs*, 25, 31.

26. Suchenwirth, *Command*, ix–x, 18–22, 115–16, 132–34.

27. Kesselring, *Memoirs*, 39–41.

28. Wheeler-Bennett, *Nemesis*, 224–25, 300, 458–59, 466; Gisevius, *To the Bitter End*, 430–31.

29. Muller, *The Army*, 71.

30. Räder, *My Life*, 241–43.

31. Galeazzo Ciano, *The Ciano Diaries 1939–1943* (Garden City, NY: Doubleday, 1946), 212.

32. Hjalmar Schacht, *Account Settled*, trans. Edward Fitzgerald (London: Weidenfeld and Nicolson, 1949), 279.

Chapter 4

1. IMT, *Trial of the War Criminals*, 1:37; IMT, *Nazi Conspiracy*, 3:295–305, 386PS; the conference of Nov. 5, 1937, the Hossbach Conference, in which Hitler laid out his plans for European aggression to his commanders-in-chief, is listed in Count One of the indictment by the IMT as a key element of the Nazi conspiracy to wage aggressive war.

2. IMT, *Trial of the War Criminals*, 21:384, 16:640–41.

3. Ibid., 17:50; Schlabrendorff, *Secret War*, 155.

4. IMT, *Trial of the War Criminals*, 28:360, 1780PS; Taylor, *Sword*, 149; Wheeler-Bennett, *Nemesis*, 365–66.

5. Keitel, *Memoirs*, 52.

6. Gisevius, *To the Bitter End*, 231–32; Wheeler-Bennett, *Nemesis*, 369–71.

7. Keitel, *Memoirs*, 16, 19.

8. Ibid., 35–36; Wheeler-Bennett, *Nemesis*, 369–70.

9. Wheeler-Bennett, *Nemesis*, 378–79; Otto John, *Twice through the Lines*, trans. Richard Barry (New York: Harper and Row, 1972), 28–29. Otto John, Lufthansa lawyer, was another anti-Nazi activist to survive; in one of his post-war assignments for the Allied Authority he was responsible for POW welfare at Camp No, 11 at Bridgend, Wales, England, where several hundred former German admirals, field marshals, generals and SS officers were incarcerated awaiting trial and/or disposition of their cases. This yielded significant insight as to their actions and attitudes which John records.

10. Guderian, *Panzer Leader*, 48–49.

11. Von Hassell, *Diaries*, 25. Von Hassell, dismissed from his post of ambassador to Rome for his anti-Nazi sentiments by von Ribbentrop, knew and worked closely with Ludwig Beck; he was executed in the aftermath of the July 20, 1944, failed coup attempt.

12. Wolfgang Förster, *Generaloberst Ludwig Beck: Sein Kampf gegen den Krieg*, (Munich: Isar Verlag, 1953), 100–105; trans. of cited passages, Gary Steiner.

13. O'Neill, *The German Army*, 154–55.

14. Förster, *Generaloberst Ludwig Beck*, 109–13.

15. IMT, *Nazi Conspiracy*, 3:306–79, 388PS.

16. Ibid., 3:316–20, 388PS.

17. Ibid., 4:364, 1780PS; O'Neill, *The German Army*, 156.

18. Förster, *Generaloberst Ludwig Beck*, 122–23; Schlabrendorff, *Secret War*, 156–57.

19. Förster, *Generaloberst Ludwig Beck*, 116–21.

20. IMT, *Trial of the War Criminals*, 20:569; John, *Twice through the Lines*, 33; Wheeler-Bennett, *Nemesis*, 402.

21. Blumentritt, *Von Rundstedt*, 37; John, *Twice through the Lines*, 32; IMT, *Trial of the War Criminals*, 20:569.

22. IMT, *Nazi Conspiracy*, 4:364, 1780PS; IMT, *Trial of the War Criminals*, 20:606; Wheeler-Bennett, *Nemesis*, 404.

23. IMT, *Trial of the War Criminals*, 19:376.

24. Ibid., 16:640–41; Förster, *Generaloberst Ludwig Beck*, 100–105, 109–13, 116–21, passim; Keitel, *Memoirs*, 45–50, 65–66; Wheeler-Bennett, *Nemesis*, 367–70, 393–404.

Chapter 5

1. Keitel, *Memoirs*, 57; Schacht, *Account Settled*, 113; IMT, *Trial of the War Criminals*, 10:504.

2. IMT, *Trial of the War Criminals*, 10:504–55; IMT, *Nazi Conspiracy*, 4:361, 1780PS.

3. IMT, *Nazi Conspiracy*, 6:911–12, C102.

4. Keitel, *Memoirs*, 59.

5. Guderian, *Panzer Leader*, 50–56; IMT, *Nazi Conspiracy*, Opinion and Judgement, 47; Manstein, *Lost Victories*, 25–26.

6. See note 5

7. Blumentritt, *Von Rundstedt*, 37. Beck represented the few who were prescient enough to see the ultimate catastrophe and strong enough to take action. Most of this small early group of Wehrmacht officers paid the supreme penalty.

8. Kesselring, *Memoirs*, 25–26, 31.

9. IMT, *Trial of the War Criminals*, 1:195; IMT, *Nazi Conspiracy*, 4:363, 1780PS.

10. IMT, *Nazi Conspiracy*, 7:923, L172; IMT, *Trial of the War Criminals*, 15:452–53, 460.

11. Keitel, *Memoirs*, 62–63; IMT, *Trial of the War Criminals*, 10:506–7.

12. IMT, *Nazi Conspiracy*, 3:316–20, 388PS.

13. Ibid., 4:363, 1780PS, 3:316–20, 388PS

14. Ibid., 4:364, 1780PS.

15. See note 14.

16. Förster, *Generaloberst Ludwig Beck*, 100–105, 109–13, 116–21.

17. Keitel, *Memoirs*, 66–68.

18. Ibid., 69–70; Manstein, *Lost Victories*, 546; Guderian, *Panzer Leader*, 270; Albert Speer, *Inside the Third Reich*, trans. Richard and Clara Winston (New York: Macmillan, 1976), 421; von Manstein was retired in 1944 and not used again; Guderian was placed on the reserve officers list in December 1941 and reactivated in 1943 to reorganize and direct the faltering tank program. Though outspoken, in the end he accommodated Hitler sufficiently so as to remain active and/or a survivor until war's end.

19. Wilhelm von Leeb, *Defense*, trans. S.T. Possony and D. Vilfroy (Harrisburg, PA: Military Publishing, 1943), 158; Keitel, *Memoirs*, 65.

20. Keitel, *Memoirs*, 65–71.

21. Neville Henderson, *Failure of a Mission* (New York: G.P. Putnam's Sons, 1940), 173, 179–80.

22. IMT, *Nazi Conspiracy*, 4:363, 1780PS, 3:316–20, 388PS; IMT, *Trial of the War Criminals*, 15:358; Wheeler-Bennett, *Nemesis*, 397.

23. IMT, *Trial of the War Criminals*, 3:46–47; IMT, *Nazi Conspiracy*, 3:324–25, 388PS.

24. IMT, *Trial of the War Criminals*, 1:196, 15:361–62, 460.

25. Ibid., 1:195, 3:75; IMT, *Nazi Conspiracy*, 3:311–12, 388PS, 4:366, 1780PS.

26. IMT, *Trial of the War Criminals*, 3:78.

27. Ibid., 3:78; IMT, *Nazi Conspiracy*, 3:658–63, 998PS.

28. Guderian, *Panzer Leader*, 57–58.

29. IMT, *Nazi Conspiracy*, 4:366; Henderson, *Failure of a Mission*, 148–75 passim.

30. IMT, *Trial of the War Criminals*, 1:197.

31. IMT, *Nazi Conspiracy*, 4:368, 1780PS.

32. Eduard Benes, *Memoirs of Dr. Eduard Benes*, trans. Godfrey Lias (Boston: Houghton Mifflin, 1954), 26.

33. IMT, *Trial of the War Criminals*, 15:461.

34. Kurt Schuschnigg, *Austrian Requiem*, trans. Franz von Hildebrand (New York: G.P. Putnam's Sons, 1946), 174–75.

35. See note 28.

36. Dönitz, *Memoirs*, 303–5.

37. Guderian, *Panzer Leader*, 60; IMT, *Trial of the War Criminals*, 20:569; Förster, *Generaloberst Ludwig Beck*, 100–105, 109–13, 116–21; John, *Twice through the Lines*, 33.

38. Keitel, *Memoirs*, 73–78; IMT, *Trial of the War Criminals*, 10:510.

39. Guderian, *Panzer Leader*, 64–66; von Papen, *Memoirs*, 376, 386.

40. Keitel, *Memoirs*, 74–75.

41. Ibid., 84–86; IMT, *Trial of the War Criminals*, 10:511.

42. Dönitz, *Memoirs*, 31, 37–43; Räder, *My Life*, 279–80.

43. See note 42.

44. Ibid.

45. Dönitz, *Memoirs*, 41–42.

46. Ibid., 52, 305–6.

47. See note 46.

Chapter 6

1. Manstein, *Lost Victories*, 148.

2. Friedrich von Rabenau, *Seeckt, Aus Seinem Leben 1918–1936* (Leipzig: Hase and Koehler, 1940), 316; trans. of citations, Gary Steiner.

3. Manstein, *Lost Victories*, 24–27; IMT, *Trial of the War Criminals*, 20:606.

4. IMT, *Nazi Conspiracy*, 3:581–86, 798PS, 665–66, 1014PS; IMT, *Trial of the War Criminals*, 1:201–2.

5. See note 4.

6. Ibid.

7. Manstein, *Lost Victories*, 30; IMT, *Trial of the War Criminals*, 21:24.

8. Manstein, *Lost Victories*, 29–31.

9. Blumentritt, *Von Rundstedt*, 43–54 passim.

10. Manstein, *Lost Victories*, 63.

11. IMT, *Trial of the War Criminals*, 15:464–65; IMT, *Nazi Conspiracy*, Sup A:1023–24, 885PS.

12. Guderian, *Panzer Leader*, 47, 82; Mellenthin, *German Generals*, 89–90; Manstein, *Lost Victories*, 63.

13. Guderian, *Panzer Leader*, 66.

14. Ibid., 85, 141; Halder, *War Diary*, 297–98.

15. Manstein, *Lost Victories*, 155–56.

16. Kesselring, *Memoirs*, 42.

17. Ibid., 39–41.

18. Ibid., 47.

19. IMT, *Nazi Conspiracy*, 7:847–54, L79; in this May 23, 1939, speech to his top commanders Hitler laid out plans for an attack on Poland at the first suitable opportunity. "We cannot expect a repetition of the Czech affair."

20. Ibid., 3:581–86, 798PS, 3:665–66, 1014PS; in two speeches to his field generals on August 22, 1939, Hitler discussed his plans for an attack on Poland "probably by Sat-

urday morning." Further, he surprised them with news of the pact with Russia. General consensus among the audience was that he was bluffing again.

21. IMT, Trial of the War Criminals, 14:178–90.

22. Ibid., 14:180.

23. Ibid., 14:187–88; IMT, *Nazi Conspiracy*, 6:887–92, C66, 6:928, C122.

24. IMT, *Trial of the War Criminals*, 1:315–17, 14:215–17, 35:235–36, 635D; IMT, *Nazi Conspiracy*, 5:1008, 3260PS.

25. IMT, Trial of the War Criminals, 14:202–3, 34:608–40, 157C.

26. Gisevius, *To The Bitter End*, 234–326 passim; IMT, *Trial of the War Criminals*, 12:202.

27. IMT, *Trial of the War Criminals*, 12:232, 300–301.

28. Ibid., 12:211–12; IMT, *Nazi Conspiracy*, Sup B:1551–53; Gisevius, *To the Bitter End*, 283–447 passim.

29. Schacht, Account Settled, 113–16; IMT, *Trial of the War Criminals*, 12:211–12.

30. IMT, *Nazi Conspiracy*, Sup B:1553.

31. Ibid., Sup B:1557–58.

32. Ibid., Sup B:1558.

33. Ibid., Sup B:1562.

34. Ibid., Sup B:3:581–86, 789PS, 665–66, 1014PS.

35. See note 32.

36. IMT, *Nazi Conspiracy*, Sup B:1571.

37. Ibid., Sup B:1563.

38. Blumentritt, *Von Rundstedt*, 103–4; Guderian, *Panzer Leader*, 142; Halder, *War Diary*, 446.

Chapter 7

1. Keitel, *Memoirs*, 93.

2. Halder, *War Diary*, 64–66.

3. Ibid., 62–67.

4. Keitel, *Memoirs*, 99–100; IMT, *Trial of the War Criminals*, 10:521.

5. S.L.A. Marshall, *World War One* (Boston: Houghton Mifflin, 1964), 55–56.

6. Halder, *War Diary*, 100; OKH was fighting the last war, whereas von Manstein, with Guderian's perceptive support, devised an innovative plan to exploit German panzer capability.

7. Guderian, *Panzer Leader*, 90; Von Leeb, *Defense*, 129.

8. See note 6; Halder, *War Diary*, 95–98.

9. Liddell-Hart, *Rommel Papers*, 4; Manstein, *Lost Victories*, 98, 124.

10. Halder, *War Diary*, 151.

11. Von Hassell, *Diaries*, 129–30; Warlimont, *Inside Hitler's Headquarters*, 101.

12. Manstein, *Lost Victories*, 78; Keitel, *Memoirs*, 35–53 passim.

13. IMT, *Trial of the War Criminals*, 15:381, 473–74; IMT, *Nazi Conspiracy*, 7D:803, L52; Manstein, *Lost Victories*, 103–5.

14. Manstein, *Lost Victories*, 71–74.

15. Blumentritt, *Von Rundstedt*, 63; Guderian, *Panzer Leader*, 91.

16. Guderian, *Panzer Leader*, 94–96; Von Leeb, *Defense*, 145.

17. Ibid., 91; Marshall, *World War I*, 55–56.

18. Manstein, *Lost Victories*, 124; Von Leeb, *Defense*, 145.

19. Liddell Hart, *Rommel Papers*, 6.

20. Mellenthin, *German Generals*, 59.

21. Guderian, *Panzer Leader*, 117.

22. Blumentritt, *Von Rundstedt*, 65, 74–77; Liddell-Hart, *German Generals*, 132–35; Milton Shulman, *Defeat in the West* (New York: Balllantine Books, 1968), 72; Liddell-Hart, *Rommel Papers*, 34; Mellenthin, *Panzer Battles*, 18; Brett-Smith, *Hitler's Generals*, 21, 45; Blumentritt, Liddell-Hart and Shulman discussed this issue with von Rundstedt, the latter two after the war; von Rundstedt maintained to them that Hitler was responsible for the "halt order."
23. Keitel, *Memoirs*, 114–15.
24. See note 22.
25. Suchenwirth, *Command*, 159–60.
26. Manstein, *Lost Victories*, 124.
27. Ibid., 148; IMT, *Trial of the War Criminals*, 20:608.
28. Raeder, *My Life*, 319.
29. IMT, *Trial of the War Criminals*, 14:184. All three twentieth-century German western attack plans involved violation of at least Belgian if not Dutch territorial neutrality: the Schlieffen Plan of 1905, the Moltke Plan of 1914 and the Manstein Plan of 1940.

Chapter 8

1. Halder, *War Diary*, 204.
2. Dönitz, *Memoirs*, 114–15.
3. Halder, *War Diary*, 227.
4. See note 3.
5. Halder, *War Diary*, 230.
6. See note 5.
7. Von Manstein, *Lost Victories*, 153–54.
8. Halder, *War Diary*, 238–39.
9. Ibid., 246–47; Confidence in Halder's conceptual, innovative and planning ability comes into question in his attempts to implement this complex operation given the schedule, limited assets, his complete inexperience in the environment and the navy's negative attitude.
10. Kesselring, *Memoirs*, 67; Liddell-Hart, *The Rommel Papers*, 106.
11. Halder, *War Diary*, 243.
12. Keitel, *Memoirs*, 116–18.
13. Kesselring, *Memoirs*, 65, 67–68, 76, 78–79, 81; IMT, *Trial of the War Criminals*, 9:207; Manstein, *Lost Victories*, 153, 157, 166–67, 169; Keitel, *Memoirs*, 116–18; Kenneth Macksey, *Kesselring: The Making of the Luftwaffe* (New York: David McKay, 1978), 65.
14. Kesselring, *Memoirs*, 41; Keitel, *Memoirs*, 80.
15. Kesselring, *Memoirs*, 42.
16. IMT, *Trial of the War Criminals*, 9:60–61, 204–5; Suchenwirth, *Command*, 35, 66, 82, 249; Kesselring, *Memoirs*, 68, 76; Ernst Heinkel, *Stormy Life*, trans. R.C. Murray and J.A. Bagley (New York: E.P. Dutton, 1956), 193–206.
17. Manstein, *Lost Victories*, 167–70.
18. Ibid., 155–56.
19. Halder, *War Diary*, 244, 406; Jak P. Mallman Showell, *Führer Conferences on Naval Affairs 1939–1945*, trans. British Govt. (Annapolis, MD: U.S. Naval Institute Press, 1990), 116–40.
20. See note 17.

Chapter 9

1. Keitel, *Memoirs*, 122–23; Blumentritt, *Von Rundstedt*, 98, 101; Liddell-Hart, *German Generals Talk*, 171–72. Defeat of the Russians west of the Dnieper was considered

critical to success so as to prevent unacceptable lengthening of logistics lines.
2. Guderian, *Panzer Leader*, 141–42; Halder, *War Diary*, 446.
3. Guderian, *Panzer Leader*, 151.
4. Keitel, *Memoirs*, 122–23.
5. Blumentritt, *Von Rundstedt*, 97, 109; IMT, *Trial of the War Criminals*, 21:25.
6. Halder, *War Diary*, 245, 297, 309, 345.
7. Keitel, *Memoirs*, 131–37.
8. IMT, *Nazi Conspiracy*, 6:887–92, C66, 6:989–91, C170; Räder, though anxious for Britain's defeat, was cool for obvious reasons toward SEALION, Hitler's proposed amphibious invasion of the British Isles in 1940.
9. Keitel, *Memoirs*, 144–45.
10. Halder, *War Diary*, 315, 400.
11. See note 10.
12. Ibid., 446; Guderian, *Panzer Leader*, 142.
13. Franz Halder, *Hitler as Warlord*, trans. Paul Findlay (Alva, UK: Cunningham and Sons, 1950), 19, 20; This is a stereotypical example of the need to compare post-war trial interrogatories and memoirs against reliable documentation.
14. IMT, *Nazi Conspiracy*, 3:626–33, 872PS.
15. Ibid., 4:374–75, 1799PS; Halder, *War Diary*, 292–97.
16. IMT, *Trial of the War Criminals*, 7:254, 268.
17. Blumentritt, *Von Rundstedt*, 103–4; Guderian, *Panzer Leader*, 256; Halder, *War Diary*, 446.
18. See note 17.
19. Gisevius, *To the Bitter End*, 468–69.
20. IMT, *Trial of the War Criminals*, 14:196; IMT, *Nazi Conspiracy*, 6:855–57, C38.
21. See note 20.
22. IMT, *Nazi Conspiracy*, Sup B:661–62.
23. Keitel, *Memoirs*, 124. Regardless of Keitel's retrospective on this point, the conventional wisdom, at least in the Army High Command at the time, projected 8 to 10 weeks to defeat the Russians (Guderian, *Panzer Leader*, 142; Halder, *War Diary*, 446).
24. See note 12.
25. Halder, *War Diary*, 225.
26. Blumentritt, *Von Rundstedt*, 112–14; Guderian, *Panzer Leader*, 256; Warlimont, *Hitler's Headquarters*, 194.
27. Keitel, *Memoirs*, 160–61.
28. Mellenthin, *German Generals*, 93–94; Guderian, *Panzer Leader*, 189, 200, 224, 226, 259; Von Leeb, *Defense*, 154.
29. Guderian, *Panzer Leader*, 142.
30. Ibid., 248, 254–55.
31. Ibid., 143–44.
32. Ibid., 190, 143. Manstein, *Lost Victories*, 297, 309, 345.
33. See note 31.
34. Guderian, *Panzer Leader*, 233–35, 237.
35. Ibid., 200; Liddell-Hart, *German Generals Talk*, 176; Halder, *War Diary*, 515–16.
36. Guderian, *Panzer Leader*, 264–71; Mellenthin, *Panzer Battles*, 212.
37. Chris Ellis, *Tanks of World War 2* (London: Octopus Books, 1981), passim.
38. Guderian, *Panzer Leader*, 278–82.
39. See note 38.
40. Ibid.
41. Ibid.
42. Ibid.
43. Ibid., 250.
44. Manstein, *Lost Victories*, 350–60; Von Leeb, *Defense*, 126–28.

45. See note 44.

46. Ibid., 361; IMT, *Trial of the War Criminals,* 20:610.

47. Manstein, *Lost Victories,* 406–7.

48. Ibid., 544–47; IMT, *Trial of the War Criminals,* 20:626; Joseph Goebbels, *The Goebbels Diaries 1942–43,* trans. and ed. Louis Lochner (New York: Doubleday, 1948), 503.

49. Manstein, *Lost Victories,* 148; G.M. Gilbert, *Nuremberg Diary* (New York: Farrar, Straus and Co., 1947), 373–74; IMT, *Trial of the War Criminals,* 21:30; Von Leeb, *Defense,* 125; Blumentritt, *Von Rundstedt,* 184. Von Rundstedt reiterated informally to the U.S. Army prison psychologist at Nuremberg, Dr. Gilbert, this earlier view of the implication of the Stalingrad debacle on the war's outcome. To the question of the necessity for the war, Rundstedt answered, "Over the lousy Corridor? Not for a minute — They could have settled that with a deal anytime.... The whole war was madness." Yet von Rundstedt persisted when he could have opted for and remained in retirement. Blumentritt, *Von Rundstedt,* 184.

50. Keitel, *Memoirs,* 131–37; Manstein, *Lost Victories,* 179–80; IMT, *Nazi Conspiracy,* 6:872–76, C50; Telford Taylor, *The Anatomy of the Nuremberg Trials* (New York: Knopf, 1992), 255–56.

51. Keitel, *Memoirs,* 144.

52. IMT, *Trial of the War Criminals,* 15:477–78; IMT, *Nazi Conspiracy,* 6:873–75, C50, 6:875–76, C51.

53. IMT, *Trial of the War Criminals,* 15:478–79; IMT, *Nazi Conspiracy,* 6:876, C52.

54. IMT, *Nazi Conspiracy,* 7:871–76, L90.

55. See note 54.

56. IMT, *Trial of the War Criminals,* 10:627.

57. Ibid., 20:609, 26:406–8, 884PS; Manstein, *Lost Victories,* 179–80.

58. International Military Tribunal (IMT), "Memorandum of Incriminating Evidence Referring to Brauchitsch, Rundstedt, Manstein and Strauss," Public Record Office, London, England, FO 371/64474.

59. IMT, *Trial of the War Criminals,* 15:308, 7:366, 26:406–8, 884PS.

60. See note 59.

61. Ibid., 15:483–91; IMT, *Nazi Conspiracy,* 3:416–17, 498PS.

62. IMT, Trial of the War Criminals, 15:336, 496, 1:57, 229.

63. Ibid., 10:626–27, 639; IMT, *Nazi Conspiracy,* 3:416–17, 498PS.

64. IMT, *Trial of the War Criminals,* 10:617–18.

65. Ibid., 10:471; Keitel, *Memoirs,* 137.

66. See note 63.

67. IMT, *Trial of the War Criminals,* 10:544.

68. IMT, *Nazi Conspiracy,* Sup B:1561.

69. Halder, *War Diary,* 232, 305, 314, 350, 506; Walter Goerlitz, *The German General Staff 1657–1945,* trans. Brian Battershaw (New York: Praeger, 1959), 385.

70. Halder, *War Diary,* 503.

71. Halder, *Hitler as Warlord,* 57.

72. Guderian, *Panzer Leader,* 233–34.

73. See note 71.

74. Halder, *War Diary,* 514–15.

75. See note 74.

76. Ibid.

77. Ibid., 497, 506; Halder, *Hitler as Warlord,* 2, 63.

78. Halder, *War Diary,* 664, 670; Halder, *Hitler as Warlord,* 2, 58; There is no indication Halder was a National Socialist advocate; instead his persistent support of Hitler's military ventures must be attributed to his apparent intense

dedication to oath, country and seemingly, above all, the legacy of the German General Staff (Halder, *War Diary,* 306).

Chapter 10

1. Dönitz, *Memoirs,* 39.

2. Räder, *My Life,* 362.

3. Gray, Edwyn. *Hitler's Battleships* (Annapolis, MD: Naval Institute Press, 1992), 186.

4. See note 3.

5. Räder, *My Life,* 363; Dönitz, *Memoirs,* 311.

6. IMT, *Trial of the War Criminals,* 14:133; The prosecution had asserted that Dönitz had been selected based on political relations and services rendered, thus this explanation by Räder.

7. Dönitz, *Memoirs,* 311–13.

8. Warlimont, *Hitler's Headquarters,* 418; Mallman Showell, *Führer Conferences,* 308–487 passim; IMT, *Trial of the War Criminals,* 13:297–98, 300.

9. IMT, *Trial of the War Criminals,* 13:299.

10. Ibid., 5:204; IMT, *Nazi Conspiracy,* 7:54–55, D443.

11. Dönitz, *Memoirs,* 114–15.

12. Ibid., 19–21.

13. See note 9.

14. Dönitz, *Memoirs,* 228, 297.

15. Ibid., 489–90.

16. Ibid., 137, 138, 333.

17. Peter Cremer, *U-Boat Commander,* trans. Lawrence Wilson (Annapolis, MD: Naval Institute Press, 1992), 215–38; IMT, *Trial of the War Criminals,* 13:295.

18. See note 17.

Chapter 11

1. Siegfried Westphal, *The German Army in the West* (London: Cassell, 1951), 100–101; General Westphal was Chief of Staff to Rommel in Africa. Accordingly his account of the campaign through El Alamein and the subsequent retreat of the German armies is authoritative and detailed; Liddell-Hart, *Rommel Papers,* 91–97.

2. Liddell-Hart, *Rommel Papers,* 98.

3. Ibid., 153–54.

4. Ibid., 175–76; Westphal, *German Army,* 109.

5. Liddell-Hart, *Rommel Papers,* 186, 195–97; Westphal, *German Army,* 107.

6. Liddell-Hart, *Rommel Papers,* 231–32; Westphal, *German Army,* 116.

7. Kesselring, *Memoirs,* 120, 124–25.

8. Liddell-Hart, *Rommel Papers,* 120, 203, 288–89; Westphal, *German Army,* 116.

9. Kesselring, *Memoirs,* 104, 120.

10. Liddell-Hart, *Rommel Papers,* 302, 327–34; Westphal, *German Army,* 117, 132.

11. Liddell-Hart, *Rommel Papers,* 321, 338; Westphal, *German Army,* 120.

12. Liddell-Hart, *Rommel Papers,* 365–66; Westphal, *German Army,* 121.

13. Liddell-Hart, *Rommel Papers,* 261.

14. Ibid., 244.

15. Westphal, *German Army,* 118.

16. Ciano, *The Ciano Diaries,* 412–13, 418, 449.

17. Liddell-Hart, *Rommel Papers,* 296.

18. Ciano, *Diaries,* 462.

19. Kesselring, *Memoirs,* 104–6.

20. Ibid., 107; Liddell-Hart, *Rommel Papers*, 192, 268–69, 272, 363, 368, 391.

21. Liddell-Hart, *Rommel Papers*, 134, 261–62.

22. Speidel, *Invasion 1944*, 164–66.

23. Ibid.

24. Kesselring, *Memoirs*, 141; Liddell-Hart, *Rommel Papers*, 192, 268–69, 272, 363, 368, 391.

25. Westphal, *German Army*, 104.

26. Kesselring, *Memoirs*, 169–70; Pietro Badoglio, *Italy in the Second World War*, trans. Muriel Currey (London: Oxford University Press, 1948), 40–41, 65–75 passim.

27. Westphal, *German Army*, 146, 168; Dönitz, *Memoirs*, 363.

28. Dönitz, *Memoirs*, 359–64.

29. British Military Court for the Trial of War Criminals, *Trial of Albert Kesselring, German National* (Venice, Italy, 1947; Public Record Office, London, England, filed as PRO/WO 235/366 through 235/376, 59 trial days, 112 exhibits, 60 documents), 2:6; note: since trial proceedings text divisions are "days," not "chapters," the trial day is indicated instead of chapter (e.g., 2:6 is Day 2, page 6); Badoglio, *Italy in the War*, 71.

30. IMT, *Trial of the War Criminals*, 9:220.

31. British Military Court, *Trial of A. Kesselring*, Exhibit 25, subexhibit A.

32. Kesselring, *Memoirs*, 232.

33. Ibid., 301–2; British Military Court, *Trial of A. Kesselring*, Exhibit 7.

34. British Military Court, *Trial of A. Kesselring*, Exhibit 9; Kesselring, *Memoirs*, 302–3.

35. British Military Court, *Trial of A. Kesselring*, Exhibit 10; Kesselring, *Memoirs*, 303.

36. British Military Court, *Trial of A. Kesselring*, Exhibit 11; Kesselring, *Memoirs*, 304.

37. British Military Court, *Trial of A. Kesselring*, Exhibit 59, 57:27.

38. Dönitz, *Memoirs*, 397.

Chapter 12

1. British Military Court, *Trial of A. Kesselring*, 1:2–3, 2:7, 3:15 (32 killed in the morning, one more died later, per Herbert Kappler)

2. The SD, *Sicherheitsdienst*, was the Nazi Party's intelligence and security force, under Heinrich Himmler; the rank, Obersturmbannfuehrer, was Lt. Colonel equivalent.

3. British Military Court, *Trial of A. Kesselring*, 3:12, 14–14, 4:9, 15, 20, 26, 57:5; Richard Raiber, "Generalfeldmarschall Albert Kesselring, Via Rasella, and the 'Ginny Mission,'" Militaergeschichtliche Mitteilungen, 56 (1997), Heft 1, 74, 75, 87, 101.

4. British Military Court, *Trial of A. Kesselring*, exhibit 1, 57:17, 58:5; Kesselring, *Memoirs*, 299.

5. British Military Court, *Trial of A. Kesselring*, 57:3–5, 58:15–15.

6. Ibid., 58:19, 21–22.

7. Ibid., 57:25–27; exhibits 10 and 11; Kesselring, *Memoirs*, 303–4.

8. British Military Court, *Trial of A. Kesselring*, exhibit 82, 46:21, 58:23.

9. Ibid., exhibits 26, 43, 56:52, 58:27–31; Kesselring, *Memoirs*, 305.

10. British Military Court, *Trial of A. Kesselring*, 58:31; Kesselring, *Memoirs*, 302; U.S. War Department, *Rules of Land Warfare*, FM27–10 (Washington, DC: U.S. Govt.

Printing Office, 1940), 87–90; U.S. Dept. of the Army, *The Law of Land Warfare*, FM27–10 (Washington, DC: U.S. Dept. of the Army, 1956), 177–78.

11. British Military Court, *Trial of A. Kesselring*, exhibit 1, 58:16.

12. Ibid., 58:19.

13. Ibid., 59:2.

14. Kesselring, *Memoirs*, 281–82.

Chapter 13

1. Blumentritt, *Von Rundstedt*, 137, 141, 151.

2. Ibid., 159–60, 183–86.

3. Ibid., 187–88.

4. Speidel, *Invasion*, 45; Liddell-Hart, *Rommel Papers*, 451–60.

5. Blumentritt, *Von Rundstedt*, 213–15.

6. Speidel, *Invasion*, 20.

7. Ibid., 24.

8. Blumentritt, *Von Rundstedt*, 226.

9. Speidel, *Invasion*, 86.

10. Speidel, *Invasion*, 37.

11. Ibid., 89–90.

12. Ibid., 51–52.

13. Ibid., 55.

14. Blumentritt, *Von Rundstedt*, 233–34.

15. Speidel, *Invasion*, 92–99; IMT, *Trial of the War Criminals*, 15:403.

16. Blumentritt, *Von Rundstedt*, 238.

17. Speidel, *Invasion*, 106; Liddell-Hart, *Rommel Papers*, 480.

18. Speidel, *Invasion*, 111.

19. Ibid., 115–17; IMT, *Trial of the War Criminals*, 10:56.

20. Speidel, *Invasion*, 29–30.

21. Ibid., 39.

22. Heinz Guderian, *Panzer Leader*, 383–87.

23. Ibid., 333.

24. Mellenthin, *Panzer Battles*, 352; Mellenthin, *German Generals*, 157–58.

25. Liddell-Hart, *Rommel Papers*, 486.

26. Wheeler-Bennett, *Nemesis*, 679–80; IMT, *Trial of the War Criminals*, 33:300–530, 3881PS; Speidel, *Invasion*, 120–26.

27. Speidel, *Invasion*, 152–56.

28. IMT, *Nazi Conspiracy*, 5:541–42, 2878PS.

29. IMT, *Trial of the War Criminals*, 13:304.

30. Dönitz, *Memoirs*, 359–64.

31. Blumentritt, *Von Rundstedt*, 241–22.

32. See note 31.

33. Ibid., 248, 264; Liddell-Hart, *German Generals Talk*, 275–78.

34. See note 33.

35. See note 33.

36. Blumentritt, *Von Rundstedt*, 272.

Chapter 14

1. Guderian, *Panzer Leader*, 400, 412; Manstein, *Lost Victories*, 153, 169; Kesselring, *Memoirs*, 98, 100, 261.

2. International Military Tribunal (IMT), *The Trial of the Major War Criminals* (Nuremberg: Allied Control Authority for Germany, 1947, 23 vols. Transcripts, 17 vols. Documents), 20:625; Samuel W. Mitcham Jr., *Hitler's Field Marshals and Their Battles* (Chelsea, MI: Scarborough House, 1990), 1, passim.

3. Guderian, *Panzer Leader*, 275; Manstein, *Lost Victories*, 73, 93; Blumentritt, *Von Rundstedt*, 233–34, 238.

4. IMT, *Trial of the War Criminals*, 20: 608–9; Manstein, *Lost Victories*, 83, 88.

5. Manstein, *Lost Victories*, 77–79.

6. Ibid., 275, 282.

7. Ibid., 88, 275–76, 280.

8. Ibid., 283.

9. Förster, *Generaloberst Ludwig Beck*, 122–23.

10. John, *Twice through the Lines*, 74.

11. Guderian, *Panzer Leader*, 431, 464–65.

12. Keitel, *Memoirs*, 111, 146, 165.

13. Speer, *Inside the Reich*, 243–44.

14. Keitel, *Memoirs*, 148, 160, 166, 169, 171.

15. Ibid., 105–10.

16. Ibid., 52.

17. Ibid., 200.

18. Ibid., 105.

19. Goebbels, *Diaries*, 142, 283, 475.

20. IMT, *Trial of the War Criminals*, 9:371.

21. Warlimont, *Hitler's Headquarters*, 254.

22. IMT, *Trial of the War Criminals*, 15:506–7.

23. IMT, *Nazi Conspiracy*, Sup B:1561.

24. Keitel, *Memoirs*, 180–81; IMT, *Trial of the War Criminals*, 15:300.

25. Robert Conot, *Justice at Nuremberg* (New York: Carroll and Graf, 1984), 188.

26. Goebbels, *Diaries*, 574.

27. Ibid., 541.

28. Mellenthin, *German Generals*, 248; Liddell-Hart, *German Generals Talk*, 278.

29. Kesselring, *Memoirs*, 265.

30. Halder, *War Diary*, 646.

31. Ibid., 428.

32. Ibid., 564.

33. Ibid., 571–73; Blumentritt, *Von Rundstedt*, 112, 238–39, 242, 279; Hitler's "no withdrawal" order, even for defensive purposes, repeatedly confounded his generals and resulted in German casualties and loss of tactical advantage.

34. See note 32.

35. Halder, *War Diary*, 636.

36. Ibid., 649; Halder, notwithstanding his periodic tactical and strategic misjudgments, attempted to maintain an orderly command structure; however, with Hitler using OKW to override OKH, he was continually frustrated.

37. Guderian, *Panzer Leader*, 166–67.

38. Ibid., 200; Liddell-Hart, *Rommel Papers*, 365.

39. Halder, *War Diary*, 80; Manstein, *Lost Victories*, 69.

40. Guderian, *Panzer Leader*, 325.

41. Ibid., 327.

42. Blumentritt, *Von Rundstedt*, 47; Westphal, *German Army*, 32; Guderian, *Panzer Leader*, 302.

43. Guderian, *Panzer Leader*, 302; Wheeler-Bennett, *Nemesis*, 201, 233, 244, 266.

44. IMT, *Trial of the War Criminals*, 20:603–4, 624; Manstein, *Lost Victories*, 544–47.

45. Manstein, *Lost Victories*, 71–74.

46. Fabian von Schlabrendorff, *They Almost Killed Hitler*, ed. Gero v. S. Gaevernitz (New York: Macmillan, 1947), 76, and *Revolt against Hitler* (London: Eyre and Spotswoode, 1948), 101.; Guderian, *Panzer Leader*, 301.

47. Guderian, *Panzer Leader*, 352; Westphal, *German Army*, 59.

48. Warlimont, *Hitler's Headquarters*, 465.

49. Speer, *Inside the Third Reich*, 421; Mellenthin, *German Generals*, 98–99.

50. Warlimont, *Hitler's Headquarters*, 512.

51. Guderian, *Panzer Leader*, 327, 378.

52. IMT, *Nazi Conspiracy*, Sup B:1285. OKW chief, Field Marshal Keitel, interrogated at Nuremberg as a defendant, describes the three-way conversation between Hitler, Rundstedt and himself held over a 2–3 day period in late 1944 concerning Hitler's plans for the recently deactivated von Rundstedt. Keitel says that Hitler, after procrastinating for this period, offered von Rundstedt the job for a second time because he decided to harness the "respect that Rundstedt enjoys with the ... services."

53. Ibid, 2:841, 6:973–74, C158; IMT, *Trial of the War Criminals*, 13:348.

54. Warlimont, *Hitler's Headquarters*, 251.

Chapter 15

1. Schlabrendorff, *Almost Killed Hitler*, v–vii.

2. IMT, *Trial of the War Criminals*, 12:226; Von Hassell, *Diaries*, 245.

3. Gisevius, *To the Bitter End*, 435; Gisevius, initially in an arm of the Gestapo, became an activist against the regime, and finally escaped to Switzerland. He was a key witness at the Nuremberg Trials.

4. Ibid., 448–49.

5. See note 4.

6. IMT, *Trial of the War Criminals*, 12:241.

7. Gisevius, *To the Bitter End*, 358–59; von Hassell, *Diaries*, 86–87, 95, 101–2; the Gestapo was the Secret State Police, instituted by the Nazis after coming to power. An arm of the SS, it was a basic instrument of repression in the Third Reich and came under Heinrich Himmler.

8. Von Hassell, *Diaries*, 130.

9. Gisevius, *To the Bitter End*, 287–88.

10. Schlabrendorff, *Almost Killed Hitler*, 74–76.

11. Schlabrendorff, *Secret War*, 186–88; IMT, *Trial of the War Criminals*, 20:625.

12. See note 10.

13. Manstein, *Lost Victories*, 187–88; IMT, *Trial of the War Criminals*, 20:625.

14. Gisevius, *To the Bitter End*, 401, 468.

15. Guderian, *Panzer Leader*, 300–301.

16. Ibid., 301; Schlabrendorff, *Almost Killed Hitler*, 76.

17. Guderian, *Panzer Leader*, 404; IMT, *Trial of the War Criminals*, 16:492.

18. Guderian, *Panzer Leader*, 426.

19. Ibid., 407; IMT, *Nazi Conspiracy*, 6:655–717, 3786PS.

20. Liddell-Hart, *Rommel Papers*, 497.

21. Speidel, *Invasion*, 158.

22. Ibid., 63–66.

23. See note 22.

24. Ibid.

25. IMT, *Trial of the War Criminals*, 12:245.

26. Liddell-Hart, *Rommel Papers*, 485–86.

27. Speidel, *Invasion*, 72–74.

28. Ibid., 70.

29. IMT, *Trial of the War Criminals*, 12:245.

30. Gisevius, *To the Bitter End*, 401, 468.

31. Ibid., 536–75 passim.

Chapter 16

1. Dönitz, *Memoirs*, 441–42; IMT, *Trial of the War Criminals*, 13:307–8.

2. See note 1.

3. Goebbels, *Diaries*, 241, 285.

4. Albert Speer, *Spandau the Secret Diaries*, trans. Richard and Clara Winston (New York: Macmillan, 1976), 297–98.

5. Ibid., 333–34.

6. See note 5.

7. Gilbert, *Diary*, 297.

8. Dönitz, *Memoirs*, 183–87.

9. See note 8.

10. Gilbert, *Diary*, 358.

11. IMT, *Trial of the War Criminals*, 13:342–43, 34:783–77, C195; IMT, *Nazi Conspiracy*, 2:842, 6:1022–23, C195.

12. See note 11.

13. Gilbert, *Diary*, 7.

14. IMT, *Trial of the War Criminals*, 17:377–81.

15. Ibid., 11:26–27.

16. IMT, *Nazi Conspiracy*, Sup B:274.

17. Taylor, *Anatomy of the Trials*, 436.

18. IMT, *Nazi Conspiracy*, Sup B:790–91.

19. U.S. Dept. of State, *International Conference on Military Trials*, Publication 3080 (Washington, DC: U.S. Govt. Printing Office, 1949), 11–12.

20. Telford Taylor, Letter to the Author dated March 20, 1995; then-General Taylor was prosecutor and subsequently Chief U.S. Prosecutor at the Nuremberg Trials; Halder, *War Diary*, 10; Mellenthin, *German Generals*, 38.

21. IMT, *Trial of the War Criminals*, 21:21–50 passim.

22. IMT, *Memo of Evidence*, 60. This dossier, PRO/FO 317/64474, was completed at Nuremberg by the office of the U.S. prosecutor and forwarded at the direction of the military governor of the U.S. Zone to the British attorney general for action. In the final analysis only von Manstein was ever tried. He was convicted by a British court and sentenced to 18 years, and freed in four; Richard Messenger, *The Last Prussian* (London: Brassey's, 1991), 258.

23. IMT, *Memo of Evidence*, 6–8; IMT, *Trial of the War Criminals*, 7:366; 26:406–8, 884PS.

24. IMT, *Memo of Evidence*, 8; IMT, *Trial of the War Criminals*, 21:25.

25. IMT, *Memo of Evidence*, 9–14; IMT, *Trial of the War Criminals*, 21:26, 44.

26. IMT, *Memo of Evidence*, 15.

27. Ibid., 33–34; IMT, *Trial of the War Criminals*, 21:45.

28. IMT, *Trial of the War Criminals*, 21:21–50 passim.

29. Ibid., 21:30.

30. Westphal, *German Army*, 193.

31. Speidel, *Invasion*, 71. Generals Speidel and Westphal, who worked closely with and for von Rundstedt, provide perceptive comments regarding his deteriorating ability to manage and innovate, and thus provide valuable insight into the man.

32. IMT, *Trial of the War Criminals*, 12:247. Gisevius, who had been an anti-Nazi activist, was considered a key prosecution witness.

33. John, *Twice through the Lines*, 91, 188. Otto John, anti-Nazi and war-time lawyer for Lufthansa, was given responsibility in 1946 for the welfare of prisoners in Camp No. 11 at Brigend, South Wales. Several hundred field marshals, generals, admirals and senior SS officers were held at Brigend, providing John a unique opportunity to attempt to assess why they had served Hitler to the bitter end.

34. IMT, *Trial of the War Criminals*, 20:626.

35. Manstein, *Lost Victories*, 470; IMT, *Trial of the War Criminals*, 20:614–16.

36. IMT, *Trial of the War Criminals*, 20:622.

37. Ibid., 4:317–19, 347–48, 20:636–37; IMT, *Nazi Conspiracy*, 3:637–39, 886PS; IMT, *Memorandum of Evidence*, 39.

38. See note 37.

39. IMT, *Trial of the War Criminals*, 20:617–40; Taylor, *Nuremberg Trials*, 246, 249, 519.

40. IMT, *Trial of the War Criminals*, 20:641–43; IMT, *Nazi Conspiracy*, Sup. A:826–8, 4064PS; Taylor, *Nuremberg Trials*, 520.

41. IMT, *Memo of Evidence*, 26–27, 63–64, 70.

42. IMT, *Trial of the War Criminals*, 4:317–19, 347–68, 20:617–40, 636–37; Taylor, *Anatomy of the Trials*, 246, 249, 519; IMT, *Memo of Evidence*, 26–27, 39, 63–64, 70; IMT, *Nazi Conspiracy*, 3:737–39, 886PS.

43. Kesselring, *Memoirs*, 307.

44. Ibid., 169–70; Ciano, *Diaries*, 174, 456, 507, 509; Badoglio, *Italy in the Second War*, 40–41, 65–75 passim.

45. Kesselring, *Memoirs*, 181.

46. Alexander P. Scotland, *The London Cage* (London: Evans Brothers., 1957), 172–86.

47. Kenneth Macksey, *Kesselring: The Making of the Luftwaffe* (New York: David McKay, 1978), 252–53.

48. Raeder, *My Life*, 272.

49. IMT, *Trial of the War Criminals*, 14:222, 5:282; IMT, *Nazi Conspiracy*, 7:153–56, D653.

50. Räder, *My Life*, 256–61.

51. See note 50.

52. Ibid., 247, 254.

53. Ibid., 265.

54. Warlimont, *Hitler's Headquarters*, 221.

55. IMT, *Trial of the War Criminals*, 9:435–36.

56. Taylor, Letter to the Author.

57. Kenneth Macksey, *Guderian, Panzer General* (London: Macdonald, 1975), 191, 206; Mellenthin, *German Generals*, 100.

58. Keitel, *Memoirs*, 56.

Conclusion

1. Speidel, *Invasion*, 13.

2. Wheeler-Bennett, *Nemesis*, 8, 86.

3. Erich Weiss, *Conversations with the Author*, May 22, 23, 1996. Erich Weiss was an Austrian expatriate and World War II British Army Interrogator of POWs.

4. Walter Goerlitz, *Paulus at Stalingrad*, trans. R.H. Stevens (New York: Citadel Press, 1963), 231.

5. Heinz Schroeter, *Stalingrad*, trans. Constantine Fitzgibbon (London: Michael Joseph, 1958), 228.

6. Walter Goerlitz, *History of the German General Staff*, trans. Brian Battershaw (New York: Praeger, 1953), 427.

7. Goerlitz, *Paulus*, 250.

8. Schroeter, *Stalingrad*, 236.

9. Ibid., 237.

10. Guderian, *Panzer Leader*, 342–50.

11. Kesselring, *Memoirs*, 281–82, 292–93; Speidel, *Invasion*, 70.

12. IMT, *Trial of the War Criminals*, 16:492.

13. Dietrich Bonhoeffer, *Letters and Papers from Prison*, trans. and ed. Eberhard Bethge (New York: Macmillan, 1971), 60.

14. Keitel, *Memoirs*, 52.

15. IMT, *Trial of the War Criminals*, 15:294.

16. Ilse Hess, *Prisoner of Peace*, trans. Meyrick Booth (London: Britons, 1954), 25.

17. Roger Manvell and Heinrich Fraenkel, *Göring* (New York: Simon and Schuster, 1962), 313–17.

18. *The British Year Book of Law 1944* (London: Oxford University Press), 69, 72–73; U.S. War Dept., *Rules of Land Warfare, FM 27–10*, para. 347; British Military Court, *Trial of A. Kesselring*, 8:5.

19. U.S. War Dept., *The Law of Land Warfare, FM 27–10*, para. 509.

20. *British Yearbook of Law*, 69, 72–73

21. Albert Speer, *Spandau: The Secret Diaries,* trans. Richard and Clara Winston (New York: Macmillan, 1976), 50, 156.

22. Halder, *War Diary*, 306.

23. IMT, *Nazi Conspiracy*, 2:817, 7:116, D640.

24. Ibid., 2:817, 5:541, 2878PS

25. H.R. Trevor-Roper, ed., *Blitzkrieg to Defeat* (New York: Holt, Rinehart and Winston, 1964), 3, 49, 212–13.

Bibliography

Primary Sources

Badoglio, Pietro. *Italy in the Second World War*. Trans. Muriel Currey. London: Oxford University Press, 1948.

Benes, Eduard. *Memoirs of Dr. Eduard Benes*. Trans. Godfrey Lias. Boston: Houghton Mifflin, 1954.

Blumentritt, Guenther. *Von Rundstedt, the Soldier and the Man*. Trans. Cuthbert Reavely. London: Odhams Press, 1952.

Bonhoeffer, Dietrich. *Letters and Papers from Prison*. Trans. and ed. Eberhard Bethge. New York: Macmillan, 1971.

Brett-Smith, Richard. *Hitler's Generals*. San Rafael, CA: Presidio Press, 1977.

British Military Court for the Trial of War Criminals. "Trial of Albert Kesselring, German National, Venice, Italy, 1947." Public Record Office, London, England, filed as PRO/WO 235/366 through 235/376. 59 trial days, 112 exhibits, 60 documents.

The British Year Book of Law 1944. London: Oxford University Press, 1944.

Ciano, Galeazzo. *The Ciano Diaries 1939–1943*. Garden City, NY: Doubleday, 1946.

Conot, Robert. *Justice at Nuremberg*. New York: Carroll and Graf, 1984.

Cremer, Peter. *U-Boat Commander*. Trans. Lawrence Wilson. Annapolis, MD: Naval Institute Press, 1992.

Dönitz, Karl. *Memoirs: Ten Years and Twenty Days*. Trans. R.H. Stevens. Annapolis, MD: Naval Institute Press, 1990.

Ellis, Chris. *Tanks of World War 2*. London: Octopus Books, 1981.

Fischer, Fritz. *Germany's Aims in the First World War*. New York: W.W. Norton, 1967.

Foley, H. *Woodrow Wilson's Case for the League of Nations*. Princeton, NJ: Princeton University Press, 1923.

Förster, Wolfgang. *Generaloberst Ludwig Beck: Sein Kampf gegan den Krieg*. Munich: Isar Verlag, 1953.

François-Poncet, Andre. *The Fateful Years*. Trans. Jacques LeClercq. New York: Harcourt, Brace, 1949.

Galland, Adolf. *The First and the Last*. Trans. Mervyn Savill. London: Methuen, 1955.

Gilbert, G.M. *Nuremberg Diary*. New York: Farrar, Straus, 1947.

Gisevius, Hans B. *To the Bitter End*. Trans. Richard and Clara Winston. Boston: Houghton Mifflin, 1947.

Goebbels, Joseph. *The Goebbels Diaries 1942–43*. Trans. and ed. Louis Lochner. New York: Doubleday, 1948.

Goerlitz, Walter. *The German General Staff 1657–1945*. Trans. Brian Battershaw. New York: Praeger, 1959.

_____. *Paulus at Stalingrad*. Trans. R.H. Stevens New York: Citadel Press, 1963.

Gray, Edwyn. *Hitler's Battleships*. Annapolis, MD: Naval Institute Press, 1992.

Guderian, Heinz. *Panzer Leader*. Trans. Constantine Fitzgibbon. New York: E.P. Dutton, 1952.

Halder, Franz. *The Halder War Diary*. Ed. Charles Burdick and Hans-Adolf Jacobsen. Novato, CA: Presidio Press, 1988.

_____. *Hitler as Warlord*. Trans. Paul Findlay. Longbank Works, UK: Robert Cunningham and Sons, 1950.

Hassell, Ulrich von. *The Von Hassell Diaries*. Garden City, NY: Doubleday, 1947.

Heiden, Konrad. *Der Führer*. Trans. Ralph Manheim. Boston: Houghton Mifflin, 1944.

Heinkel, Ernst. *Stormy Life*. Trans. R.C. Murray and J.A. Bagley. New York: E.P. Dutton, 1956.

Henderson, Neville. *Failure of a Mission*. New York: G.P. Putnam's Sons, 1940.

Hess, Ilse. *Prisoner of Peace*. Trans. Meyrick Booth. London: Britons Publishing, 1954.

International Military Tribunal (IMT). "Memorandum of Incriminating Evidence Referring to Brauchitsch, Rundstedt, Manstein and Strauss." Filed with Public Record Office, London, under FO 371/64474.

_____. *Nazi Conspiracy and Aggression*. Washington, DC: U.S. Govt. Printing Office, 1946. 10 volumes.

_____. *The Trial of the Major War Criminals*. Nuremberg: Allied Control Authority for Germany, 1947. 23 volumes of transcripts, 17 volumes of documents.

John, Otto. *Twice through the Lines*. Trans. Richard Barry. New York: Harper & Row, 1972.

Keitel, Wilhelm. *The Memoirs of Field Marshal Keitel*. Trans. David Irving. New York: Stein and Day, 1966.

Kesselring, Albrecht. *The Memoirs of Field-Marshal Kesselring*. Trans. Lynton Hudson. London: William Kimber, 1953. Reprint. Novato, CA: Presidio Press, 1989.

_____. *Soldat bis zum letzten Tag*. Bonn: Athenaeum-Verlag, 1953.

Keynes, J.M. *The Economic Consequences of the Peace*. New York: Harcourt, Brace and Howe, 1920.

Leeb, Wilhelm von. *Defense*. Trans. S.T. Possony and D. Vilfroy. Harrisburg, PA: Military Publishing, 1943.

Liddell-Hart, B.H. *The German Generals Talk*. New York: Morrow/Quill Paperbacks, 1979.

_____. *The Rommel Papers*. Trans. Paul Findlay. New York: Harcourt, Brace, 1953.

Macksey, Kenneth. *Guderian, Panzer General*. London: Macdonald, 1975.

_____. *Kesselring: The Making of the Luftwaffe*. New York: David McKay, 1978.

Mahan, Alfred Thayer. *The Influence of Sea Power upon History 1660–1793*. Boston: Little, Brown, 1890.

Manstein, Erich von. *Lost Victories*. Trans. Anthony Powell. Novato, CA: Presidio Press, 1982.

Manvell, Roger, and Fraenkel, Heinrich. *Göring*. New York: Simon and Schuster, 1962.

Marshall, S.L.A. *World War One*. Boston: Houghton Mifflin, 1964.

Massie, Robert K. *Dreadnought: Britain, Germany, and the Comng of the Great War*. New York: Random House, 1991.

Mellenthin, F.W. von. *German Generals of World War II*. Norman: University of Oklahoma Press, 1977.

_____. *Panzer Battles*. Trans. H. Betzler. Norman: University of Oklahoma Press, 1956.

Messenger, Richard. *The Last Prussian*. London: Brassey's, 1991.

Mitcham, Samuel W., Jr. *Hitler's Field Marshals and Their Battles*. Chelsea, MI: Scarborough House, 1990.

Müller, Klaus-Jürgen. *The Army, Politics and Society in Germany, 1933–45*. Manchester: Manchester University Press, 1987. New York: St. Martin's Press, 1987.

Naumann, Friedrich. *Central Europe*. Trans. Christabel M. Meredith. London: P.S. King and Son, 1916.

O'Neill, Robert J. *The German Army and the Nazi Party 1933–1939*. New York: Heineman, 1966.

Oppenheimer, Heinrich. *The Constitution of the German Republic*. London: Stevens and Sons, 1923.

Papen, Franz von. *Memoirs*. Trans. Brian Connell. London: Andre Deutsch, 1952.

Rabenau, Friedrich. *Seeckt, Aus Seinem Leben 1918–1936*. Leipzig: Hase and Koehler, 1940.

Raeder, Erich. *My Life*. Trans. Henry W. Drexel. Annapolis, MD: U.S. Naval Institute, 1960.

Raiber, Richard. *Generalfeldmarschall Albert Kesselring, Via Rasella, and the "Ginny Mission."* Militaergeschichtliche Mitteilungen, 56 (1997), Heft 1.

Rommel, Erwin. *Attacks*. Vienna, VA: Athena Press, 1979.

Ruge, Friedrich. *Der Seekrieg*. Trans. M.G. Saunders. Annapolis, MD: U.S. Naval Institute Press, 1957.

Schacht, Hjalmar. *Account Settled*. Trans. Edward Fitzgerald. London: Weidenfeld and Nicholson, 1949.

Schlabrendorff, Fabian von. *Revolt against Hitler*. London: Eyre and Spotteswoode, 1948.

_____. *The Secret War against Hitler*. Trans. Hilda Simon. New York: Pitman, 1965.

_____. *They Almost Killed Hitler*. Ed. Gero v. S. Gaevernitz. New York: Macmillan, 1947.

Schroeter, Heinz. *Stalingrad*. Trans. Constantine Fitzgibbon. London: Michael Joseph, 1958.

Schuschnigg, Kurt. *Austrian Requiem*. Trans. Franz von Hildebrand. New York: G.P. Putnam's Sons, 1946.

Scotland, Alexander P. *The London Cage*. London: Evans Brothers, 1957.

Seager, Robert, II. *Alfred Thayer Mahan, the Man and His Letters*. Annapolis, MD: Naval Institute Press, 1977.

Showell, Mallman. *Führer Conferences on Naval Affairs 1939–1945*. Trans. British Government. Annapolis, MD: U.S. Naval Institute Press, 1990.

Shulman, Milton. *Defeat in the West*. New York: Ballantine Books, 1968.

Smith, Woodruff D. *The Ideological Origins of Nazi Imperialism*. New York: Oxford University Press, 1986.

Speer, Albert. *Inside the Third Reich*. Trans. Richard and Clara Winston. New York: Macmillan, 1976.

_____. *Spandau the Secret Diaries*. Trans. Richard and Clara Winston. New York: Macmillan, 1976.

Speidel, Hans. *Invasion 1944*. Trans. Theo R. Crevenna. Chicago: Henry Regnery, 1950.

Suchenwirth, Richard. *Command and Leadership in the German Air Force*. Ed. Harry R. Fletcher. New York: Arno Press/U.S. Historical Division, Air University, 1969.

Taylor, Telford. *The Anatomy of the Nuremberg Trials*. New York: Knopf, 1992.

Trevor-Roper, H.R., ed. *Blitzkrieg to Defeat*. New York: Holt, Rinehart and Winston, 1964.

United States. Department of State. *International Conference on Military Trials*. Publication 3080. Washington, DC: U.S. Govt. Printing Office, 1949.

_____. War Department. *Rules of Land Warfare, FM27-10*. Washington, DC: U.S. Govt. Printing Office, 1940. Reprint. 1956.

Warlimont, Walter. *Inside Hitler's Headquarters 1939–45*. Trans. R.H Barry. Novato, CA: Presidio Press, 1964.

Westphal, Siegfried. *The German Army in the West*. London: Cassell, 1951.

Wheeler-Bennett, John W. *The Nemesis of Power*. London: Macmillan, 1953.

Further Sources

Adenauer, Konrad. *Memoirs 1945–53*. Trans. Beate Ruhm von Oppen. Chicago: Henry Regnery, 1965.

Barnett, Correlli. *Hitler's Generals*. Ed. Correlli Barnett. New York: Grove Weidenfeld, 1989.

Bentley, James. *Martin Niemöller*. New York: Free Press, 1984.

Bormann, Martin. *The Bormann Letters*. Ed. H.R. Trevor-Roper. London: Weidenfeld and Nicolson, 1954.

Chuikov, Marshal Vasili Ivanovich. *The Battle for Stalingrad*. Trans. Harold Silver. New York: Holt Rinehart and Winston, 1963.

Clark, Alan. *Barbarossa, the Russian-German Conflict, 1941–45*. New York: Quill, 1985.

Deutsch, Harold C. *Hitler and His Generals*. Minneapolis: University of Minnesota Press, 1974.

Dietrich, Otto. *Hitler*. Trans. Richard and Clara Winston. Chicago: Henry Regnery, 1955.

Dirksen, Herbert von. *Moscow, Tokyo, London*. Norman: University of Oklahoma Press, 1952.

Dodd, William E. *Ambassador Dodd's Diary*. Ed. William E. Dodd Jr. and Martha Dodd. New York: Harcourt, Brace, 1941.

Eich, Hermann. *The Germans*. Trans. Michael Glenny. New York: Stein and Day, 1980.

Eyck, Erich. *A History of the Weimar Republic*. Trans. Harlan P. Hanson and Robert G.L. Waite. New York: John Wiley and Sons, 1967.

Fest, Joachim C. *The Face of the Third Reich*. Trans. Michael Bullock,. New York: Pantheon Books, 1970.

_____. *Hitler*. Trans. Richard and Clara Winston. New York: Vintage Books, 1975.

Fragen an die Deutsche Geschichte (Questions on German history). Bonn: German Bundestag Press, 1984.

Fritzsche, Hans. *The Sword in the Scales*. Trans. Diana Pike and Heinrich Fraenkel. London: Allan Wingate, 1953.

Gilbert, G.M. *The Psychology of Dictatorship*. New York: Ronald Press, 1950.

Goerlitz, Walter. *Paulus and Stalingrad*. Trans. R.H. Stevens. New York: Citadel Press, 1963.

Goebbels, Joseph. "Final Entries 1945." *The Diaries of Joseph Geobbels*. Ed. H.R. Trevor-Roper. Trans. Richard Barry. New York: G.P. Putnam's Sons, 1978.

_____. *The Goebbels Diaries: 1939–1941*. Trans. and ed. Fred Taylor. Middlesex, UK: Penguin Books, 1984.

Guderian, Heinz. *Achtung Panzer*. 1937. Reprint. Trans. Christopher Duffy. London: Brockhampton Press, 1999.

Gulick, Charles A. *Austria, from Habsburg to Hitler*. Vols. 1 and 2. Berkeley: University of California Press, 1948.

Hanfstaengl, Putzi. *Hitler, the Missing Years*. London: Eyre and Spottiswoode, 1957.

Hildebrand, Klaus. *The Foreign Policy of the Third Reich*. Trans. Anthony Fothergill. Berkeley: University of California Press, 1973.

Hitler, Adolf. *Hitler's Secret Book*. Trans. Salvator Attanasio. New York: Grove Press, 1961.

_____. *Mein Kampf*. Trans. Ralph Manheim. Boston: Houghton Mifflin, 1971.

Hoene, Heinz. *Canaris*. Trans. J. Maxwell Brownjohn. New York: Doubleday, 1979.

Hoffman, Henrich. *Hitler Was My Friend*. Trans. R.H. Stevens. London: Burke, 1957.

Hoffman, Peter. *German Resistance to Hitler*. Cambridge, MA: Harvard University Press, 1988.

Höss, Rudolf. *Commandant of Auschwitz*. Trans. Constantine FitzGibbon. New York: World Publishing Company, 1959.

Jacobsen, H.A., and Rohwer, J., eds. *Decisive Battles of World War II: The German View*. Trans. Edward Fitzgerald. New York: G.P. Putnam's Sons, 1965.

Kelley, Douglas M. *22 Cells in Nuremberg*. New York: Greenberg, 1947.

Kohl, Helmut, et al. *Reflections on July 20th, 1944*. Mainz: von Hase and Koehler Verlag, 1984.

Lang, Serge, and Schenck, Ernst von. *Memoirs of Alfred Rosenberg*. Trans. Eric Posselt. Chicago: Ziff-Davis, 1949.

Laval, Pierre. *The Unpublished Diary of Pierre Laval*. London: Falcon Press, 1948.

Liddell-Hart, B.H. *History of the Second World War*. New York: G.P. Putnam's Sons, 1970.

Lukacs, John. *The Hitler of History*. New York: Knopf, 1997.

Maser, Werner. *Hitler's Letters and Notes*. Trans. Arnold Pomerans. New York: Harper and Row, 1973.

Moltke, Helmuth James von. *A German of the Resistance*. London: Oxford University Press, 1948.

Musmanno, Michael A. *The Eichmann Kommandos*. London: Peter Davies, 1962.

Namier, Lewis. *In the Nazi Era*. London: Macmillan 1952.

Neave, Airey. *On Trial at Nuremberg*. Boston: Little, Brown, 1978.

Paget, R.T. *Manstein, His Campaigns and His Trial*. London: Collins, 1951.

Rauschning, Hermann. *The Revolution of Nihilism*. New York: Alliance Book Corporation, 1939.

_____. *The Voice of Destruction*. New York: G.P. Putnam's Sons, 1940.

Reimann, Viktor. *Goebbels*. Trans. Stephen Wendt. New York: Doubleday, 1976.

Ribbentrop, Joachim von. *The Ribbentrop Memoirs*. Trans. Oliver Watson. London: Weidenfeld and Nicolson, 1954.

Rothfels, Hans. *The German Opposition to Hitler*. Trans. Lawrence Wilson. London: Oswald Wolff, 1961.

Ruge, Friedrich. *Rommel in Normandy*. Trans. Ursala R. Moessner. San Rafael, CA: Presidio Press, 1979.

_____. *The Soviets as Naval Opponents 1941–1945*. Annapolis. MD: Naval Institute Press, 1979.

Sajer, Guy. *The Forgotten Soldier*. New York: Brassey's, 1967.

Salomon, Ernst von. *Fragebogen*. Trans. Constantine FitzGibbon. New York: Doubleday, 1955.

Schacht, Hjalmar. *The End of Reparations*. Trans. Lewis Gannett. New York: Jonathan Cape and Harrison Smith, 1931.

Schweppenburg, Geyr von. *The Critical Years*. London: Allan Wingate, 1952.

Seeckt, Hans von. *The Future of the German Empire*. Trans. Oakley Williams. New York: E.P. Dutton, 1930.

Sereny, Gitta. *Albert Speer, His Battle with Truth*. New York: Knopf, 1995.

Snyder, Louis L. *Roots of German Nationalism*. New York: Barnes and Noble, 1978.

Strasser, Otto. *Flight from Terror*. New York: National Travel Club, 1943.

Taylor, Telford. *Sword and Swastika*. Chicago: Quadrangle, 1952.

Thyssen, Fritz. *I Paid Hitler*. Trans. Cesar Saerchinger. New York: Farrar and Rinehart, 1941.

Trevor-Roper, H.R. *The Bormann Letters*, Trans. R.H. Stevens. London: Weidenfeld and Nicolson, 1954.

_____. *Hitler's Secret Conversations, 1941–44*. New York: Farrar, Straus and Young, 1953.

_____. *Hitler's Table Talk*. London: Weidenfeld and Nicolson, 1953.

_____. *The Last Days of Hitler*. New York: Macmillan, 1947

Walters, F.P. *A History of the League of Nations*. London: Oxford University Press, 1967.

Weitz, John. *Hitler's Diplomat*. New York: Ticknor and Fields, 1992.

Weizsaecker, Ernst von. *The Memoirs of Ernst von Weizsaecker*. Trans. John Andrews. London: Victor Gollancz, 1951.

Weygand, Maxime. *Recalled to Service*. Trans. E.W. Dickes. London: Heinemann, 1952.

Wheeler-Bennett, John W. *Hindenburg, The Wooden Titan*. London: Macmillan, 1936.

_____. *Munich, Prologue to Tragedy*. London: Macmillan, 1963.

Wiskemann, Elizabeth. *Czechs and Germans*. London: Oxford University Press, 1938.

Additional Recommended Reading

Air Ministry. *The Rise and Fall of the German Air Force 1933–45,* St. Martin's Press, New York, 1983.

Aron, Robert. *The Vichy Regime 1940–44.* Trans. Humphrey Hare. Boston: Beacon Press, 1969.

Berghahn, V.R. *Modern Germany*. Cambridge: Cambridge University Press, 1982.

Bernadotte, Folke. *Instead of Arms*. Stockholm: Bonniers, 1948.

Bloch, Marc. *Strange Defeat*. New York: W.W. Norton, 1968. Reprint. 1999.

Bonhoeffer, Dietrich. *A Testament to Freedom*. (Papers of D. Bonhoeffer.) Ed. Geoffrey Kelly and Burton Nelson. San Francisco: Harper, 1990.

Bragadin, Marc Antonio. *The Italian Navy in WWII.* Annapolis, MD: U.S. Naval Institute, 1957.

British Air Ministry. *The Rise and Fall of the German Air Force, 1933–45.* New York: St. Martin's Press, 1983.

Bullock, Alan. *Hitler, a Study in Tyranny*. Abridged. New York: Perennial Library, 1971.

Dahrendorf, Ralf. *Society and Democracy in Germany*. New York: Doubleday/Anchor Books, 1969.

Daladier, Edouard. *In Defense of France*. New York: Doubleday, Doran, 1939.

Frieser, Karl-Heinz. *The Blitzkrieg Legend*. Annapolis, MD: U.S. Naval Institute Press, 2005.

Frischauer, Willi. *Göring*. London: Odhams Press, 1950.

_____. *Himmler*. Boston: Beacon Press, 1953.

Gehlen, Reinhard. *The Service: The Memoirs of General Renhard Gehlen*. Trans. David Irving. New York: World Publishing, 1972.

German Democratic Republic. *Brown Book: War and Nazi Criminals in West Germany.* n.p.: National Council of the National Front of Democratic Germany, Verlag Zeit Im Bild, 1965.

Goldensohn, Leon. *Nuremberg Interviews*. New York: Knopf, 2004.

Heiden, Konrad. *A History of National Socialism*. New York: Knopf, 1935.

Irving, David. *Göring, a Biography*. New York: Morrow, 1989.

Junge, Traudl. *Until the Final Hour*. Trans. Anthea Bell. New York: Arcade, 2003.

Kleine-Ahlbrandt, W. Laird. *Appeasement of the Dictators*. New York: Holt, Rinehart and Winston, 1970.

Klotz, Helmut. *The Berlin Diaries*. New York: Morrow, 1934.

Messenger, Charles. *Hitler's Gladiator*. London: Brassey's, 1991.

Mommsen, Wolfgang J. *Imperial Germany, 1867–1918*. New York: Arnold, 1995.

Nolte, Ernst. *Three Faces of Fascism*. Trans. Leila Vennewitz. New York: Holt, Reinhart and Winston, 1965.

Paxton, Robert O. *Anatomy of Fascism*. New York: Knopf, 2004.

Pflanze, Otto. *Bismarck and the Development of Germany*. Princeton, NJ: Princeton University Press, 1963.

_____. *The Unification of Germany 1848–1871*. Melbourne, FL: Krieger, 1968.

Redlich, Fritz. *Hitler, Diagnosis of a Destructive Prophet*. New York: Oxford University Press, 1998.

Reynaud, Paul. *In the Thick of the Fight*. Trans. James D. Lambert. New York: Simon and Schuster, 1955.

Reynold, Nicholas. *Treason Was No Crime*. London: Kimber, 1976.

Riefenstahl, Leni. *A Memoir*. New York: St. Martin's, 1993.

Schellenberg, Walter. *The Schellenberg Memoirs*. Trans. Louis Hagen. London: Andre Deutsch, 1956.

Shtemenko, S.M. *The Soviet General Staff at War 1941–45*. Trans. Dudley Hagen and Francis Longman. Moscow: Progress Publishers, 1986.

Swallow, Alan, ed. *Readings on Fascism and National Socialism*. Denver: University of Colorado Press, 1948.

Turner, Ashby, Jr. *Hitler, Memoirs of a Confidant*. Trans. Ruth Heim. New Haven, CT: Yale University Press, 1985.

United States. Department of the Army. *Operations of Encircled Forces, German Experiences in Russia*. Washington, DC: U.S. Govt. Printing Office, 1952.

Van Roon, Ger. *German Resistance to Hitler*. London: Van Nostrand Reinhold, 1971.

Index

Numbers in *bold italics* indicate pages with illustrations.